The Socialist Party of Argentina
1890–1930

Latin American Monographs, No. 42
Institute of Latin American Studies
The University of Texas at Austin

The Socialist Party
of Argentina 1890–1930
by Richard J. Walter

Institute of Latin American Studies
The University of Texas at Austin

International Standard Book Number 0-292-77539-3 (cloth)
0-292-77540-7 (paper)
Library of Congress Catalog Card Number 77-620003

The Latin American Monographs Series
is distributed for the Institute of
Latin American Studies by:
  The University of Texas Press
  P. O. Box 7819
  Austin, Texas 78712

To the memory of my father

Contents

Tables

Map

Acknowledgments

I would like to thank Washington University for providing me with generous support during an academic leave for 1970–1971, when I conducted the bulk of the research for this study. I am also indebted to the Social Science Research Council for financial assistance during my field work in Buenos Aires.

In Argentina, Sr. Juan Lamesa, director of the Biblioteca Obrera 'Juan B. Justo,' was especially helpful in permitting me to use the facilities of the Socialist Party library. Socialist leader Américo Ghioldi took time from his busy schedule to submit to a series of questions in a lengthy interview, for which I am most grateful.

In the United States, David Zubatsky and William Kurth of the Olin Library, Washington University, greatly assisted me in gathering research materials on Argentine politics. I owe a special debt of gratitude to Ms. Joanne Fox Przeworski, who performed much of the heavy and tedious work involved in organizing the occupational data included in Appendix A. Peter H. Smith of the Department of History, University of Wisconsin, read the manuscript and provided me with advice and encouragement at a time when they were sorely needed. Thomas F. McGann of the Department of History, University of Texas, and Carl Solberg of the Department of History, University of Washington, also read the manuscript, and I have benefited greatly from their comments and suggestions.

Finally, my wife, Vincenza, helped me collect the information on the popular theater noted in chapter four and served beyond the call of duty in working with me to compile the occupational information in Appendix A. She has aided me in other ways too numerous to mention.

Any errors in fact and interpretation in what follows are my responsibility.

Preface

At the end of the nineteenth century and the beginning of the twentieth, socialist parties, in one form or another, appeared throughout most of Latin America. Influenced by European examples, they sought to mobilize the working classes and to represent their interests in the political arena. Usually adopting a reformist posture, they enjoyed little real success in organizing the proletariat in pre-industrial societies or in achieving social betterments through the political process in countries with weak democratic-constitutional traditions. However, they did manage to introduce the potent idea of a socialist alternative to the prevailing capitalism of the period, to stimulate a greater public awareness and consideration of social problems, and to encourage the growth of labor unions.[1]

Argentina's Socialist Party, established in 1895, was one of Latin America's first modern political parties. Its founders formulated a specific program, drew up detailed statutes for organization and membership, and maintained a stable structure and leadership. From 1896 the Socialists entered every national election for Congress and from 1916 every presidential election. Between 1896 and 1930 they registered an ever-increasing growth in members, voters, and officials elected to office. Throughout these years they were an important factor in the politics of the Argentine Republic. By 1930, moreover, the Argentine Socialist Party was the most successful socialist party in Latin America.

The emergence of modern political parties has been one of the most significant and, at the same time, least studied developments in twentieth-century Latin American history.[2] There are few detailed investigations of specific parties within specific historical contexts, and generalized essays on the overall nature and role of parties in Latin America suffer from this deficiency.[3] Little scholarly attention has been paid to socialist parties in particular, although the Argentine party has been described briefly in some general works in English. These descriptions, however, fail to provide extensive information on party organization and function within the larger framework of Argentine political history.[4] Excessive partisanship and scholarly myopia frequently mar Argentine histories of the party.[5]

With these considerations in mind, the purpose of this study is to describe in detail the evolution of Argentina's Socialist Party between 1890 and 1930. Although the party persists into the 1970s, I have chosen to concentrate on its origins, its expansion during a difficult period of repression, and its participation in an eighteen-year era of uninterrupted civilian, democratic rule. Following electoral reform in 1912, Argentina embarked on an experiment in democracy with an expansion of the electorate and reasonably honest and free elections. In 1930 this experiment came to an end, replaced by endemic military interventions and fraudulent political practices. The 1912–1930 interval, therefore, provides a consistent and coherent span in which to gauge the Socialist Party's effectiveness under relatively normal, stable conditions of political competition.

Between 1912 and 1930 the Partido Socialista (PS) (Socialist Party) and the Unión Cívica Radical (UCR) (Radical Party) were the two main competitors for political office in the federal capital of Buenos Aires. Accordingly, I have tried to present as much information as possible on the Radicals to compare and contrast them with the Socialists. In so doing I have focused especially on the principal arenas of combat: election campaigns and the national Congress.

In addition to describing Socialist interaction with other political parties, I have also considered party relations with groups representing special interests. Of major concern have been the party's contacts and influence with organized labor, particularly in the light of Socialist competition with anarchists, syndicalists, and Radicals for the political allegiance of the working classes. Also, I have looked at Socialist attitudes and actions with regard to wealthy landowning groups and industrial and commercial interests.

Although I have presented information on Socialist Party activities throughout Argentina, the major concentration has been on the federal capital. It was in the city of Buenos Aires that the party originated, organized, and enjoyed its greatest strength. Although Socialist activities in areas outside of Buenos Aires were important and interesting, limitations of time, space, and documentation necessitate the focus on the capital.

Considerable attention has been paid to the inner workings of the party itself. At the same time that the Socialists competed with other parties for votes and political office, they competed with each other to represent the interests of Argentina's working classes and to implement socialism in the Argentine Republic. An understanding of internal party politics is crucial to an understanding of the party's actions and role on the larger national stage.

In this study I have compiled and presented as much factual information as possible. I have done so for a variety of reasons. First, because the basic political history of this period has been told only in broad outline in most secondary accounts. Second, because it is my belief that North American scholars should give the same careful, close, and detailed attention to political history in the Latin American setting as is given to the political histories of the United States and Europe. In so doing they will capture the nuances of political developments in the area and avoid some of the misconceptions that have plagued general studies based on inadequate monographic material. Third, because I believe that a concentrated focus on personalities, programs, elections, and activities within governmental institutions best describes the great complexity of Argentine political history. Fourth, because through detail I hope to transfer to the reader, particularly the North American reader, a sense of the flavor of politics in Argentina: its motion, its rhetoric, and its meaning. To this end I have frequently described political meetings, campaigns, and debates and have quoted often from newspapers, periodicals, and public records.

The bulk of this study is narrative description. However, I have attempted to analyze election results through the use of quantitative data and information on the occupational composition of the Buenos Aires electorate. I have also compiled information on the occupational status of Socialist Party leaders and members at large. Furthermore, although this study is basically a political history, I have included material on social and economic developments in the republic, developments that had a direct bearing on the politics of these years. Especially have I concentrated on the emergence of social problems and issues in Argentina and the response of political parties and politicians to these.

The material presented here should help shed light on some important questions of general interest to all students of Latin American politics and history. For example, what factors contributed to the relative success of Argentina's Socialist Party in this period when compared with the frustrations of similar parties elsewhere in the area? And, although relatively successful, why was the Argentine party unable to form a mass base and achieve executive power? How does the Argentine experience relate to the applicability and adaptability of socialism in Latin America in general? Finally, what is the relationship between

the historical development of Argentina's Socialist Party and that country's major political phenomena of the twentieth century, Juan Perón
and Peronism?

In sum, I intend in this work to present a case study of a Latin American political party, stressing factual information and description. Although the major concentration has been on the Socialist Party, I have
tried to depict the overall framework of Argentine political history in
these years, focusing on the interaction of political parties in national
elections and national government. In so doing, I hope to fill gaps in
and add to the scarce literature available on Argentine political history
during a period of party emergence, increased electoral activity, and
growing citizen involvement in government.

The Socialist Party of Argentina
1890–1930

1. Emergence: 1890–1895

> On one side is the Avenida Alvear, and on the other
> an immense barrio of conventillos. . . . On one side
> a rich and indolent class, whose only occupation is to
> vary and display its insolent luxury, contrasted with
> a working class that after a life-time of labor has no
> other prospect than misery.
>
> *La Vanguardia*, April 7, 1894

Argentina's Socialist Party emerged in the 1890s against the background of important changes in the social and economic aspects of national life. In the economic realm, Argentina was, by the end of the nineteenth century, Latin America's wealthiest nation. Economic expansion began in mid-century with the introduction of various technological advances designed to stimulate the production of agricultural goods. For the period prior to 1890 these goods were primarily cereals. After 1890 livestock products became the chief export commodity and contributed to an economic boom of unprecedented proportions. Latin America's most extensive rail system carried grains and meats from the interior plains to the port city of Buenos Aires for shipment abroad.[1]

Massive government-sponsored foreign immigration was an important concomitant to economic growth. Beginning with a yearly average of 5,000 in the 1850s, by 1889 the number of immigrants to Argentina in a single year reached 260,909. For the period 1857 to 1895 a total of 2,117,570 foreigners entered the country. Not all stayed; some came only seasonally, others left when unable to find land or work, still others made their fortune and returned to their homeland. But the balance of immigrants to emigrants by 1895 was nevertheless a respectable 1,484,164. Also, by 1895 immigrants had arrived in such numbers that they represented one-fifth of Argentina's nearly four million inhabitants.[2]

3

Immigrants made a significant contribution to the overall growth of the republic's population, which more than doubled between the time of the first national census of 1869 and the second national census of 1895. Moreover, immigration had considerable impact on the distribution of the population. Most foreigners settled in the large cities along the banks of the Río de la Plata after finding ownership of the rural areas monopolized by already established native landowners. Between 1869 and 1895 the percentage of the total population living in cities of over 2,000 grew from 25 percent to 37 percent.[3] The process of urbanization and the contribution of foreign immigrants to this development was seen most clearly in the city of Buenos Aires. In 1895 the total population of the city, which had become the federal capital in 1880, was 663,854 (from an estimated 177,787 in 1869), of whom more than half, 345,493, were foreign born.[4]

Economic expansion, immigration, population increase, and urbanization affected the growth of various occupational categories in the republic. As table 1 shows, there were significant increases in all categories, but growth was most notable in those groups that formed the bulk of Argentina's emerging middle class—commerce, public administration, jurisprudence, education, fine arts, science, and letters. The total numbers in these categories grew four and five times between 1869 and 1895.

All these developments fed the pride of the nation's leaders, who by the end of the century foresaw Argentina's destiny as a potential world power. However, there were several serious flaws in this generally bright picture. In the economic sphere, much of the growth of this period was due to a heavy inflow of foreign capital investment, especially in the transportation sector. Major investors were British, who after 1852 directed most of the construction and control of railroads, public utilities, and port facilities. Loans and credits for Argentine investors and the government itself were provided by United Kingdom lending institutions. England also served as a major market for the republic's exported agricultural goods and in turn supplied many of the country's imports.[5]

In addition to this dependence on Great Britain, certain other imbalances were evident. One of the most noticeable was that between the city and province of Buenos Aires and the interior. Continuing a process begun in the eighteenth century, wealth, political power, intellectual and scientific expertise, and population increasingly centered in the capital city and its environs. Long the major port in the country, Buenos Aires's influence grew with the economic expansion of the nation.[6]

TABLE 1

TOTAL POPULATION OF THE REPUBLIC, FOURTEEN
YEARS OF AGE AND ABOVE, BY OCCUPATIONS, 1869 AND
1895

Occupations	1869	1895	Increase
Production of primary material	187,923	393,948	206,025
Industrial production	280,540	366,087	85,547
Commerce	39,815	143,363	103,548
Transport	29,429	63,006	33,577
Movable and immovable real estate	5,389	28,445	23,056
Services	120,162	222,774	102,612
National defense	9,062	13,102	4,040
Public administration	4,294	23,934	19,640
Religion	1,473	3,013	1,540
Jurisprudence	1,232	5,661	4,429
Medicine	2,548	4,946	2,398
Education	5,229	18,358	13,129
Fine arts	570	2,598	2,028
Science and letters	508	2,479	1,971
Ambulatory professions	2,787	8,186	5,399
Day laborers without fixed work	163,989	342,493	178,504
Personnel in charge of another	2,217	3,337	1,120
Total with profession	857,167	1,645,830	788,663
Without profession	156,908	805,931	649,023
Total	1,014,075	2,451,761	1,437,686

Source: República Argentina, *Segundo censo*, II, p. *cxlii*.

Another imbalance was between agriculture and industry. Manufacturing to produce consumer goods had not kept pace with agricultural growth in a nation where landowning interests and their trade-
oriented allies controlled government and politics. Although there was
some expansion of light industry around Buenos Aires at the end of the
nineteenth century, official policy did little to encourage or protect native manufacturers. The resultant need to depend on imports, both for
heavy equipment and consumer goods, produced twenty-two yearly
trade deficits between 1864 and 1890, deficits that were only overcome
in later years by massive increases in exports.[7]

Finally, the wealth and income from economic expansion were not
evenly distributed among the population. Economic power and profits
rested primarily in the hands of a small elite. This power was based on
the ownership of extensive tracts of land. The concentration of land in
a few hands had begun following independence from Spain in 1810 and
had accelerated throughout the century.[8] Beyond the large estates, and

particularly in the geographic extremes of the northeast, the northwest, and the far south, oppressive rural poverty remained the lot of the majority.[9]

Despite dependence, imbalance, and inequities, significant changes in economic and social structures had occurred in the nineteenth century. In the political realm, however, for most of the century there were few similar developments.

Following independence from Spain, Argentina underwent two decades of chaos while liberal *unitarios* (unitarists) struggled with conservative *federalistas* (federalists) for control of the new republic. In the 1830s strongman Juan Manuel de Rosas initiated a long period of dictatorial rule, finally broken in 1852. In 1853 the Argentine Constitution, similar in many respects to that of the United States, was promulgated to serve as the governing document of a democratic republic. From 1862 to 1880 three men who had struggled against Rosas, Bartolomé Mitre, Domingo Sarmiento, and Nicolás Avellaneda, served as presidents. These men consolidated the nation, stabilized politics, and oversaw the social and economic growth of the republic. In 1880 Julio A. Roca assumed the presidency and marked the appearance of a new political generation in Argentina. The so-called Generation of Eighty dominated the country's national life until 1916. Roca and his successors continued to promote immigration, investment, economic growth, and the centralization of power in Buenos Aires. Using the strong executive authority inherent in the Constitution, the presidents of this period also employed electoral fraud and administrative corruption to control the nation's political life. This control, used in alliance with economic power, furthered the interests of a tightly-knit elite known as the "oligarchy," composed of landowners, bankers, bureaucrats, and public office-holders, both local and national!.[10]

The Constitution of 1853 said little about elections beyond brief phrases related to the selection of national executive and legislative officials. The formulation of election procedures was left to the national Congress, which in a series of legislative measures sought to lay out the regulations for participation in the political process. Basically, as this legislation evolved through the late nineteenth century, the details of elections became the responsibility of local officials. Voting, which was voluntary and public, was restricted to male citizens eighteen years of age or over. There were no educational or property restrictions. An important feature of the election system was the *lista completa* (complete list) to choose representatives to the Chamber of Deputies. According to this procedure, a list of candidates that won a simple plurality in an electoral district was awarded all of the seats contested.

Although certain aspects of these laws were relatively liberal in comparison with those of other Latin American states, they did not promote significant voter mobilization or participation. The first national census of 1869 listed 333,725 citizens eligible to vote, but it is doubtful that national elections ever attracted more than 10 percent of that number to the polls. Oligarchical control of the electoral system discouraged higher voter turnout.

Another characteristic of nineteenth-century political life in Argentina was the absence of stable and permanent political parties to articulate the interests of competing groups. Politicians, bureaucrats, landowners, lawyers, and merchants coalesced around certain ideas or personalities in loose-knit groups of generally like-minded individuals. But after elections these coalitions often disintegrated until new issues or personalities appeared to renew the pattern once again. Candidate selection usually took place among small groups of men sharing similar backgrounds, points of view, and interests. Political bargaining occurred within the institution of the *acuerdo*, or gentlemen's agreement. Most *acuerdos* were worked out in private between two or three acknowledged leaders or representatives of loosely-formed coalitions.

The major political coalition in the latter part of the nineteenth century, and the closest thing to a stable party, was the Partido Autonomista Nacionalista (PAN) (Nationalist Autonomist Party). Like most such organizations, the PAN had little in the way of a concrete program beyond supporting the status quo. Created by Julio A. Roca, its structure was dependent upon control of the government and personalistic leadership.

In 1890 the tensions between social and economic change and the relative stagnation of the Argentine political system produced a critical turning-point in the country's history. The immediate background to the events of 1890 was an ever-worsening economic situation that the executive leadership could not ameliorate. The President at that time was Roca's brother-in-law, Miguel Juárez Celman. Under Juárez, speculation in land, generous concessions to foreign capital, and a devaluation of the peso produced runaway inflation by the end of the 1880s.[11]

Widespread discontent with Juárez brought to the surface various groups with grievances against the regime implanted in 1880. They included young professionals closed out of the political system, idealistic university students concerned with political reform, federalists who opposed centralization of authority, Catholics who objected to anti-clerical measures enacted under Roca, some *estancieros* (owners of *estancias* or large estates) of newly-acquired wealth, and some military men who had personal ties with the civilian opposition.

These disparate groups found leadership in Leandro N. Alem, a charismatic lawyer and congressman, who throughout the 1880s had spoken out against government corruption and waste. In 1889 Alem and others formed the Unión Cívica de la Juventud (UCJ) (Civic Union of Youth), which determined to support all efforts to assure free suffrage and honest elections, to respect the principle of provincial autonomy, and to advocate efficiency in government.[12]

In 1890 the UCJ acquired additional support, including the backing of former President Mitre. Changing the name of their organization simply to Unión Cívica (UC) (Civic Union), the leaders of the opposition mobilized in mid-year to force the overthrow of the government. On July 26, 1890, Alem, with the backing of some military units, massed his followers in central Buenos Aires, issued a manifesto, and vowed to replace the Juárez regime with a revolutionary leadership that would call new and honest elections. The rebellion lasted only three days, finally defeated under pressure from troops loyal to the government.[13]

"El Noventa," as the uprising came to be known, did produce the resignation of Juárez Celman on August 6. The oft-quoted post mortem statement of Senator Manuel Pizarro, "The revolution, Mr. President, is beaten. But the government is dead," was only partially true. The government of Juárez Celman might have been dead, but the government of the oligarchy was very much alive. Vice President Carlos Pellegrini assumed the presidency in August 1890, included some members of the opposition in his cabinet, and granted amnesty to the rebels. He stabilized finances, created the Bank of the Nation in 1891, and restored the first favorable trade balances for the republic since the early 1880s.[14]

Unlike many previous opposition movements, the Unión Cívica persisted in its activities following the unsuccessful revolt of 1890. In 1891 the Unión split into two camps. Those who followed Bartolomé Mitre and favored some sort of accommodation with the Pellegrini government formed the Unión Cívica Nacional (UCN) (National Civic Union). Those who followed Alem and opposed accommodation formed the Unión Cívica Radical (UCR), more commonly known as the Radical Party.

In the 1890s Leandro N. Alem struggled with his nephew and political associate, Hipólito Yrigoyen, for control of the UCR. After another attempt at armed rebellion failed in 1893, Alem tried to gain Yrigoyen's support for one more revolutionary uprising but found his relative and protegé unwilling to cooperate. Increasingly depressed by his failures to achieve his political aims, and burdened with personal problems, Alem committed suicide on July 1, 1896. The death of Aristóbulo del

Valle, another Radical leader, in that same year, left Yrigoyen as un-disputed head of the Unión Cívica Radical.

Few political movements have been so dominated by one man as was the Radical Party of Argentina under Hipólito Yrigoyen, who indelibly stamped his personality and his philosophy on the UCR. Yrigoyen was born in 1852 in a suburb of Buenos Aires. As a young man he spent some time in the law school of the University of Buenos Aires, the usual training ground for national political leaders, but never received the degree. In the 1870s and 1880s Yrigoyen held a number of posi-tions: police commissioner, school teacher, bureaucrat, and even na-tional deputy from Buenos Aires between 1880 and 1882, most of them gained through the influence of his uncle. There is little evidence that he distinguished himself in these occupations. His major achievements and principal education took place in the realm of politics. Yrigoyen worked side by side with Alem to learn the essentials of political or-ganization. In the 1880s he acquired landed properties that provided him with a substantial income, and this in turn gave him the financial independence to devote most of his time and attention to politics. In 1897 he became a member of the Jockey Club, the oligarchical social institution *par excellence*, and, although not a frequent visitor, never-theless remained a member until his death.[15]

Although Yrigoyen had the ability to move among the upper social circles, he rarely did so. Unlike his gregarious uncle, he seldom attend-ed public functions. He preferred the solitude of his apartment or his *estancia*. He shared few of the social conceits of the oligarchy, dressed modestly, lived with little luxury, and avoided the vices of drinking and smoking. The base of his political strength was an ability to sway peo-ple to his side through face-to-face personal contacts. An atrocious speaker, he only occasionally appeared on the public platform. But in the backroom maneuvering that is often the stuff of politics, Yrigoyen excelled. By the mid-1890s he had used these tactics to gain the adher-ence of most of the younger members of the UCR and had developed a strong base of support in the province of Buenos Aires.

Once Yrigoyen gained control of the UCR in 1896–1897, he com-pletely rejected the "acuerdista" argument and established instead a policy of "intransigence." As Yrigoyen saw it, the existing political sys-tem was hopelessly corrupt and totally under the control of the ruling oligarchy. Therefore, participation in elections and agreements with existing political groups were useless. The UCR would maintain its intransigent position from outside the present framework, applying pressure for change through sheer growth in numbers, increased or-ganization, and the continued use or threat of armed rebellion.

Within UCR ranks considerable controversy swirled around the nature and orientation of the organization. For Yrigoyen and his idealistic and intransigent followers—the *rojos* (reds)—Radicalism represented an ethical, regenerative movement rather than simply a political party. They saw it as a moral crusade, a "cause" that was locked in struggle against the corruption and immorality of the oligarchical "regime." For many *rojos* a political party meant an organization similar to the PAN. The more pragmatic members of the UCR—the *azules* (blues)—stressed the need for structure as a party and eventual participation in elections.

Despite the avowed resistance of Yrigoyen and the *rojos*, the Radical movement gradually acquired the characteristics of a political party. Committees and clubs that had been formed in late 1889 and early 1890 remained as bases for further organization. A January 1891 convention of the Unión Cívica was the first of its kind in Argentina and served as a forerunner for other meetings to choose candidates and to set policy.[16] In November 1892, at another convention, the UCR issued a national charter that set out the details for party structure. The preamble stated that "The Unión Cívica Radical [is] essentially an impersonal political association, into whose ranks may enter all citizens who wish to adhere to its program. . . ." The party's ultimate authority rested with a national convention, which met every six years to choose presidential and vice-presidential candidates, formulate party principles, and amend, if necessary, the charter. Delegates were chosen from provincial conventions and a convention in the federal capital. A national committee oversaw the day-to-day direction of the UCR. Located in the city of Buenos Aires, it was composed of sixty representatives, four each from the fourteen provinces and four from the capital.[17]

With regard to a program, the UCR never spelled out a comprehensive set of goals much beyond support for free suffrage, honest elections, and local autonomy. Radical programmatic vagueness resulted in part from the heterogeneous nature of the UCR. The loosely-stated goals of political honesty and respect for local rights appealed to a broad, national sector of the population, cutting across geographic and class lines. Rarely did the Radicals say anything specific with regard to social-economic conditions or suggest reforms in those areas. Especially in the 1890s and up to 1912 their principal concerns were political. They voiced little dissatisfaction with the basic social and economic structure of the nation, only with its management. And it was primarily political control of this management that they sought.

In sum, although the Radicals lacked a clearly articulated program and some members resisted the appellation of political party, the UCR was clearly different from the political coalitions of the past. With a

permanent organization at the national and local level, a structure designed to survive transitions in leadership, and a determination to take
control of national decision-making through mobilization of the populace, the Unión Cívica Radical bore the earmarks of one of Argentina's
first stable and lasting political parties.[18]

In later years the Radicals gradually came to attract members of
Argentina's emerging middle class. A larger and potentially more
powerful class remained generally isolated from the national political
maneuvering of the 1890s, but also began to organize in these years.

A glance at the occupational figures for 1869 and 1895 in table 1
shows very substantial increases in those categories in which working-
class representation was strong. Between 1869 and 1895 those persons
employed in industrial production increased from 280,540 to 366,087,
in commerce from 39,815 to 143,363, in transportation from 29,429 to
63,006, and in services from 120,162 to 222,774, and those without fixed
employment increased from 163,989 to 342,493.

The bulk of industry and its workers concentrated around Buenos
Aires. Most industrial establishments, and other activities wherein
large numbers of working-class employees could be found, were ordinarily connected with some aspect of the agricultural-export economy.
They usually performed a service function of one kind or another for
the grain and cattle raisers of the interior. The leading industries were
food processing, construction, clothing and furnishing, and metallurgy.
There were no heavy industries such as steel or iron production, and
few mining activities. Most factories were small-scale, employing only
a handful of workers.[19]

By using census figures for 1895 and the categories that will be employed later for voting analysis, some statistical estimate of the size of
the working class in the city of Buenos Aires can be made.

According to table 2, almost 70 percent of the occupied male population of Buenos Aires belonged to categories A and B. Category A included mostly unskilled workers. For example, 27,707 or 35.39 percent
of the total for that category in 1895 included day laborers. Category B
included mostly skilled workers, with masons, carpenters, blacksmiths,
tailors, and shoemakers numbering 49,421 or a little more than 50 percent of the total. Of great future significance for Argentina's Socialist
Party was the fact that 83 percent of those persons in categories A and
B were foreign-born and hence ineligible to vote in national elections.

Beginning in the 1890s, opposing sides debated the state of the living
and working conditions of the proletariat. For the spokesmen of the
oligarchy, when they bothered to consider social problems, claims
of working-class leaders for improved conditions were considered exag-

TABLE 2
ARGENTINE AND FOREIGN MALES OVER 14 YEARS OF AGE BY OCCUPATIONAL CATEGORY, FEDERAL CAPITAL, 1895

Category	Argentine	Percent Total	Percent Category	Foreign	Percent Total	Percent Category	Total	Percent
(A) Manual worker	12,383	19.7	15.8	65,897	34.8	84.2	78,280	31.0
(B) Artisan and small merchant	17,054	27.1	17.3	81,288	42.9	82.7	98,342	39.0
(C) Employee	13,684	21.8	46.8	15,569	8.2	53.2	29,253	11.6
(D) Owner	2,864	4.6	29.0	7,000	3.7	71.0	9,864	3.9
(E) Professional	10,071	16.0	60.2	6,668	3.5	39.8	16,739	6.6
(F) Various and without profession	6,762	10.8	34.4	12,906	6.8	65.6	19,668	7.8
TOTAL	62,818			189,328			252,146	

Source: República Argentina, *Segundo censo*, II, pp. 47–50. For information on the specific occupations included in each category, see Appendix A.

gerated and unfounded. They pointed out, and with some justification, that wages were higher, food was more plentiful and cheaper, and mobility was easier in late nineteenth-century Argentina than in most European and American countries. Why else, they argued, should immigrants continue to arrive at the republic's shores in ever-increasing numbers? In the face of growing labor agitation and organization in the 1890s, conservatives responded with apparently sincere assertions that the basic social and economic causes of class conflict simply did not exist in a prosperous Argentina where all who worked hard lived well. Their answer to a rash of strikes after 1890 was to blame them on "outside agitators" who found cause for grievances where none actually existed.[20]

Critics of these assertions noted that real wages had been cut in half by inflation in the 1880s and 1890s. Although food was cheap and accessible, housing was crowded and inadequate and rents double and triple the value of accommodations. Immigration continued, they affirmed, because the government heeded the demands of agriculturists and industrialists to provide a constant flow of cheap labor. Ignoring advice that immigration be made spontaneous, the government propagandized, paid for passages, and resorted to other less-than-honest devices to attract newcomers to Argentina. Finally, the depth of feeling and commitment on the part of organized workers to suffer as much as four months on strike without pay indicated that the need to improve conditions was a real one and not, as one socialist put it, just the "response to senseless propaganda from a few foreign ringleaders."[21]

It is difficult to judge the exact validity of these opposing points of view in the 1890s. No doubt conservatives and critics both, facing one another from opposite sides of the barricades, tended to exaggerate their respective positions. Nevertheless, the weight of available evidence suggests that those who criticized existing social and economic conditions were more often in the right than their opponents.

The contrast between the living conditions of the oligarchical minority, which had benefited most from the economic boom of the late nineteenth century, and those of the wage-earning majority was seen in the clearest form in the city of Buenos Aires. In the 1880s and 1890s the capital became the showplace of the nation, a city that would be favorably compared with Paris by the time of the republic's centennial celebration in 1910. The profits accrued from foreign trade were directed in part to modernizing and beautifying Buenos Aires. Enjoying this growth were the oligarchs, men of landed wealth who constructed permanent residences in the capital, many modeled after European estates and some covering an entire city block. In the capital they belonged to exclusive private clubs, lavishly furnished and decorated. For vacations they traveled either to Europe or to the beach resort of Mar del Plata some 250 miles to the south.

Most of the new homes of the oligarchs were located in the northern part of the city. To the south and spreading out to the west were the residences of the working classes. The most common proletarian dwelling was a *conventillo* or tenement. These were often wooden buildings two or three stories high with zinc roofs; they contained an interior courtyard for communal cooking, washing, and sanitation. Crowded, unsanitary, lacking municipal services, the *conventillos* were breeding grounds for disease, crime, and social discontent.

Salaries for unskilled workers ranged between two and three pesos a day or between 75 and 125 a month (the peso was valued at about three to the dollar). Skilled workers might receive between three and five pesos daily, barely adequate to provide basic necessities. With the inflation of the 1880s and 1890s and the resulting devaluation of the peso, real salaries in terms of buying power declined by more than fifty percent.[22] This decline forced the wage earner to add more hours to what was often a ten-hour day, and one more day to what was usually a six-day week. In many cases not even overtime was sufficient to sustain a family, and women and children were forced to find employment as well.[23]

Despite the fact that immigrants poured into Argentina in the 1890s, there were many who poured out at the same time. Some wrote of their experiences in Argentina and warned their fellow countrymen preparing to leave the Old World not to expect much better conditions in the New. An Italian immigrant, complaining of his treatment in Argentina at the hands of employers and officials, concluded that "in America there is no justice for the poor, less than in Europe, and the avarice of the rich is nearly criminal as they fill their pockets at the expense of the poor."[24]

In sum, although conditions for workers in Argentina might not have been as bad as in other countries of America and in Europe, they were still far from good. Comparative and relative arguments probably meant little to those who were working long hours for an inadequate salary, which barely if at all provided food, shelter, and clothing. In one sense the conservatives were correct. Much of the social agitation of the 1890s and after was due to the influence of "outside agitators," articulate spokesmen for European socialist and anarchist philosophies. But the grievances voiced and the proletarian nerves touched were not figments of the imagination. To a great degree they were the result of actual conditions, produced by oligarchical policies and largely ignored by oligarchical statesmen.

Throughout the second half of the nineteenth century certain immigrants brought to Argentina not only their skills and labor but also ideas at variance with what were then considered the republic's traditions. Many had participated in European social and political struggles and as a result of their activities had been forced to find refuge in the New World. Influenced by the works of Marx, Engels, Stirmer, Kropotkin, Bakunin, and others, they began to organize in Argentina, particularly in Buenos Aires and Rosario, groups that espoused communism, socialism, and anarchism.

It should be pointed out that militant immigrants were only a small minority among those foreigners who came to Argentina. Those who were militant, however, often exerted influence beyond their numbers. They found in Argentina many of the conditions they had sought to change in Europe and they set about to raise the revolutionary consciousness of the working class. One of their major instruments was the press. Often two- or three-man operations, journals oriented toward the working man and social conditions began to appear with consistency in the 1860s. But if appearance was consistent, so, too, was disappearance. Distribution was limited, few contained advertising, and editors were men of humble means and could keep their publications alive only through sympathetic contributions or personal funding.[25]

The first important socialist organization was the Club Alemán Vorwarts (German Workers' Club), founded in Buenos Aires in 1882. Its journal, written in German and entitled *Vorwarts*, appeared with regularity after its first issue in 1886. The aim of the club was to imitate in Argentina the success of Germany's Social Democrats, but in practice the group had little appeal or following beyond the confines of the German immigrant community.[26]

From the 1870s the ideological struggle that was to mark much of Argentina's radical history was joined. Opposed to the often inchoate and poorly-expressed socialism of this period was a growing anarchist movement. A number of anarchist journals, as short-lived as their socialist counterparts, appeared in the 1870s and 1880s. In 1890 an anarchist newspaper, *El Perseguido* (The Persecuted), made its appearance and soon was publishing 4,000 copies.[27]

The development of working-class organizations along occupational lines paralleled the growth of socialist and anarchist groups. In 1857 typographers in Buenos Aires formed Argentina's first mutual aid society. In 1878 the society evolved into the Unión Tipográfica (Typographers' Union) and carried out the republic's first successful strike action for shorter hours, higher wages, and an end to piecework. In the 1880s and 1890s other groups followed suit and increasingly resorted to militant strikes to achieve their demands.[28]

Against this background of growing labor organization and activity, representatives from various unions met in March 1890 to plan for the first time in the republic's history the celebration of May 1 as the official holiday of the working class. Forming the Comité Internacional Obrero (International Workers' Committee), the representatives also determined to organize a national labor federation, found a newspaper, and present a petition for social and economic reform to Congress.

The May 1 meeting was held in one of the central plazas of the federal capital. Several thousand people heard speeches given in Spanish, Italian, French, and German by men with surnames as diverse as Winiger, Kühn, Mauli, Jakel, Sánchez, Uhle, Gilbert, and Ragazzini, underscoring eloquently the multi-national character of the workers' movement at this time.[29]

A petition to Congress soon followed, signed by more than 7,000 sympathizers. Demands included the eight-hour workday, restrictions on and regulation of child and female labor, abolition of most night work, an uninterrupted thirty-six-hour rest weekly for all workers, prohibition of piecework, state safety inspection of workshops and factories, state sanitary inspection of workers' housing, controls on the sale of food and drink to guard against adulteration, state- and employer-supported insurance against on-the-job accidents, and provisions for collective bargaining. These demands emphasized what the workers' committee viewed as the real and prevailing living and working conditions in the republic. Unfortunately, the conservative congressmen did not agree and the petition was sent to the archives without consideration.[30]

The Comité's aim of organizing a central labor federation was realized in June 1890 with the formation of the Federación de los Trabajadores de la Región Argentina (Federation of Workers of the Argentine Region). However, despite the form of a central labor organization, the reality of unifying the proletariat remained a distant hope. Although workers were generally concentrated in a particular geographic area, differences of nationality and the lack as yet of a real identification with Argentina hindered the formation of a cohesive national federation. Moreover, within the labor movement anarchist and socialist struggles for working-class affiliation proved additional obstacles to cooperation and confederation. Socialists dominated the leadership of the central organization, but anarchists controlled most individual unions. Therefore, when the resolutions of the second congress of the Federación included as one of its aspirations "the possession of political power for the working class," the alienation of the apolitical anarchists was assured, and the federation dissolved in late 1892.[31]

One of the most significant contributions of the federation during its two-year existence was to stimulate the production of a newspaper, El Obrero (The Worker). Begun in December 1890, El Obrero was an important instrument in spreading socialist ideas and publicizing the cause of the working class in Argentina. Many socialists gained valuable journalistic experience and El Obrero's articles and essays forecast themes and issues that would be adopted and expanded later by the Socialist Party. Appearing weekly for two years, El Obrero ceased publication in September 1892 at approximately the same time as the disintegration of the Federación.[32]

Despite the ultimate demise of the national federation of workers and El Obrero, socialists continued to organize in the early 1890s. French and Italian socialists formed groups in 1891 and 1894 respectively. The Spanish-speaking and Argentine socialist element appeared in December 1892 as the Agrupación Socialista (Socialist Group), which in 1893 published six issues of a newspaper entitled El Socialista (The Socialist), intended as a continuation of El Obrero. On July 14, 1894, its members inaugurated official headquarters, located, like the offices of most socialist groups, on the near south side of the city of Buenos Aires. At that time the group changed its name to the Centro Socialista Obrero (CSO) (Socialist Workers' Center). Two months later the center issued a four-point program that stated that: 1) the CSO was a political association whose program was based on the tenets of the international socialist movement, with adjustments for local circumstances; 2) the center would disseminate socialist ideas through publications, lectures, and a library; 3) it would support all efforts at union organization; and 4) "It will attempt as soon as possible to transform itself into the Socialist Workers' Party of the Argentine Republic."[33]

While the Agrupación Socialista was making its gradual transformation to the CSO, the Spanish-speaking members of the socialist community in Buenos Aires tried once again to produce a periodical reflective of their interests. On August 2, 1893, a meeting was called for this purpose at a downtown café. Those who attended were mostly members of the Agrupación Socialista who had been connected with the publication of the now defunct El Obrero and El Socialista. They included two Spanish immigrants, Esteban Jiménez, a typographer and journalist, and Isidro Salomó, a carpenter. Augusto Khün, a type-smelter, was a German immigrant. Víctor Fernández represented the barrelmakers' union. The final figure, and the most important, was Juan B. Justo, an Argentine-born doctor who had recently affiliated with the socialist group.

From the meeting of these men a new socialist periodical was born, *La Vanguardia* (The Vanguard). Like many of its forerunners, *La Vanguardia* was initiated and operated on a shoestring. To get the paper started, Khün contributed 300 pesos and Justo sold the carriage he used to make his medical rounds. The first presses were borrowed from a friendly printer and set up in Khün's house. Despite these difficulties, the first edition appeared on April 7, 1894. Unlike its predecessors, *La Vanguardia* maintained a regular schedule, weekly until 1905 and daily thereafter, as the principal journalistic organ for Argentine socialism.[34]

Juan Bautista Justo was the first editor of *La Vanguardia* and the driving force behind not only its production but also the eventual founding of the Socialist Party. Although he would have objected to the comparison, Justo imposed his personality and philosophy as securely and as profoundly on the Socialists as Hipólito Yrigoyen did his on the Radicals.

Justo was born in Buenos Aires in 1865. His parents were also Argentines, although descended from Spanish and Italian immigrants. His father was a professional administrator of various *estancias*, on which young Juan spent much of his early life. In 1882 Justo entered the medical school of the University of Buenos Aires, where he soon displayed many of the characteristics that would mark his political career: enormous industry and self-discipline, together with a wide-ranging and inquisitive mind that could comprehend a variety of subjects far removed from his immediate specialization.

In 1888 Justo graduated from the medical school, winning the gold medal for his thesis. Deciding to specialize in surgery, he made the first of several trips to Europe in 1889. Visiting Paris, Vienna, and Rome, he concentrated on perfecting his knowledge of advanced surgical techniques. Returning to Argentina, he won another prize for a paper dealing with cranial surgery. In 1892 he was appointed professor of surgery in the Faculty of Medicine and in that same year also became head of the surgical clinic of a major hospital in Buenos Aires. As chief of the clinic Justo introduced basic procedures of personal hygiene and sanitization and sterilization of surgical equipment in a hospital where surgeons often went from examining a diseased cadaver to operating on a still-living body without bothering to wash their hands. Justo, as he saw it, attempted to inculcate modern scientific methods into a backward Argentine medical practice, much as he would later similarly see his role as a practitioner of socialism.

His strong belief in the rightness of what he was doing, his concern for the well-being of his patients and later of the proletariat, and his frustration with those who did not agree with him often produced a brusque and cynical reaction from Justo, not only as a doctor but as a politician. An intense, serious, and sober man, Justo usually resorted to humor only to make an ironical point or to underscore some contradiction. His physical appearance—a stocky, heavy-set frame topped with a bearded and mustachioed face, his short hair parted and brushed to one side, his dress, like that of most *porteños* (citizens of Buenos Aires), dark and conservative—added to the general somber impression of a man with a mission.

Like many Argentine and Latin American doctors, Justo cultivated an active interest in politics. In 1890 he became a member of the directive committee of the Unión Cívica de la Juventud. In that year, however, he opposed military action of any kind and instead suggested a peaceful and purely civilian movement. Justo later claimed to have been ignorant of the planning and inception of the July 26 revolt until the troops had already concentrated. Justo served the cause of the Unión Cívica in the July days by tending to the wounded, but took no part in the fighting. The ultimate result of his opposition to "El Noventa" was to disassociate himself from the Civic Union. As he later put it, "That dishonest and sterile factional struggle [the 1890 uprising] filled to overflowing the measure of my disdain for *la política criolla* [traditional politics] and it was then for the first time that I began to approach a small number of workers already organized in the Agrupación Socialista." [35]

Justo said later that he became a socialist without having read Marx. His original commitment to socialism apparently was motivated primarily by sentiment. As a doctor, he wrote, he dealt with the victims of "misery, fatigue, exploitation, and alcohol." As he saw endless numbers of patients suffering from ills induced by their living and working environment, he questioned whether as a doctor his duty was to treat only the symptoms or instead to attack the causes of these ills. Was it his responsibility, Justo asked, simply to patch over the wounds he treated and send his patients once again to fall into "the gears of a social organization that . . . justified privilege and oppression," or to change the nature of that social organization? [36]

Justo joined the Agrupación Socialista in 1893 and soon became a

prominent speaker before working-class audiences. In 1894 he participated in the establishment of *La Vanguardia* and in 1895 he embarked
on another trip to Europe, this time to study the operations of socialists rather than surgeons. In Europe, Justo held discussions with Emile
Vandervelde and was impressed with the organization of the Belgian
Socialist Party and the development of the cooperative movement in
that country. In Paris he attended sessions of parliament, where he
heard the great French socialist Jean Jaurès, who sixteen years later
would be Justo's guest in Buenos Aires. While in Madrid, Justo completed the first Spanish translation of *Das Kapital*, indicating his now
intimate knowledge of the writings of Marx.[37] It was during this period
that he wrote to his friend and colleague Nicolás Repetto that after
undergoing a "crisis of sentiments" he was planning to devote his life
fully to socialist politics. Returning to Buenos Aires in late 1895, he
turned his considerable intellectual and physical energies to the organization of a socialist political party in Argentina, a party that would
draw upon European experience but be molded to fit Argentine conditions.[38]

Justo's thinking as he entered the socialist movement was a blend
of ideas based on European influences and personal experiences. Although he was attracted to workers' organizations by idealistic sentiments of human betterment, his professional and scientific training
had great influence in formulating his particular brand of socialism.
Like many of his generation he had been greatly influenced by positivism, with its emphasis on evolutionary development, analysis and
structuring of society along scientific lines, and use of scientific and
empirical knowledge to formulate laws concerning human and social
behavior. For Justo, the most important figure in determining his adherence to socialism was not Karl Marx but Herbert Spencer, whose
Social Darwinism owed much to positivism. Justo used Social Darwinism to explain society's evolution into competing and antagonistic
classes. The same philosophy, with a different interpretation, had been
employed by the oligarchical leadership to rationalize political order
and economic progress in the 1880s and 1890s.[39]

Justo strongly favored peaceful political organization and participation. He saw these as the proper means of promoting the interests of
the proletariat and the transition from capitalism to socialism. He drew
inspiration from the successful example of the German Social Democrats and found himself philosophically allied with the revisionism of
Eduard Bernstein and the moderation of Jean Jaurès. In Argentina he
opposed the violent tactics of some anarchists as self-defeating and
counterproductive and the revolutionary and intransigent bent of the

Radicals as a throwback to caudillismo and the worst aspects of traditional politics. Speaking to a socialist group on May 1, 1894, he stated firmly that to realize its ideals and goals the working class must shake itself from its former indifference and enter fully into the political life of the republic.[40]

This call for political action reflected a growing concentration of Argentina's disparate socialist centers into a single political party. In April 1894 representatives of the Agrupación Socialista and French and Italian groups met to form the Partido Socialista Obrero Internacional (PSOI) (International Socialist Workers' Party). The Club Vorwarts and the Centro Socialista Universitario (Socialist University Center) also joined. On April 13, 1895, fifteen representatives, three from each center, met to draw up a charter and to issue a minimum program. José Ingenieros, a nineteen-year-old representative from the university center, presided over the meeting. The charter that emerged from the assembly designated a central committee as the directing organ of the party. The purposes of the PSOI echoed those of the earlier-established Agrupación Socialista: basically, to organize politically, to spread socialist ideas, and to support the labor union movement.[41]

The Central Committee sat in Buenos Aires, met twice a month, and chose presiding officers from among the delegates selected by the adhering centers. Membership dues covered expenses. The committee was independent of the centers, as they were in turn independent of the committee in all matters except those of general interest. The committee called conventions for the selection of candidates for national and local elections, resolved disputes between affiliated groups, and assembled national party congresses.

The PSOI's minimum program placed political reforms at the top of the socialist agenda. Specific articles demanded universal and unrestricted suffrage for national and local elections, including the extension of the vote to females; a shortening of residence requirements for the naturalization of foreigners to one year; the establishment of a proportional electoral system with minority representation; municipal autonomy; abolition of the death penalty; separation of church and state, with suppression of the prerogatives of the clergy and confiscation of their possessions; suppression of standing armies and "militarized" police; and abolition of laws blocking divorce. The social-economic part of the program repeated the original points of the workers' committee petition of 1890, with additional provisions favoring state-supported, free and obligatory, scientific and secular education; state support for the aged, infirm, and orphans; abolition of indirect taxes; and establishment of direct progressive income taxation.[42]

By 1895, then, there were two political parties organized in Argentina to dispute the rule of the oligarchy and the PAN—the Unión Cívica Radical and the Partido Socialista Obrero Internacional. Both shared certain characteristics. They were concerned with political change, they opposed the status quo, and they stressed political organization through chartered groups. Various aspects of their thinking coincided: universal and unrestricted suffrage, a proportional electoral system with minority representation, and respect for municipal autonomy.

But their differences were more significant. First, the Socialist program went much beyond that of the Radicals. Suffrage for women, easier naturalization of foreigners, anti-clerical measures, divorce provisions, and suppression of the military were measures which the UCR not only did not share with the Socialists but actively opposed. Second, the enunciation of the clearly-written program that included provisions for social and economic change set the Socialists sharply apart from the Radicals. Third, the Socialists, who planned to participate in the admittedly corrupt political process with the aim of changing from within and by example, opposed the UCR policy of intransigence and revolution. In sum, the Socialists sought political power not for its own sake but rather to effect significant modifications in Argentine national life. As a party they also hoped to provide a model for modern political organization and activity, a model that would serve to alter permanently the prevailing political culture in the republic.

2. Organization and Recruitment: 1895–1900

> Fundamentally different from other parties, the Socialist Workers' Party does not say it struggles for pure patriotism, but [rather] for legitimate interests; it does not pretend to represent the interests of everybody, but [does represent] those of the working people, against the oppressive and parasitic capitalist class; it does not lead the people to believe that it is possible to arrive at well-being and liberty from one moment to another, but assures them the triumph if they decide for a persevering and tenacious struggle; it expects nothing from fraud or violence, but everything from popular intelligence and education.
>
> From the first electoral manifesto of the
> Socialist Party, February 29, 1896

"El Noventa" and the emergence of Radical and Socialist opposition shook but by no means destroyed the foundations of conservative power in Argentina. For the last decade of the nineteenth century, men representing the views of the PAN and conservative forces generally continued to monopolize the legislative, judicial, and executive branches of government and to control political and economic decision-making. Conservative presidents Carlos Pellegrini (1890–1892), Luis Sáenz Peña (1892–1895), José Evaristo Uriburu (1895–1898), and Julio A. Roca (1898–1904), the dominant figure of the period, concerned themselves primarily with the reestablishment of political order and stability and the recuperation of the financial and economic structure of the nation.

The Radicals, under the direction of Yrigoyen, maintained their intransigent position. Refusing to join coalitions or to participate in

23

elections, the UCR virtually withdrew into itself in these years. By 1898 there remained only one effective UCR organization in the republic, that of Buenos Aires province. For several years, until 1904 and the first meeting of the national committee since 1897, the UCR almost disappeared as a viable national political force.

For the Socialist Party, the late 1890s were years of continued expansion in organization and activity. In April 1896 the executive committee met to plan the first constituent congress, scheduled for June of that year in Buenos Aires. On May 9 the committee presented a report on the state of the party for submission to the congress. It noted in its preamble the shifting and uncertain nature of Argentine socialism in those years, exemplified by the dissolution of the French socialist group and the withdrawal from the party of the Italian socialist group in 1895. Nevertheless, the report noted, organization of adherent groups was proceeding successfully in the federal capital and the provinces of Buenos Aires, Santa Fe, and Entre Ríos. The total number of groups adhered to the party was seventeen. The eleven that had submitted membership figures counted a total of 803 associates, of whom, according to available figures, 348 were Argentine citizens.[1]

The constituent assembly met at 8:30 in the morning on June 28 at the headquarters of the Club Vorwarts. The hall was decorated with red flags representing the participating groups and surrounded with wall hangings bearing the names of socialism's founders. Thirty-five groups with eight-five delegates were in attendance. Representation at the congress was a mixture of middle-class professionals and working-class union leaders, with the direction of both the assembly and the party firmly in the hands of the former.

After the selecting of presiding officers, the first order of business was to consider the party's statutes, declaration of principles, and minimum program. Juan B. Justo, the architect of these documents, introduced them to the congress, stressing that the Socialist Party represented mainly the working class but nevertheless was open to members of other strata willing to subordinate their interests to the interests of the proletariat. The socialist movement, he continued, aimed at the economic betterment of the working class. The party that spearheaded this movement was to be egalitarian and democratic in its internal structure, as provided in its statutes. Beginning thirty years after the European socialist parties, Justo emphasized, the party in Argentina should model itself after continental examples and benefit from the successes and failures already marked. Socialists in Argentina, he observed, should be revolutionaries in the true sense of the word: that is, to seek not just a change of national leadership on the political level but also a profound change in social and economic conditions in the republic. The implementation of the minimum program would bring about this revolution, even though "the scarce political education of the Argentine people obligates us to be modest, and to present only the reforms most comprehensible to all, and of the easiest and most urgent realization."[2]

Following Justo's presentation the assembly approved in general his proposals. The declaration of principles stressed the division of Argentina into two classes: the exploited and oppressed proletariat, living in misery and insecurity and without political power, and the owners of the means of production, living in ostentatious luxury and monopolizing political power. These divisions, in turn, were aggravated by the greed of the wealthy and "the ignorance of the people." The advent of new technology and the use of more machines increased the exploitation of the workers, who could either continue to accept oppression or organize to defend their own interests with the ultimate aim of collectivizing and socializing ownership of the means of production. The declaration concluded "that while the bourgeoisie respects political rights and amplifies them by means of universal suffrage, the use of these rights and the organization of the resistance of the working class will be the means of agitation, propaganda, and betterment that will serve to prepare that force." The wording of the declaration implied political organization and action, working through existing procedures, although more violent means were not excluded if the bourgeoisie should *not* respect present political rights.

The minimum program, composed of twenty-one articles, combined the principal features of the 1895 political and economic programs of the Partido Socialista Obrero Internacional. These included demands for an eight-hour workday (the first article), equal compensation for men and women employed at the same tasks, state safety inspection of factories, monetary and tax reforms, suppression of artificial stimulation of immigration, and universal suffrage for all elections.[3]

The statutes approved by the assembly, subsequently modified, established the general framework within which the party initially developed. With regard to organization, the party was composed of all "political groups, labor societies, circles of social studies and of propaganda, mutual aid societies and cooperatives" that formally adhered to the socialist program and enrolled ten or more members. Affiliated labor groups were urged to become part of a national federation. Three or more groups in a municipality and five or more in a province were urged to form local federations. Article 7 stressed the importance of acquiring Argentine citizenship and underscored the socialist commitment to give women a voice in politics. It read that "only members of the party who have political rights, and the women adhering, divested of these rights by law, will resolve political questions (attitude of the party in elections, designation of candidates, etc.). The other members of the party [those without citizenship] will have their field of action in propaganda, in administrative tasks of the groups, etc." Article 8 ordered expulsion from the party of those who allied with bourgeois parties or candidates.

A general vote was the ultimate authority in directing party matters. Then, in descending order, power was invested in the ordinary and extraordinary congresses, the national executive committee, and provincial or local committees. The general vote took place when three or more groups presented to the executive committee a proposal requiring party approval. The committee then presented the proposal to all groups, any one or several of which could offer amendments. After two months of deliberation, the affiliates of each group voted on the proposal, sending their totals to the national committee. The majority decision became the position of the party. All affiliates decided nonpolitical matters that came to a general vote. These usually dealt with internal structural matters. Only those who possessed political rights voted on political questions.

National congresses were held every two years. Each group sent one delegate for each 100 members. The duties of the congress included hearing and approving the national committee's two-year report on party activities and electing new members to that committee. The decisions of the congress, as of the general vote, were final and binding on the party.

The seven-man executive committee conducted the day-to-day business of the Socialist Party. This committee proved in the long run the most powerful administrative unit within the organizational structure. Members served on the committee for two years, were liable to recall, and were eligible for re-election. Members had to possess national political rights. Committee officers were the secretary-general, treasurer, and two secretaries. The committee carried out the resolutions of the congress or the general vote, organized congresses, handled the mechanics of general votes, administered funds, directed propaganda, assured membership respect for the party program, and established relations with similar parties and organizations in other countries. Local and provincial organizations were also directed by executive committees, members of which had to possess citizenship. Their duties corresponded to those of the national committee.

Official Socialist newspapers and periodicals had to be recognized as such by the national party congress. The executive committee oversaw the publication of the central organ of the party, *La Vanguardia*. That journal was directed by a five-man editorial board elected by the party congress. This board was not part of the executive committee, although the editor-in-chief chosen from its number did have a voice in committee meetings. Any disputes between the editorial board and the committee were resolved in a joint meeting of the two bodies by a majority vote, the seven-member executive committee enjoying an inherent advantage in such contests.

A lengthy article, number 36, dealt with the responsibilities of party members elected to the Argentine national Congress. After election, the legislator submitted his salary to the national committee, which determined proper reimbursement for the deputy, usually about 50 percent of the original compensation. During those periods when Congress was not in session, the Socialist representative was at the disposal of the national committee, which sent him wherever necessary to fulfill his "obligation to dedicate himself to propaganda in favor of the political struggle."

Statutes on party finances stipulated that each group make a regular contribution to the national party treasury. This meant a monthly sum equivalent to ten centavos per adherent. Those members not belonging to a particular group were to submit monthly dues of fifty centavos. The payment of dues was stamped in a member's party card, which became invalid for non-excused failure to pay dues. The balance of the party treasury was published monthly, and each two years a special committee reviewed party accounts. Provisions were established to pay a percentage (usually half) of the traveling expenses for deputies on propaganda missions and for delegates to national congresses.

Disciplinary statutes were the final provisions of the charter. These soon became the most controversial of the party's rules and regulations. They implied very strict adherence to a high norm of private and public behavior, seen by the party's founders as an integral part of socialist action within the Argentine Republic. Articles 56 through 58 obligated all Socialist Party members "to guard within it good administration," to respect the Socialist program, and to report violators of these. Such accusations, if proved, could lead to the expulsion of the violator. The accuser, however, if proved wrong, had to issue a public apology or find himself expelled. A two-thirds vote of a group allowed the non-appealable expelling of an adherent who violated the program or method of action. Articles 59 and 60 established provisions for separating from the party entire groups for similar violations. Article 61 stated that "no affiliate of the party can accept a challenge of arms to resolve personal questions of any kind, being in contrary case separated from the party."[4]

With the approval of its principles, program, and statutes in 1896 the Socialist Party of Argentina emerged as the republic's most clearly articulated and tightly organized political group. There was no doubt as to the party's aims, its philosophy, or the details of its organization. The statutes represented an ideal guide to action. Designed to provide initial flexibility, considerable federalist autonomy, and protection and encouragement for individual expression, their ultimate goal was consolidation of opinion and highly disciplined behavior within certain prescribed regulations. As a theoretical framework to conciliate divergent positions and to maximize effectiveness, the statutes seemed particularly well-suited to an organization made up of different philosophical interests and still small in numbers and influence. As the party developed and entered fully and more actively into national and local politics, the strains between practice and theory led to revisions and modifications of statutory provisions. Nevertheless, the basic intent and framework of the charter remained intact, and much of the political success the party enjoyed in the early decades of the twentieth century was in large part due to its original organization.

The Socialist Party aimed to achieve socialist goals through political means. To this end, in the late 1890s, the party entered candidates and campaigned in three contests: the election of deputies to the national Congress from the federal capital in 1896, 1898, and 1900. Although the results were meager in terms of votes, the experience gained through defeats laid the groundwork for future victories.

The election campaign to renew five of the capital's deputy seats on March 8, 1896, was the first entered, even prior to the formulation of statutes and program. Candidates were selected at a general meeting held on February 9 at the headquarters of the Club Vorwarts. Those in attendance and those selected were restricted to Argentine citizens. Although the details of candidate selection underwent many changes in later years, the Socialists pursued throughout a commitment to a democratic method in this process. In 1896 each group proposed five candidates, not necessarily members of that particular group. Juan B. Justo, for example, was a candidate from almost every adhering center. The party assembly then chose the final candidates by majority vote. The list for 1896 was composed of Juan B. Justo (doctor), Juan Schaeffer (shoemaker), Adrián Patroni (painter), Germán A. Lallemant (engineer), and Gabriel Abad (fireman). Argentine electoral custom required that parties participating in elections make up their own candidate lists to serve as ballots. For these first elections it was the custom of the Socialists to note the professions of their candidates, presumably to underscore the mixture of proletarian and middle-class professional backgrounds.

The election platform, divided into two parts, repeated the principal aspects of the minimum program. At the top of the "Parte Política" was "Universal and unrestricted suffrage for national and local elections, extended to women," and leading the "Parte Económica" was the "Workday of eight hours for adults, and six for those between 14 and 18, and the abolition of work for those less than 14."

This original campaign contained many of the characteristics of subsequent efforts. Despite scarce financial resources, the Socialists threw themselves into pre-electoral activity with furious enthusiasm and energy. They published and distributed 20,000 copies of their program and several thousand lists of their candidates, and affixed 8,000 posters to fences, walls, and sides of buildings in the federal capital. They tried to hold a number of pre-election rallies and lectures, but difficulties in acquiring access to assembly halls produced only three such meetings, one each in the working-class districts of San Cristóbal, Barracas, and La Boca. *La Vanguardia* was an important campaign tool. It published articles and editorials on the importance of voting and political participation and provided detailed information as to election laws and procedures. In a typical pre-election editorial, *La Vanguardia* urged all Socialists and workers to vote and argued that the casting of ballots would make the Argentine working class "awaken to the consciousness of its rights" and upset for the *clase rica* (wealthy class) of Argentina "the tranquility with which until now it has surrendered itself to the easy task of exploitation."[5]

The final results of the elections were as expected. The "acuerdistas," or Mitre-Roca coalition, received 6,965 votes and captured all five seats contested. The Radicals won 5,258 votes, and in the "various" category were 570 votes, 138 belonging to the Socialist list. In the nine parishes where the election was held, Socialist totals ranged between 5 and 20. The conservative press agreed with the radical press that the March 8 balloting had been a "typical" Argentine election, that is, marked by fraud, bribery, coercion, and an indifference that produced only 12,793 votes in a city with a population estimated at close to 700,000 inhabitants.[6] As it so often did after elections, *La Vanguardia* urged Socialists to concentrate on educating workers on the hows and whys of their exploitation, getting foreigners nationalized, improving the means of propaganda, and increasing socialist solidarity.[7]

Despite the lopsided results of 1896, the party continued to present

candidates in congressional contests. In late March 1898 fifteen Socialists were chosen for deputy elections the following month. The
platform was again a distillation of the party's minimum program,
topped by a demand for the eight-hour day. Preelectoral activity paralleled that of 1896. Party manifestoes and programs were printed,
some 5,000 for pasting on walls, some 15,000 for hand-to-hand distribution. Three lectures were held on the Sunday before the election. The
party stressed voter education and provided a center for electoral information in each of the six parishes where voting was scheduled. *La
Vanguardia* published in full those articles of existing electoral laws
that had special relevance for the Socialist constituency.

The results of the April 10, 1898, contest were disappointing for the
Socialists, who received only 105 votes in six parishes. Once again the
kind of fraud that led Hipólito Yrigoyen to adopt a stance of non-
participation prevailed.

Disappointed but undaunted, the Socialist Party entered a list of
candidates for the congressional elections of March 11, 1900. Although
the party continued to campaign faithfully and vigorously for its candidates, editorials in *La Vanguardia* suggested that these activities were
carried out more to provide experience and an educational example
than in hopes of actual victory. On the day preceding the election a
La Vanguardia editorial "to the people" began, "Citizens: Even when
fraud is not going to be avoided, the best protest is to demonstrate to
the corrupt politicians that one fraction of the people does not renounce the exercise of the vote, that it is disposed to continue coura-
geously in the task of bringing political education to the masses so that
some day soon we shall not be offered the sad spectacle of the so-called
política criolla."[8] After another "typical" election, in which the Socialists received 135 votes to the acuerdistas' 15,618, *La Vanguardia* stated
optimistically that, although "today our votes are few, tomorrow they
will be more and afterwards much more, until we form, like our European comrades, an immense phalanx of workers ready to oppose corruption and fraud and to make these conditions disappear."[9]

The corrupt electoral system was not the only stumbling block to
Socialist political effectiveness. The party encountered serious difficulties in convincing foreigners, who composed the bulk of the working
class, to become naturalized citizens and hence eligible to vote. During
the late 1890s Juan B. Justo wrote a series of articles on this subject,
primarily in response to arguments in foreign-language newspapers
that advised immigrants to retain their European citizenship. These
sentiments were particularly strong within the Italian community, the

largest foreign group in Argentina. Italian-language papers asked why the Italian should renounce his most cherished possession, his nationality, to enter into a political system where many natives had no voice or vote. Justo's reply was obvious. Only by acquiring political rights, he argued, could the immigrant hope to change a system whose abuses affected all who lived in Argentina. There was little sense, for example, in complaining about national monetary policies that had a detrimental effect on the working class unless the foreign members of that class were equipped at least with the minimal requirement to change those policies—the right to vote.[10]

Justo's exhortations and other efforts had little impact. Many foreigners who arrived in Argentina at this time planned to remain only long enough to earn their fortunes and return to Europe. Moreover, immigrants enjoyed the protection of the Argentine Constitution in most particulars (except for the right to vote and to hold public office) even without citizenship. Although the qualifications for naturalization were simple (two years of residence), the procedures were complicated and became more so in later years. Also, by the first decade of the twentieth century, citizenship for males implied obligatory military service. Finally, the argument of the Socialist Party for naturalization, that is, its effectiveness politically, had little influence among those recently arrived who neither spoke the language nor as yet identified with the nation. Those who were aware of the political realities in the republic were dubious that much could be accomplished in a situation of limited suffrage and oligarchical control.[11]

Accordingly, the number of foreigners who adopted Argentine citizenship remained pitifully low. The second national census of 1895 counted only 1,638 naturalized Argentines.[12] By 1904 this figure for the federal capital, where most naturalization occurred, was only 5,133, and by 1909 it stood at a mere 8,149 in a total city population of 1,231,698.[13]

Another problem for the Socialists in mobilizing the proletariat politically was the increasing influence of anarchists in the labor movement. The Socialists viewed the anarchists as disorganized and disorderly romantics whose activities only served to heighten official repression. Nevertheless, in the late 1890s the anarchists began to sway many politically-minded workers in their direction.

Anarchism, like socialism, was first introduced into Argentina and sustained primarily by foreigners. From the 1870s and 1880s a strong stress on individualism marked Argentina's anarchists, many of whom advocated direct and violent action against institutions and persons representing the authority of the state. In 1885 Italian anarchist Enrico

Malatesta arrived in Buenos Aires for a four-year stay, during which he tried to move Argentine anarchists away from reliance on individual action and toward collective organization and federated activity.[14] Another Italian anarchist, Pietro Gori, arrived in Buenos Aires in 1898. Gori continued the work of Malatesta and urged Argentina's anarchists to concentrate their efforts on working-class organization rather than sporadic, individualistic acts.[15]

Gori's call for organization found a sympathetic response with anarchist leaders like Inglan Lafarga and Antonio Pellicer Paraire. Lafarga was a Spanish-born cabinetmaker who in 1897 helped to found and edit the principal anarchist newspaper, *La Protesta Humana* (Human Protest), which in 1909 changed its title simply to *La Protesta*. Pellicer Paraire was born in Barcelona, the center of Spanish anarchism, in 1851. Forced into exile for his radical activities, he settled in Argentina in 1891 after traveling in Mexico, Cuba, and the United States. A typographer by profession, he became one of the leading figures in Argentine anarchism and along with Gori, Lafarga, and others helped to lead the shift from individual effort to labor union organization at the turn of the century.[16]

Although the individual emphasis remained as an important ingredient of Argentine anarchism, and occasionally produced isolated attempts on the lives of public officials, from 1900 the organizational strain dominated. The goal of the anarchists was to use working-class organization as a revolutionary tool to destroy the state. The main instrument of action to achieve this goal was the general strike, which would paralyze the economic activities of Argentine society and eventually undermine the foundations of government. At the same time, the anarchists also worked for specific and immediate improvements in the social-economic position of the workers affiliated with their organizations.

As Socialists and anarchists struggled for working-class support in the 1890s, another contender entered the fray. Reflecting the spirit of Pope Leo XIII's famous encyclical, *Rerum novarum*, Catholics in Argentina began to form their own working-class groups as alternatives to those inspired by radical thought. The first such group, the Círculo Central de Obreros (Central Workers' Circle), was founded in Buenos Aires in February 1892. The circle stated that its aim was "to defend and to promote the material and spiritual well-being of the working class, in marked opposition to the baneful propaganda of socialism and impiety, which, by making deceitful promises of ephemeral happiness, leads the worker to temporal and eternal ruin and transports to all society incalculable evils." The activities of this first circle, and of those that followed, included the provision of aid, particularly medical, for its members, elementary and professional education with a "solid and religious" base, lectures on themes of interest to the proletariat, promotion of unions, and the convening of congresses to formulate "points of common interest."[17]

Father Federico Grote was the driving force behind the founding of the workers' circles. Born in Germany in 1853, he arrived in Buenos Aires in 1884 and devoted his first attention to studying social conditions. He devised the circles as instruments "to form Christian workers, strong in the faith of Catholic morality and duly prepared for a good individual, familiar, and social life." Between 1892 and 1900 Catholic worker circles were set up in various districts of the capital and in principal cities of the interior. Beginning with one unit of 60 associates in 1892, their numbers grew to forty circles with 10,400 members by 1900. In 1898 thirty-three of these met in the first congress of the Catholic workers' circles, where they discussed needed social legislation. The next year, 1899, they presented a proposal to the national Congress for the promulgation of a law of obligatory Sunday rest for all workers.

Grote frequently debated Socialists and anarchists in public meetings.[18] Their arguments added to a swelling national discussion over the nature of social conditions in Argentina and the means to their amelioration. Moreover, Catholic concern with the plight of the republic's proletariat served to stimulate sympathetic public figures to initiate and support progressive social legislation. Catholic workers' organizations did not openly endorse candidates or engage in overt political activity, but they did have close contacts with certain influential public men. These politicians, in turn, represented Catholic interests in the legislative and administrative branches of government.

The 1890s in Argentina were years of mounting intellectual activity and excitement. As the country tightened its economic ties with Europe and continued to hold its doors open for foreign immigrants, almost every conceivable philosophic and literary mode and movement entered the country and influenced a young and receptive Argentine intelligentsia. And Buenos Aires was the focal point of this growing intellectual life. It was in the capital that intense and energetic young men met in classrooms, cafés, and salons to discuss and to argue the new world of thought opening up in the republic. It was in Buenos Aires that plays were produced, poetry read, novels written, and a growing number of literary and philosophic journals published.

Several key figures of the young intelligentsia associated with the

Socialist Party during the late 1890s. Three of the most important were Roberto J. Payró, José Ingenieros, and Leopoldo Lugones, all beginning notable careers as men of letters who would enjoy continent-wide reputations in later years.[19] All three participated in the constituent congress of the Socialist Party in 1896 and were prominent as lecturers, essayists, and journalists for various Socialist publications.

In 1897 Lugones and Ingenieros co-edited a short-lived journal entitled *La Montaña*, which during its brief existence attacked the national leadership in shocking and spectacular terms. In addition, both Lugones and Ingenieros disagreed with the reformist orientation of the Socialist Party and tried to move it toward a more revolutionary position. In one *La Montaña* article, for example, Ingenieros castigated those Socialists who sought to play down the revolutionary consequences of socialist thought and action to attract petit bourgeois elements to the party. "Socialist and revolutionary," he concluded, "are two inseparable qualities." [20]

Within a few years after the 1896 constituent assembly, Ingenieros, Lugones, and Payró all severed their connections with the Socialist Party. Although each had his own reasons for breaking his ties with the party, in the cases of Lugones and Ingenieros disagreement with its reformist philosophy and the rigid application of disciplinary statutes were important considerations. However, at the same time these three left the party, other able young men entered. Two in particular, Enrique Dickmann and Nicolás Repetto, were to share with their close friend and ally, Juan B. Justo, the leadership of the socialist movement in Argentina in the early twentieth century.

Dickmann and Justo first met in November 1895. Both had attended a meeting that the police had disrupted, arresting those they could capture. Sleeping on the same jail-cell floor for three days and nights, the two men established a friendship that was to last for more than thirty years.[21]

As Justo came to know Dickmann he must have been impressed by his new-found friend's biography. Born in a small town in northern Russia of Jewish parents in 1874, Dickmann was forced to leave his homeland as a young man to escape poverty and religious persecution. He elected to emigrate to the New World. He arrived in Argentina penniless and alone in November 1890. In the early 1890s he cooperated with three other men in farming one hundred hectares of virgin land on a Jewish-owned-and-administered agricultural colony in the province of Entre Ríos. Working as a rural laborer, Dickmann came to know the social and economic conditions of the republic's interior. By 1894 he had saved enough money to provide food and shelter for his mother, father, and three younger brothers, who arrived in Argentina in that year. With his family ready to take over his farming chores, Dickmann decided to leave Entre Ríos and seek an education in Buenos Aires. He arrived in the capital in May 1895 and sought entrance to the university. Told he must first receive the graduation certificate from a secondary school or *colegio,* Dickmann completed the necessary examinations in three years and entered the medical school of the University of Buenos Aires in 1898. After six years of study, marked by summers working in the fields of Entre Ríos and a student's penury that often reduced him to a weekly diet of oranges, Dickmann graduated with honors in 1904. In 1905 he assumed a position as chief of clinic in the San Roque Hospital, which post Juan B. Justo had held a decade earlier.

In the space of fifteen years Enrique Dickmann had realized the dream of many immigrants. Through hard work and perseverence he had received a university education and by 1905 was embarked upon what seemed an assuredly successful professional career. Married in December 1904 to Luisa Campodónico, daughter of Italian immigrants, he opened his own medical office in 1905. But his professional career alone was not sufficient for Dickmann. Parallel with his commitment to medicine was an equally strong commitment to the republic's fledgling socialist movement. While a student he had spent one of his hard-earned pesos on a subscription to *La Vanguardia.* On June 1, 1895, he became a member of the Centro Socialista Obrero. In 1896 he contributed the first of many articles to *La Vanguardia* and also gave the first of many lectures.

Dickmann's early publications and talks stressed the non-violent and evolutionary aspects of the Argentine socialist movement. He had become a socialist, he later remembered, primarily from an innate sentiment "to defend the weak." As he studied philosophy, theory, and medicine under the guidance of Justo, he formed a scientific base for his thinking, echoing the positivist socialism of his mentor.[22]

In 1897 Dickmann acquired Argentine citizenship. The following year, his younger brother, Adolfo, became a member of the Socialist Party while still a student. Graduating in 1905 with a degree in dentistry from the medical school of the University of Buenos Aires, Adolfo Dickmann also became a Socialist activist and rose to influential positions within the party organization. As politics and eventual election to local and national office began to take up the majority of their time, the Dickmann brothers paid less and less attention to their medical careers. As with many of their Socialist colleagues, working for the party became their real and consuming profession.

Nicolás Repetto was born in Buenos Aires in 1871. His parents were Italian immigrants from Genoa and, according to Repetto, were of the hard-working "petite bourgeoisie, of no substantial fortune."[23] They were of substantial enough fortune, however, to enroll their son in the medical school of the University of Buenos Aires in 1888. For most of his university career Repetto was a Radical Party sympathizer and affiliated with a student branch of the UCR. As a student, however, he came into contact with Dr. Juan B. Justo, who impressed upon him the connection he saw between socialism and the practice of medicine.

Repetto was not immediately converted to socialism, but his initial exposure to this philosophy through Justo was the first step toward eventual commitment. Between 1894 and 1897 Repetto traveled in Europe and amplified his knowledge of advanced European medical techniques. Like Justo, he specialized in surgery. In 1895, while in Switzerland, Repetto received a letter from his mentor confirming Justo's intention of devoting his full attention to socialist activities. This news stimulated further Repetto's curiosity with regard to socialism, and he began to study pertinent literature in Europe. Returning to Argentina in 1897, he recalled subsequently that "I felt that the Radical Party no longer satisfied me. I did not find in it precise, clear, fundamental goals that could move a man to true political action."[24] Consequently he began to participate in Socialist Party activities. After receiving his medical degree in 1898 he aided Justo in the publication of a socialist newspaper, El Diario del Pueblo (The Newspaper of the People), and in 1900 became an official party member.

In addition to Enrique Dickmann and Repetto, two other medical students from the University of Buenos Aires contributed to party development in the 1890s. Angel M. Giménez was born in Buenos Aires in 1878. He received his degree in medicine in 1901, writing his thesis on working-class hygiene. As a student he helped José Ingenieros form the Centro Socialista Universitario and was a delegate to the constituent congress. In 1898 he organized the Sociedad Luz, which aimed to educate the working class through the popularization of subjects of particular proletarian interest. Located in the heart of the working-class district of Barracas, the Sociedad Luz underscored the Socialists' desire to provide inexpensive and accessible educational opportunities for the workingman, not only to recruit adherents and voters but also to offer different experiences and open new horizons for a class commonly confined by the walls of factory or conventillo.

One of the most active participants in the Sociedad Luz was Augusto Bunge, who joined the Centro Socialista Obrero in 1896 while a third-year medical student. Bunge was born in Buenos Aires in 1877, the son of a supreme court justice and member of a distinguished and wealthy *porteño* family. He received his medical degree from the University of Buenos Aires in 1900 and, like his Socialist contemporaries, held various teaching and hospital positions in addition to his political activities. Within the party and through the Sociedad Luz he lectured on topics related to the physical and mental health of the working class, particularly concentrating on the problem of alcoholism.

Augusto Bunge, Angel Giménez, Nicolás Repetto, Enrique Dickmann, Adolfo Dickmann, and Juan B. Justo, then, were all either students at or graduates of the medical school of the University of Buenos Aires. Their affiliation with the Socialist Party stemmed from a variety of factors. Some, like Justo and Repetto, became Socialists in part because of disaffection and disagreement with the Unión Cívica Radical. The personality and philosophy of Juan B. Justo influenced Repetto and Dickmann. Moreover, the often unstated but powerful motivations of political ambition, the desire to belong to a romantic and somewhat exotic movement, an idealistic concern for the underdog, and youthful rebellion against the conventional probably also played roles. But one underlying factor that all seemed to share was the influence their actual medical training and experience had on their decision to join the Socialist Party. To one degree or another they saw themselves, as students or doctors, dealing only with the results rather than the causes of social ills, with curative rather than preventive medicine. Internship and public health service had given them a close look at the products of an Argentine social system in which they, with the exception of the Dickmanns, held privileged positions. They began to question their roles within that system and determined to change those conditions that produced human misery and suffering. Real preventive medicine, they concluded, implied social and political action. As Repetto put it, "The implementation of the eight-hour workday has improved the physical and mental state of the masses to a much greater extent than would have been possible with the application of numerous hygienic precepts and individual cures. . . . "[25]

It should also be noted, however, that although doctors were a significant segment of the Socialist Party leadership, Socialist doctors were only a tiny minority within their profession. The national census of 1895 listed a total of 646 "médicos" and 71 "dentistas" in the federal capital, and of these only a handful were associated with Socialist politics. Moreover, the influx of medical men in the 1890s, and their assumption of important positions, should not overshadow the fact that many others who affiliated with the party during this period were of humbler backgrounds and working-class professions. A partial listing, for example, includes Eugenio Albani (commercial employee), José D. Castellanos (customs clerk), Francisco Cúneo (electrician), Domingo de Armas (typographer), Felipe Di Tella (tailor), José M. Lemos (mechanic), Manuel T. López (employee), Jacinto Oddone (wood-lathe operator), Basilio Vidal (commercial employee), and Antonio Zaccagnini (typographer, railroad employee).

The Socialist Party in the late 1890s engaged in recruitment, the development of internal party organization, and the continued formulation and fulfillment of programmatic attitudes and activities. Recruitment was carried out through individual effort and influence, the holding of regular lectures and meetings—usually in the evenings or on Sundays—and electoral campaigns. The Socialists established offices, ordinarily in private homes, where interested individuals or groups could adhere to the party. These locations were published periodically in *La Vanguardia*, which began to expand its format in these years and to serve also as an important means of attracting new members.

Party membership during these years fluctuated considerably. In 1896 the party listed a total of nineteen adhered groups, but in 1898 this figure had dropped to eleven. By 1900 the number rose to sixteen. Nine of these groups were located in the interior and reflected the gradual expansion of the socialist movement out from Buenos Aires. *La Vanguardia* listed agents for the newspaper in such major interior cities as Azul, Bahía Blanca, Junín, Mercedes, Mar del Plata, and Quilmes in Buenos Aires province and the cities of Córdoba, Rosario, and Santiago del Estero. The total number of affiliates was not published, largely because of irregular and inconsistent statistical reporting from the constituent groups, but dues-paying members probably numbered between 1,000 and 1,500 by the turn of the century.[26] The number of members who participated actively in party affairs, however, was no more than 10 to 15 percent of the total. General votes listed in *La Vanguardia* for 1898 and 1899 varied from approximately 100 to 200 Socialists, the lower figure being the most frequent.

While the Socialists saw to the details of organization, they continued to express concern for the position of the proletariat with the hope of mobilizing them politically. One tactic in this regard was to publicize working-class conditions. Articles in *La Vanguardia*, for example, described the low pay and long hours of the laborers in the customs houses or the personnel of the British-owned streetcar companies. In October 1898 *La Vanguardia* began regularly to list reported on-the-job accidents, noting the name of the worker and the extent of his injury and keeping a running tally of the total number for the week, month, and year. The party also expanded its celebrations of May 1, holding rallies and publishing special editions of *La Vanguardia* printed on red paper. Finally, the Socialists supported and occasionally collaborated in various strikes. The most important of these was an 1896 walkout by railroad employees at the works in Sola, Junín, and Campana in Buenos Aires province. This strike, for an eight-hour workday and an end to piecework, lasted four months. Socialist collaboration included the raising of finances, the publication in full of grievances and actions, and the printing of special editions on the strike, with proceeds from their sale going to the strike fund.

Although Enrique Dickmann later remembered that "the Socialists had a very active and efficacious participation" in the 1896 walkout, the party's programmatic attitude toward strike action underwent important modifications at this time.[27] During the railroad stoppage *La Vanguardia* forecast this change, stating that Socialists did not provoke or encourage strikes as such but, once strikes had been called, joined to provide leadership and encouragement and to prevent the strikers from being inspired by "some fanatic," an obvious reference to anarchist influence.[28]

Juan B. Justo argued that to go on strike was better for the workers than submission to unjust conditions. Strikes did produce a sense of proletarian solidarity and showed a willingness to resist capitalist exploitation. "But the strike," Justo concluded, "is a rudimentary form of struggle, it is a passive, negative action; in a strike the workers unite only to do nothing. For this reason the results are so meager, and obtained at the cost of so many sacrifices. Only in active effort, only in the political struggle and in cooperative association, can the working class acquire the knowledge and the discipline, which they now lack, to achieve their emancipation."[29] With these problems in mind, the third Socialist congress of 1900 amended the statutes of the party to state "the duty of adherents to support and develop union societies," while also resolving that "the party will not lend its support to strikes that are declared [when] the societies that initiate them are not in conditions to confront them."[30]

The Socialists based their strike position on sound principles. Walkouts should be well planned, well executed, and adequately financed. They should promote solidarity and serve to concentrate rather than diffuse efforts, to achieve solid benefits, not to increase or aggravate existing miserable conditions. If these criteria were not met, the Socialists reasoned, strikes should not be initiated or, if initiated regardless, then not supported. Despite the soundness of this position on strike action it contained definite conservative connotations for a growing and increasingly militant working class just beginning to flex its muscles in the economic and political arena. The Socialists' cautious attitude on the advisability of strike action clearly handicapped the party when competing with anarchists, syndicalists, and independents for working-class support. Although the Socialists held sway in the ranks of organized labor in the late 1890s, their predominant position was soon to fall to their more militant rivals.

Another central concern for the Socialists in these years was the complex problem of national monetary policy. From the fall of Rosas in 1852 to the end of the nineteenth century the national legislative and executive branches attempted to impose some order and stability on a very confused and disorderly monetary structure. The establishment of a national banking system over these years brought some uniformity and control, but another major problem—the lack of a sound and consistent metallic base for the Argentine peso—plagued the economy and public administration. The falling value of paper money, particularly in the 1890s, drastically reduced the real wages of the middle and working classes. Finally, in 1899, the national executive initiated and the legislature, after bitter debate, agreed on a conversion law to stabilize the peso. A government bureau, the Caja de Conversión (Conversion Office), was established to convert pesos to gold or vice versa at the set rate of one paper peso to 0.44 centavos of one gold peso.

Exporters, who benefited directly from the controversial reform, received conversion favorably. Importers, who paid for goods abroad in gold, resisted the measure.[31] So, too, did Socialists, who viewed the conversion law and establishment of the gold standard as a direct attack on the buying power of the wage-earning classes. Socialists argued not so much against the fact of pegging the peso to gold, since stability implied at least some control on speculation and inflation, but against the rate of conversion, 44 centavos gold to one paper peso. This, they argued, was an arbitrary and unrealistic figure that further depressed salaries and increased the cost of living.

On monetary policy, as well as on most other issues, Juan B. Justo was the Socialist Party's chief spokesman.[32] His thinking was most often expressed in public lectures or the pages of *La Vanguardia*. For a short while, however, from October 1, 1899, to November 30, 1899, he published his own newspaper, *El Diario del Pueblo*. Its first editorial stated that *El Diario* "will combat the *política criolla* of the inept and rapacious oligarchy that burdens the country. Will defend the working people of the cities and the countryside. . . . Will sustain a foreign policy of free and pacific commerce, the democratization of military institutions, [and] the entrance of the foreign population into national politics."[33]

Articles in *El Diario* forecast future areas of Justo's political concern. Particularly did he state his opposition to the conversion law, to the artificial stimulation of native industry through special privileges and protection, and to government encouragement of foreign immigration. Indicating a change he himself would introduce into the national Congress, Justo also criticized the lack of legislative attention to the formulation and approval of the national budget, which, he argued, "is the most important function of legislative assemblies in all civilized countries. While this has not been fulfilled, they [legislatures in 'civilized' countries] do not consider any other issue. Here it is reversed. The legislators first occupy themselves with all kinds of things and, at the tail end of all other issues, vote the budget quickly . . . [with] no other purpose than to obtain favors for their clients."[34]

Socialist criticisms of the oligarchy and its political representatives, be it the colorful prose of the young literati or the acerbic phrases of Justo, were only minor irritations for national administrations in the late 1890s. Although police harassed Socialist meetings and the Congress suggested legislation restricting political activities, on the whole the party organized, developed, and functioned free from official restraints. The laissez-faire attitude of the government was largely due to the party's small size and reformist position. After the turn of the century, when an increase in labor militancy produced bloody general strikes, anarchist-influenced direct action, and a renewed revolutionary attempt by the Unión Cívica Radical, conservative officialdom reacted to any and all opposition, peaceful or violent, with stern repressive measures. Socialist Party development during this period would be frustrating and difficult, but it would proceed.

3. Repression and Growth: 1900–1910

Like a resounding sea the multitude advances,
Perpetual energy creative and destructive,
The multitude passes destructive and creative,
With their faith, their strength, their hymn, their flag.
And during the combat that their clamor shatters
The pampas become silent, the city becomes silent
And even life itself stops and waits.

> From a poem by Mario Bravo, "Canción a la huelga general" (Song of the general strike)

Political action is for us one of the means we consider useful for the emancipating work we have undertaken, an instrument that the bourgeoisie has placed at our reach and of which it would be stupid not to take advantage.

> From a pre-election editorial in *La Vanguardia*, July 15, 1905

The first years of the twentieth century in Argentina saw a continuation of economic expansion and conservative political control. In the economic realm Argentina recorded its most impressive growth to date. Exports of cereal products, coupled with a monumental increase in the overseas sale of frozen beef (from 24,590 tons in 1900 to 245,267 tons in 1910) produced ten years (1900–1910) of consistently favorable trade balances. For these same years railroad mileage, another indicator of growth, increased from 16,563 kilometers to 27,994 kilometers. After a hesitant start at the beginning of the century, immigrants poured into the country at a rate far surpassing all previous years. In

43

1900 a total of 105,902 foreigners entered Argentina, while 55,417 emigrated, leaving a balance of 50,485. Ten years later, in 1910, 345,275 entered, 136,405 left, with a resulting balance of 208,870. Public works, port improvements, and the spread of telegraph and telephone lines proceeded apace.

Within this framework of economic growth, and despite the challenges of the new political parties that had appeared in the 1890s, the conservative oligarchy still monopolized politics and government. Conservative kingpin Julio A. Roca was president of the republic from 1898 to 1904. Conservative Manuel Quintana, born in Buenos Aires and a graduate of the University of Buenos Aires law school, succeeded Roca in the presidency. Like other presidents of this period, Quintana had acquired considerable legislative and administrative experience prior to becoming chief executive, having served as deputy and senator in the national Congress and as Minister of the Interior under President Luis Sáenz Peña. As Interior Minister, Quintana played a crucial role in defending the government during the Radical revolt of 1893. Seventy years old in 1905, Quintana found the strains of office too much for his health and resigned in 1906 in favor of his vice-president, José Figueroa Alcorta. Figueroa Alcorta, a lawyer and politician from Córdoba, had been a national senator before his election as vice-president. Stern and unyielding, he proved a strong opponent of political and social reform and a staunch supporter of conservative interests.

During their administrations, Roca, Quintana, and Figueroa Alcorta were compelled to deal with increasing political and social discontent and dissent. In the early years of the new century the Radicals recovered from their earlier divisions to grow in numbers and to pose new threats to conservative omnipotence. Of equal concern for the oligarchs was the growing militance of urban labor, which, under anarchist influence, frequently resorted to the general strike and acts of violence against proprietors, public officials, and the police.

Government reaction to labor agitation in the 1890s had been to ignore labor demands and to depend on employers and the police to handle strikes and demonstrations. By the turn of the century, however, the number of workers engaged in strike action, the aggressiveness with which they pressed their demands, and the damaging effects their movements produced for the national economy led the national administration to a more active policy of official repression of radical elements. One method was the state of siege, a power granted to the executive branch to suspend constitutional guarantees under unusual circumstances. In the early twentieth century conservative administrations applied this instrument to deal with anarchist-inspired general strikes and perceived threats to national stability resulting from individual violence. From 1902 to 1910 the state of siege was imposed in Argentina five different times for a total period of eighteen months.

The state of siege allowed the government to severely restrict freedom of assembly and expression. In practice, this meant the police were given unlimited authority to prohibit public demonstrations, in these years usually related to strikes, and to prevent the appearance of the opposition press. However, the suspension of individual rights was basically an ex post facto measure, intended to halt the spread of already initiated agitation. In 1902 and 1910 conservatives introduced two legislative measures designed to strengthen and supplement the state of siege and to discourage radical action. On November 22, 1902, following a widespread and successful general strike, both houses of Congress approved the first of these, the "Ley de Residencia" (Residence Law). Introduced by conservative Senator Miguel Cané, who patterned the law on European measures to restrict anarchist and labor agitation, law 4,144 gave the executive branch the authority to "order the expulsion [from Argentina] of any foreigner whose conduct threatens national security or disturbs public order." The chief executive could also prohibit the entrance into the republic of any foreigner with "antecedents" that indicated he might disrupt "public order."[1]

In later years government spokesmen claimed that the Residence Law was an efficacious instrument, used sparingly, carefully, and only when absolutely necessary. However, by 1910 conservatives agreed that the Residence Law was no longer sufficient to meet the challenges of the day. Congress approved a more comprehensive measure to deal with "outside agitators," the "Ley de Defensa Social" (Social Defense Law), on June 28, 1910. The law was passed in the space of a few hours after a bomb exploded in Buenos Aires's Teatro Colón. Police blamed the explosion on an anarchist named Romanoff, although the case against him was never proved. Nevertheless, in the emotion-charged atmosphere following an attack upon one of the oligarchy's proudest monuments, restrictive legislation to prevent further such outrages met only token opposition from those who questioned the constitutionality of some of its clauses.

The initial article of law number 7,029 prohibited the entrance into the republic of "anarchists and other persons who profess or preconceive an attack by whatever means of force or violence against public officials or governments in general or against the institutions of socie-

ty." Article four allowed the executive branch to expel from the country any non-citizen who succeeded in entering the country in violation
of this law or the Residence Law. Other articles prohibited "all association or meeting of persons who have as an object the propagation
of anarchist doctrines" and the use of "emblems, standards, or flags"
representing anarchist sympathies. As with the Residence Law, the
new provisions broadened the scope of executive action and singled
out anarchists for specific attention.[2]

Within the legal framework established during this period, the
police had the major responsibility in enforcing the provisions of the
state of siege and the Residence and Social Defense laws. Most militant
activity took place within the federal capital, and the police of the
capital were most often at the forefront of government repression of
these activities. The national executive chose the chief of police for
the capital and directed him through the Ministry of the Interior. Between 1896 and 1912 four of the five capital police chiefs were from
military backgrounds.[3] These men developed police forces and tactics
especially to control public demonstrations associated with protest activity. Special squadrons, mostly on horseback, were crucial for crowd
control and dispersal. The cavalry, often composed of Indians and
mestizos from the northern provinces, skillfully employed steeds and
sabers in their intimidations of or charges against the largely foreign
demonstrators. When the number of demonstrators or strikers grew
beyond the ability of the police to handle them, or when strikes spread
throughout the republic, the national government called on the army
and navy to aid in the restoration of order.

The overall pattern of police-labor-radical relations in the early
twentieth century was one of mutual antagonism. For the police, in the
words of one chief, anarchist associations were "true schools of crime,"
and the Socialists, although more respectable and pacific, also served
to produce a "tendentious incitation in favor of class hatred" just as
dangerous to public order.[4] For the Socialists, the police represented
the cutting edge of official repression and the protectors of the capitalist class. Not content with simply enforcing restrictive laws, Socialist
spokesmen contended, the police actively hindered protest activity by
denying out-of-hand permission for peaceful demonstrations and encouraging *agents provocateurs* to disrupt labor meetings or to urge a
violent course sure to lead to increased repression. Jacinto Oddone,
himself active in the socialist movement at the beginning of the century, observed that "the police were constantly an element of disturbance, of corruption, of confusion and of obstruction. . . . "[5]

During a decade when Argentine society appeared inextricably locked in a vicious circle of violent action and reaction, the basically reformist and non-violent Socialist Party often found itself trapped in the middle between the extreme measures of the anarchists and the constraining tactics of the conservatives. Particularly in trying to attract working-class support did the party find it difficult in this period to achieve the proper political stance.

For the first years of the twentieth century the anarchists prevailed within working-class groups. Moving actively into established unions and helping to form new ones, anarchists speeded the pace of working-class organization and broadened the concept of labor action to include use of boycotts and the general strike. They enjoyed particular success with port workers, both in Buenos Aires and Rosario. Soon they inspired a number of successful strikes. In November 1902 in Buenos Aires the fruit handlers in the central fruit market and in Barracas struck for the recognition of their union and a series of benefits. When employers refused to accept their demands, other unions, including the port workers and teamsters of Buenos Aires, struck in solidarity. The strike soon became generalized in the capital and spread to Rosario and other cities in the interior. On November 22 the government responded with the first state of siege designed to deal with a labor disturbance and the enactment of the Residence Law.

The position of the Socialist Party in this first general strike underscored the difficulties of a middle-of-the-road posture in a period of increasing polarization. Although the Socialists opposed the actions of employers and the government and sympathized with worker demands, they could not accept the general strike. Basing their objections on principles enunciated in the 1890s, they argued that the general strike, in the long run, would prove of little value and serve as an excuse for further government repression. During a period of high unemployment, as was the case in 1902, to add to this unemployment by walking off the job weakened rather than strengthened the workers' economic position. A party manifesto deplored "the attitude assumed by some unions upon declaring themselves on strike for the simple spirit of solidarity with the handlers, stevedores, and teamsters, an attitude that is determined by anarchist propaganda and is counterproductive." The best way to show solidarity, the manifesto told the workers, was to stay on the job and contribute part of their salary to the strike fund.[6]

Caught in a situation not of its making but to which it had to respond, the Socialist Party first offered to serve as mediator between the strikers and the government. When the national administration imposed the state of siege and enacted the Residence Law, the party argued against a more widespread general strike and instead advocated a continuous opposition through political action.

The government directed most of its repressive measures against the anarchists. Several were slated for deportation. Others left the country before the deportation order could be effected, many going into exile in Montevideo. Still others were imprisoned without charge or trial and subjected to severe physical punishment. Police raided anarchist headquarters, forced them to close, and prohibited publication of journals like the anarchists' *La Protesta Humana.*

Although the Socialists were not made specific targets, they also suffered from the general repressive policies. Police imprisoned Socialist workers, shut down Socialist centers, and forbade the appearance of *La Vanguardia* during the state of siege, although the paper continued to publish clandestinely in defiance of the law. Also in 1902 police closed the Socialist periodical *La Luz,* published in the sections of the city where many worker-police confrontations took place.

Despite the divergence of their tactics, then, Argentina's anarchists and Socialists were thrown together in joint suffering at the hands of officialdom. The year 1904 offered further examples of that involuntary entanglement. On May 1, Socialists and anarchists held separate meetings of celebration in Buenos Aires. The Socialist gathering, which *La Vanguardia* claimed some 40,000 people attended, took place without incident. The anarchist demonstration, beginning as usual with an assembly in one plaza and a march to another, was halted en route when an incident between marchers and a streetcar provoked what appeared to be a pre-planned police charge. A mounted squadron, wielding sabers and firing revolvers, attacked a tightly-packed crowd, including women and children, and left a toll of one worker dead and many wounded. Although not a Socialist but an anarchist rally had been attacked, the Socialists responded as though they themselves had been the objects of the police charge. The party condemned the violent action in a public manifesto against the "barbarous assault" of May 1, labeling it a "violation of fundamental rights, as well as the expression of a contemptible hate toward the Argentine proletariat on the part of the police, before which the Socialist Party cannot remain indifferent. . . . "[7]

In the second half of 1904 a number of strikes occurred in the tense atmosphere that followed the May Day tragedy. In the federal capital the Socialist Party supported and sometimes even encouraged these actions. Responding in part to growing anarchist strength among organized labor, the Socialists advocated well planned and well financed "partial strikes." These were to be realized with the "greatest decorum and order on the part of the workers" so as not to provoke police or government intervention. In November 1904 *La Vanguardia* reported current Socialist-supported strikes among a number of unions.[8]

In that same month a strike of commercial clerks in Rosario for the eight-hour day and Sunday holidays produced a police reaction that resulted in several workers killed and wounded. The incident touched off a widespread demand for a nation-wide general strike. Anarchists quickly began to organize the protest. The Socialists planned their usual demonstration and manifesto, but when the Buenos Aires police chief refused them permission to hold their meeting they too adhered to the general strike call. Urging all members to support the strike and counseling workers to proceed with "the necessary calm and tranquility" to avoid "the repressive action of armed force," the party termed its participation in the strike a necessary political act in a time of crisis when all other channels of protest had been closed.[9] The strike, which made its greatest impact on Rosario and Buenos Aires, causing a shutdown of most commercial and industrial activities in the two cities, lasted for forty-eight hours through December 1 and 2. The Socialists saw the general walkout as a demonstration of the political power of a united proletariat and underscored the need to continue a political as well as economic struggle. They viewed the general strike as a measure of last resort to be used sparingly and with caution and control.

In February 1905 the Socialists once again were submitted to a blanket government repression prompted by a development not of their own making. The Unión Cívica Radical, quiescent since the mid-1890s, had slowly reorganized under the leadership of Hipólito Yrigoyen. In late 1904 and early 1905 Yrigoyen planned a third UCR uprising against the government. Counting on the support of some sympathetic army units, the Radicals initiated a series of attacks against public offices and transportation-communication centers in the republic's principal cities. The rebels failed, however, to gain control of the key area in the country, and the area where they were politically strongest—the province of Buenos Aires. Swift government action in the province forced Radical units in the interior to surrender with little resistance. The whole rebellion lasted only a few hours of February 4, 1905. For the Radical leaders, participation in this abortive uprising meant short terms in prison or foreign exile in nearby Chile or Uruguay until a general amnesty was proclaimed in 1906.[10]

The Socialist Party condemned the February revolt. Blaming the

national government for creating conditions that produced such violence, and equally blaming the Radicals for resorting to violence, the
party urged the working class to remain apart from "these quarrels
provoked by an unmeasured thirst for power and petty ambitions" and
to conserve their energies in the "fortifying and consolidating of your
economic and political organization with the object of obtaining your
most rapid liberation."[11]

Socialist opposition to the rebellion notwithstanding, the government included the party in the general reaction that followed the
February outbreak. On the day after the uprising, February 5, the
national administration imposed a ninety-day state of siege, closed
Socialist and labor headquarters, prohibited meetings, and deported
militants. La Vanguardia did not appear from February 11, 1905, until
May 13, 1905. With some justification the Socialists complained that
they had been forced to pay a higher price for the Radical rebellion
than the Radicals themselves.

The pattern continued unabated from 1905 to 1910. Probably the
most serious confrontation occurred on May 1, 1909, when police under
the direction of Chief Ramón L. Falcón attacked an anarchist demonstration in the capital, leaving scores of wounded and eight dead. All
radical groups, including the Socialists, responded to the attack with
a call for a general strike to demand the resignation of Falcón. From
May 3 to May 8 normal activities in Buenos Aires came to a halt. Shops
were closed, transportation facilities ceased to function, and municipal
services were cut to a minimum. Clashes occurred between strikers and
police, and when these threatened to escalate into a civil war the army
was called in to patrol the streets of the city. The national Department
of Labor estimated that 150,000 workers left their jobs during the
course of the strike.[12]

Finally, on May 8 strike leaders met with government representatives to resolve the conflict. The government refused to force the resignation of Falcón but did accede to other demands and released imprisoned workers, allowed the reopening of labor halls closed by the
police during the strike, and abolished certain municipal work regulations seen by union leaders as anti-labor. The strikers agreed to return
to work on May 10. One of Argentina's most serious civil disturbances
in the twentieth century, the "General Strike of the Week of May,"
was over.[13]

The Socialist Party had been active during the strike. The executive
committee and La Vanguardia had done an effective job of rallying
and organizing strike support. Socialist lawyers were at the forefront
of legal actions connected with strike activity and served as interme-

diaries between labor and government, forecasting a task often undertaken by attorneys connected with the party during periods of working-class agitation. The Socialist Party, often accused by anarchists of remaining passive when repression increased, or of standing aside when the going became hot and violent, stood its ground against police intimidation and harassment, held meetings forbidden by official decree, and saw leaders like Juan B. Justo arrested for strike activity. Although the party still disavowed the general strike as an acceptable weapon, the Socialists proved their willingness to resort to this measure if the circumstances so demanded and to accept the consequences of such action.

While the Socialists continued to eschew violence as a method of political opposition, other groups and individuals did not. On November 14, 1909, the Argentine radical movement's principal *bête noir*, Police Chief Falcón, accompanied by his secretary, Juan Lartigau, returned from a funeral at the Recoleta Cemetery. As his carriage reached an intersection, a young man approached and hurled a bomb into the interior, killing Lartigau outright. Falcón was rushed to a nearby hospital but died on the operating table. The assassin was an eighteen-year-old Russian immigrant, Simón Radowitsky, employed as a mechanic and known to be an anarchist sympathizer. In his trial Radowitsky claimed to have been incensed by the police massacre of demonstrators on May 1, 1909, and had determined to do "something practical" to avenge the working class.[14]

The assassination of the chief of police of Buenos Aires, a major symbol of Argentine law and order, was one of the most spectacular events of this bloody period. Following on the heels of the May week, the act strengthened the hand of those who favored renewed and increased official constraints. The assassin himself was sentenced to perpetual imprisonment. The government's opponents again suffered the consequences of the state of siege, imposed for sixty days beginning November 14. Once more headquarters were closed, newspapers censored, meetings forbidden, and militants deported. At one point during this fourth suspension of constitutional guarantees, all the personnel of *La Vanguardia* were jailed. The Socialists again, as they had after the three previous states of siege, sharply criticized the government for resorting to this measure instead of considering the basic social-economic conditions that produced grievances and led to extreme acts. After the lifting of the suspension of guarantees, the party issued a manifesto that disassociated the Socialists from the assassination of Falcón but that also attacked the government for its repressive response. A Socialist-organized rally to protest government actions was held on January 23, 1910, and was attended by some 20,000 people.[15]

Manifestoes and meetings, however, proved of little avail during this period of growing tension. In the early months of 1910 another confrontation loomed as Argentina prepared to celebrate the centennial of the republic's independence, a centennial to be attended by statesmen from neighboring countries as well as visiting European royalty. The anarchist-led Federación Obrera, in a petition to the Minister of the Interior during the first week of May, demanded the abrogation of the Residence Law, a lifting of the penalty for those who violated the law of obligatory military enrollment, and an amnesty for those jailed or exiled because of radical-labor activities. If these demands were not met, the Federación planned to call a general strike during the centennial celebration.

The official response was predictable. On May 14 the Congress declared a three-month state of siege. On that same day, groups of private citizens, composed primarily of young members of the oligarchy, armed themselves and prepared to attack opposition headquarters as soon as the state of siege was announced. Fearing such an attack, the Socialists requested police protection, and a picket of security forces was sent to guard the editorial offices of La Vanguardia. However, when a group of young "patriots" arrived to sack the offices the police mysteriously disappeared. To cries of "¡Viva la patria!" the attackers overturned the presses of La Vanguardia. They then moved on to party headquarters, where they wreaked similar havoc, destroying files and furniture and setting fire to books collected for the Socialist library.

Juan B. Justo rushed to police headquarters for assistance as soon as these attacks began. Told by the police that there was no one around to help him, Justo returned to the offices of La Vanguardia to repel the attackers as best he could, and, in what must have seemed to him a nightmare, found himself arrested for disturbing the peace. As La Vanguardia put it, "In the local police station the only one detained for the assault on and destruction of our newspaper was its director!"[16]

This reactionary decade served to accentuate and accelerate the divisions and rivalries between Socialists and anarchists, despite their momentary periods of alliance. Nowhere were these divisions clearer or more acute than in the development of organized labor.

At the turn of the century various labor leaders, mostly Socialist in their sympathies, again attempted to achieve greater working-class solidarity through the creation of a unified, national central labor confederation. After some preliminary groundwork, a meeting for this purpose was held in the capital on May 25, 1901. Attending were forty-nine representatives of twenty-seven different organizations, including anarchists Pietro Gori and Héctor Mattei and Socialists Francisco Cúneo and Adrián Patroni. Although no spirit of compromise permeated the gathering, sufficient flexibility produced the outlines of a new central entity, the Federación Obrera Argentina (FOA) (Argentine Workers' Federation). The principles of the FOA reflected the belief that the new body could remain viable only by rejecting any connection of any kind with any political group, anarchist or socialist. The Federación recognized the general strike as "the supreme base of the economic struggle," but also approved working-class pressures to urge Congress to enact social legislation. The administrative committee of the Federación included Socialist Cúneo and anarchist Mattei.[17]

The temporary alliance did not last long. At the next congress of the FOA, in April 1902, a procedural debate over the seating of a delegate from La Plata led the Socialist members of nineteen unions representing 1,789 workers to walk out of the meeting, leaving the congress and the central organization in anarchist hands. Twenty-nine organizations representing 7,630 workers remained in the federation. Those who remained represented a mixture of skilled and unskilled workers, with the two largest groups being stevedores (3,200) and coach-drivers (1,200). The second congress reaffirmed the importance of the general strike to achieve working-class demands and added the boycott and sabotage as means to bring about "efficacious results for the workers' cause."[18] In a subsequent congress in 1904 the FOA changed its title to the Federación Obrera Regional Argentina (FORA) (Argentine Regional Workers' Federation) and in 1905 voted 54 to 2 to approve the following resolution: "That it [the fifth congress of the FORA] approves and recommends to all its adherents the broadest propaganda and illustration, in the sense of inculcating into the workers the economic and philosophic principles of anarchic communism [by which was meant anarchism]."[19]

From 1902 to the end of the first decade of the century the FORA remained anarchist. Some of those who left the Federación in 1902 regrouped the next year to form a rival organization, the Unión General de Trabajadores (UGT) (General Union of Workers). Meeting in March 1903, seventy-five delegates representing forty-one unions gathered at the Club Vorwarts to draw up statutes and principles. The UGT took a more moderate stance on the general strike, which, the Unión stated, "can be an efficacious means of struggle [only] when it is declared [in light of] previous organization that offers possibilities of triumph; that it can be useful in questions that directly affect working people and as an act of resistance and of protest; that it [the UGT] absolutely rejects the general strike any time it is intended for the ends of violence and revolt, considering that far from favoring the proletariat it determines in all cases violent reactions from the capitalist class, which contributes to the weakening of the workers' organization."[20] Although the congress stressed that the Unión had no ties with any political group, it was clearly under Socialist influence and numbered among its directors Socialists Francisco Cúneo, Alejandro Mantecón, Luis Poggi, and Basilio Vidal.

During the social agitations of 1903 and 1904 the actions and ideas of the UGT and the Socialist Party often coincided. Party and Unión speakers shared the same platform, issued similar manifestoes, and joined in collective protest against government repression. At the third congress of the UGT in August 1905, however, the ties between the Unión and the Socialist Party weakened. Reflecting a growing split within the party itself, the increasingly influential syndicalist faction largely replaced Socialist leadership. Drawing upon many of the same European intellectual roots as the anarchists, the syndicalists sought to divert the labor movement from politics to a concentration on working-class organization. Syndicalists agreed with socialism's analysis of history and society and socialism's major goals, but believed "that the revolutionary action of socialism rested fundamentally in the syndical organization of the workers." Referring to the Socialist Party's emphasis on politics and parliamentarianism, the syndicalists argued that "no action at the margin of this force [working-class organization] can be considered . . . genuinely socialist."[21] With this emphasis as a foundation, the third congress of the UGT approved a resolution that sought to overcome differences between Socialist and anarchist organizations and pave the way for joint action with the FORA.

The fourth congress of the Unión General de Trabajadores, held in December 1906, marked the definitive syndicalist takeover of the organization. Outnumbered by the Socialists in terms of delegates, the syndicalist representatives outmaneuvered their adversaries procedurally. They instituted votes in the congress on the bases of total number of adherents, wherein they represented the majority. Again the issue of the general strike defined the lines between those who would lead Argentine labor. The syndicalists forced through a resolution echoing anarchist sentiment and rejecting the more cautious approach of the Socialists. After describing the contributions of the general strike to working-class solidarity, the resolution concluded: "The Fourth Congress declares that the general strike is an efficacious instrument, and advises the proletariat to empower itself to exercise it, without limits of any kind, since it should surge spontaneously in the moments and circumstances when it is required." The new officers of the UGT were all syndicalists, thereby effectively ending Socialist control of the Unión, although Socialists continued to adhere and to participate.[22]

By 1906, then, the anarchists and syndicalists had closed out any significant Socialist leadership in the two major central labor organizations of the day. The implications for the Socialists were serious. For the moment, at least, Argentina's organized workers seemed more attracted to an emphasis on revolutionary action, independent and apolitical union organization, and immediate and concrete social-economic improvements than to the gradualist, parliamentary approach of the Socialists, particularly in a period of repression and continued tight oligarchical control over political life. These difficulties would persist for the party, to one degree or another, for several years to come.

The general congruence of goals and tactics between the UGT and the FORA prompted another attempt to fuse disparate syndicates of the nation into a central organization. Anarchists and syndicalists, representing by this time the majority of organized labor in the republic, met in Buenos Aires in March 1907 to consider fusion. Socialist representatives and independents also attended. The results of the meeting disappointed those who sought increased solidarity. The FORA spokesmen demanded adherence to anarchist principles, Socialists continued to defend parliamentarianism, and syndicalists rejected partisan philosophies and politics for a concentration on pure trade-union organization and action. As Jacinto Oddone summarized it: "After each congress of fusion, working-class forces remained more divided than before."[23]

A September 1909 congress made a final attempt at unification. The refusal of the FORA even to attend doomed the meeting to failure. The change of name from UGT to Confederación Obrera Regional Argentina (CORA) (Argentine Regional Workers' Confederation) was the only real achievement of this gathering. Syndicalist in its leadership and sympathies, the CORA proclaimed itself "purely economic," opposed to "all political and religious parties," and seeking "a free federation of free associations of free producers."[24]

In sum, confusion, complexity, and frustration characterized the history of Argentine labor organization at the turn of the century. Statistics on union affiliation reflect these characteristics. Although no comprehensive figures are available for this period, anarchist Diego Abad de Santillán claimed that the FORA contained forty-two groups with 15,212 members in 1903 and sixty-six groups with 32,893 members in 1904.[25] Socialist Jacinto Oddone traced the number of unions attached to the UGT from forty-one in 1903 to a peak of ninety-five in 1906 to a low of twenty-six in 1909.[26] The national Department of Labor surveyed a number of unions in the federal capital to gauge membership. A summary for 1908 disclosed forty-five workers' associations in Buenos Aires, with a combined membership of 23,438 dues-paying adherents out of 214,370 workers in the represented professions.[27]

These statistics show uneven and fluctuating union affiliation. Overall, the organized central federations probably did not represent more than 10 percent of the total work force. The difficulties union leadership faced in attracting more members paralleled those of the Socialist Party in seeking to mobilize the proletariat for political action. Conflicts among competing ideologies, the cosmopolitan nature of the proletariat, and the need to pay dues, even the relatively small fee of fifty centavos, undoubtedly discouraged many from affiliating with newly-established organizations.

Despite the low percentage of workers who actually belonged to unions, however, it should be mentioned that at moments of crisis many non-affiliated members joined in protest actions. Speaking of the Federación Gráfica Bonaerense (Buenos Aires Printers' Federation), one of the most successful unions in the capital, the Department of Labor noted that "in times of agitation this last figure [1,974 active members of about 6,200 in printing trades] grows a great deal, and when a strike breaks out . . . almost all workers in this profession obey the determinations of the Federación. . . . "[28]

Between 1907 and 1910 the Department of Labor also collected statistics on strikes in the federal capital. These showed a total of 785 strikes with the participation of 204,146 strikers, a marked increase over previous years. The increased incidence of strikes, however, did not always mean a corresponding efficacy of strike action. The department divided strikes into three categories: "Favorable," wherein all the demands of the strikers were met; "Partial," wherein some of the demands were met; and "Unfavorable," wherein none of the demands were met. For the 1907–1910 period, 278 strikes involving 20,337 strikers were classified as "Favorable"; 95 with 3,682 participants were "Partial"; and 412 with 180,127 strikers were "Unfavorable." The failure of labor agitation to end with a higher percentage of favorable results stemmed from the inability of poorly-financed unions to support long walkouts, the greater political and financial power of management, and the successful repression of labor and its allies.[29]

Despite states of siege, repressive legislation, police and right-wing harassment, and the continued use of electoral fraud and corruption, the Socialist Party grew in size and organization in these years. The holding of regular congresses provided one proof of party viability. The Socialists held six ordinary congresses and one extraordinary congress between 1901 and 1910.

These congresses dealt with both general national issues and specific party concerns. The resolutions that emerged focused on the restrictive policies of the government and how best to respond to them. The convened party members collectively criticized the laws of Residence and Social Defense and called for their abrogation. The fourth congress recognized "the importance of the general strike" but the sixth congress rejected by a vote of 1,232 to 238 a proposed amendment to the declaration of principles that read, "without omitting recourse to violence in case it be necessary." The Socialists determined to distinguish themselves on this issue from anarchists, Radicals, and the government, rejecting violent action and placing their reliance on the ultimate efficacy of peaceful political participation.

The seventh ordinary party congress considered the struggle with the syndicalists. The rival ideology had been first introduced into Argentina by an Italian journalist, Walter Mocchi, who in 1903 and 1904 used guest columns in La Vanguardia to expound the syndicalist point of view. At about the same time, party adherents who had been exposed to syndicalism in France tried to convince their Argentine colleagues of its efficacy. In 1906, the syndicalists finally managed to gain control of the UGT. In the seventh congress the Socialist Party, by a vote of 822 to 222, approved the following resolution: "The Seventh Congress would be pleased to see the group of affiliates titled Syndicalists constitute themselves into an autonomous party, with the object of realizing the experimental proof of their doctrine and tactics." The syndicalists, along with several centers, accepted this politely-worded invitation and withdrew from Socialist ranks. Those who remained noted, as they would in subsequent years when further schisms occurred, that the separation was "healthful" for the party because it allowed the Socialists "to follow their normal and organic route" and "demonstrated in practice how false and illusory were their [the syndicalists'] doctrines and methods."[30]

The revision of party organization also took place within national congresses. An important reform was a 1903 resolution that foreigners who entered the party, to remain in good standing, had to acquire Argentine citizenship within one year of entrance. The 1908 congress changed the name of the party to Partido Socialista, dropping the word Argentino from the title.[31]

Between 1901 and 1910 the number of groups adhering to the Socialist Party grew from twenty-one (ten in the capital, eleven in the interior) to thirty-six (fourteen in the capital, twenty-two in the interior).[32] Outside the capital the larger cities of the province of Buenos Aires contained the greatest number of Socialist groups. The southern port of Bahía Blanca had the first Socialist center in the province in 1897. It was followed by other centers in Tres Arroyos and Avellaneda (1899), Junín (1900), Lobos (1901), Morón and San Nicolás (1902), San Pedro (1903), Tigre (1904), Quilmes, Mar del Plata and Pernal (1907), and Azul (1910), many of which, it should be noted, were close to the federal capital.[33]

During this period Socialist centers also appeared in major interior cities like Rosario, Córdoba, and Tucumán. Mendoza, farthest removed of any from the capital, saw the establishment of a Socialist group in April 1900. Thirty-three affiliates, a mixture of artisans and intellectuals, met in a local restaurant to found the Mendoza branch.[34]

The major concerns of Socialist groups in the interior paralleled those of the central party: to organize for participation in the political process, to win elected office, and to enact legislation that would better the lot of the working class. Generally, groups in the provinces faced greater difficulties in achieving these goals than did their comrades in Buenos Aires. Electoral fraud and corruption seemed to increase proportionately the farther removed one was geographically from the capital. Local leaders, usually associated with the conservative apparatus, exercised nearly dictatorial control over their bailiwicks. *Estancieros* found it a simple task to discourage those who lived or worked on their land from organizing politically. The great distances of the provinces and the scattered and basically apolitical nature of the rural working classes compounded Socialist difficulties. Nevertheless, seemingly unconquerable obstacles never prevented the Socialists from trying. In 1900 the Socialist committee of La Plata, the capital of the province of Buenos Aires, put forth Juan B. Justo as candidate for the senate of the province. After a campaign in the fashion of the capital centers—lectures, pamphlets, posters—their efforts came to naught, for Justo did not gain a single vote according to the official tabulation, even though various affiliates had voted for him. Provincial groups, nevertheless, continued to present slates and programs for local and national elections. They failed to gather many votes or victories but prepared themselves for better days ahead and established a permanent presence on the political scene.[35]

The growth of the Socialist Party in the interior implied an inclusion of new elements and concerns. The party's major focus remained on the city of Buenos Aires and the urban proletariat. But to attract rural workers to the cause, the party began to make some program-matic adjustments to include agricultural problems in its philosophic and tactical overview. Many leaders realized that if the Socialists did not attract agricultural workers and small farmers and develop a base in the provinces, where the majority of the general population still resided despite the growth of the metropolis, the party had little chance of seizing national political power.

Juan B. Justo first called attention to rural problems. At the turn of the century, Justo spent two years as a country doctor in the small provincial town of Junín, located in the center of a large agricultural region in the province of Buenos Aires. In Junín, Justo helped to or-ganize a Socialist center, a mutual aid society, and a cooperative. But as important as Justo's impact on Junín was Junín's impact on Justo. There, through personal observation and long conversations with owners, tenants, and workers, he learned first-hand the sometimes grim facts of rural life. In April 1901 Justo presented a lecture on "El pro-grama socialista del campo" (The Socialist rural program) in which he described and analyzed contemporary agricultural conditions as he saw them. The overwhelming fact of rural life, he argued, was the ownership of large tracts of land by a few. Eighty percent of those who worked the land were not owners but tenants, dependent for their livelihood not only on the caprices of nature but also on the caprices of the *estancieros*. The Socialist program on these matters, he con-cluded, should aim toward assuring the security of the renter by re-ducing, through progressive taxation of land, the power and the hold-ings of the owners.[36]

At the fourth party congress, the first to be held outside of Buenos Aires (La Plata, July 7–8, 1901), Justo introduced changes in the minimum program to deal with agricultural matters. Approved by the congress, these included, "Abolition of taxes that encumber agricul-tural and livestock production," "Direct and progressive taxation on income from land," "Exemption from direct taxation for small rural property," "Indemnization for renters who leave capital improvements in the fields they use," "Hygienic regulation of industrial and agricul-tural labor," and "Obligation to provide hygienic lodging to rural workers."[37] Later congresses approved resolutions referring to specific improvements for agricultural workers, and electoral programs for provincial elections included these above-mentioned measures at the top of their list.

Although the Socialist Party spread into interior cities in the 1900–1910 period, the groups in the federal capital remained the party's most enduring and important source of strength. The Buenos Aires centers first appeared in the 1890s in the various parishes into which the city had been divided for both ecclesiastical and electoral purposes. An electoral reform law, first tested in 1904, redivided the capital into twenty *circunscripciones* (similar to municipal wards in the United States) that corresponded roughly to the original parish lines. (See map.) In these years the party had affiliated centers located in almost every one of the twenty subdivisions. Within their areas of jurisdiction they provided the keystones for party organization and activity. Each center was organized autonomously with its own administrative officers and statutes. They engaged in numerous activities designed to recruit members and to spread socialism. These included regular lectures, debates, picnics, raffles, and concerts to raise funds, and the establishment of libraries for members and the general public. The larger and more active centers published their own newspapers. These journals were intended to supplement *La Vanguardia*. They appeared more irregularly than the party organ, usually on a monthly basis. They were also smaller in size and coverage. Although they printed news of general party concern, and like the main journal usually published the party program and declaration of principles, their major attention centered on local matters.

Centers and the press continuously stressed recruitment to the Socialist cause. During the first years of the century the party attracted able and committed young men, many of whom quickly assumed important positions of leadership. Whereas in the 1890s doctors joined the party, in the following decade young lawyers were among the most important new adherents. Four lawyers in particular, Mario Bravo, Enrique del Valle Iberlucea, Antonio de Tomaso, and Alfredo L. Palacios, the last-named to be discussed in more detail in the following chapter, joined the Socialist Party between 1900 and 1910 and made an immediate and lasting impact.

Mario Bravo was one of a number of *provincianos* attracted to the cultural, intellectual, and political life of Buenos Aires at the turn of the century. Born in Tucumán in 1882, Bravo arrived in the capital in 1899, seeking public employment. A budding poet, he entered the literary world of Buenos Aires and made friends with Leopoldo Lugones, Roberto Payró, and José Ingenieros.

Soon after his arrival, Bravo entered the law school at the University of Buenos Aires. While a student he made his first contacts with the Socialist Party, visiting headquarters to acquire pamphlets on general matters of social concern. At that time the party made little impression on him. It was only when he returned to Tucumán in the summer and became involved in a sugar workers' strike that he read the pamphlets

BUENOS AIRES BY CIRCUNSCRIPCION
CIRCA 1918

1 Vélez Sarsfield	11 Balvanera Norte
2 San Cristóbal Sud	12 Concepción
3 Santa Lucía	13 Monserrat
4 San Juan Evangelista	14 San Nicolás
5 Flores	15 San Bernardo
6 San Carlos Sud	16 Belgrano
7 San Carlos Norte	17 Palermo
8 San Cristóbal Norte	18 Las Heras
9 Balvanera Oeste	19 Pilar
10 Balvanera Sud	20 Socorro

he carried. "It was necessary," he later recalled, "that a social fact of singular proportions for my spirit should awaken me to reality."[38] In 1905 he graduated from the university, having written his thesis on labor legislation, and in that same year he became a member of the Socialist Party in Tucumán. Returning to Buenos Aires in 1906 he attended the party congress of that year and joined the staff of *La Vanguardia*. Rising rapidly in Socialist ranks, he was elected to the executive committee in 1907 and served ably as secretary-general during the difficult "Strike of the Centennial" in 1910.[39]

Enrique del Valle Iberlucea, one of the most important and one of the most neglected figures in the early history of the Socialist Party, was born in Spain in 1878. Although little biographical information on del Valle Iberlucea's early years is available, he apparently arrived in Buenos Aires with his parents in 1882. After spending some time in school at Santa Fe, he entered the law school of the University of Buenos Aires and received his degree in 1902. In that same year he joined the Socialist Party, either by then being or soon after becoming a naturalized Argentine citizen.[40] Like Bravo, he quickly made his mark: he was selected several times as a candidate for the national Chamber of Deputies and in 1906 was chosen as president of the sixth party congress.

Antonio de Tomaso was born in Buenos Aires in 1889. His parents were Italian immigrants, his father a bricklayer and his mother a seamstress. Showing much of the same dogged determination as Enrique Dickmann, he graduated from a secondary business school in three accelerated years rather than the customary six. As a young man he affiliated with the Socialist Party and served on the staff of *La Vanguardia* while still a student. In 1914 he received his law degree from the University of Buenos Aires.[41]

Although young lawyers were among the brightest stars attracted to the party in these years, the majority of new affiliates represented a more heterogeneous cross-section of Argentine society. Eugenio Albani, born in Genoa, Italy, in 1882 and later a naturalized Argentine citizen, joined the party in 1900. He was a commercial employee and his first socialist activity had been to found a bread cooperative in the district of Barracas. José F. Grosso, born in Buenos Aires in 1890, began his professional life as a manual laborer, a commercial clerk, and finally a secondary school teacher. He entered the Socialist Party in 1907, affiliating with the center of *circunscripciones* six and nine, where he held the position of secretary-general from 1909 to 1913. Agustín S. Muzio, like Grosso, was born in the federal capital in 1890. He began his activity in 1904, joining a Socialist youth group. Muzio entered the party through the center of the second *circunscripción* in 1909, and from that date was an active Socialist representative in the tanners' union (Unión de Obreros Curtidores), which he helped to establish. José F. Penelón, also born in Buenos Aires in the year of "El Noventa," in 1908 founded the Juventud Socialista (Socialist Youth) in sections twelve and thirteen. A typographer active in his union, he also organized the Agrupación Gráfica Socialista (Socialist Printers' Group) in 1911. José Rouca Oliva, born in 1889, was attracted to the party in 1907 through his journalistic interests and an invitation from Mario Bravo to join the staff of *La Vanguardia*.[42]

These brief biographies suggest certain general patterns of recruitment, patterns that persisted throughout the first decades of the twentieth century. First, although the Socialist Party was theoretically a working-class party, it attracted a significant number of middle-class people and professionals, particularly doctors and lawyers, who, like Justo, Repetto, Dickmann, del Valle Iberlucea, Bravo, and others, quickly assumed positions of leadership. Nevertheless, men of more humble occupational status—lithographers, electricians, bookbinders, salesmen, mechanics—also joined the party and served in important secondary positions of leadership. Party composition, then, was a mixture of middle class and skilled working class. Notably absent were representatives from the extremes of the spectrum, bankers and *estancieros* on the one hand and unskilled workers, for example, day laborers, on the other.

Second, many of those who enrolled did so in their youth. The average new member was in his twenties, and several established contacts with or actually joined the party while still teenagers. The Socialists formed special youth branches to interest students and young workers in their philosophy and activities. Added to the work of *La Vanguardia* and the centers, these youth groups successfully supplemented recruitment.

Third, more and more native-born Argentines joined the party. There were important foreign-born members—Adolfo and Enrique Dickmann, Esteban Jiménez, and Enrique del Valle Iberlucea to name a few—but much of the leadership by the turn of the century consisted of men born in Argentina, principally (with the important exception of Mario Bravo) in the federal capital. The party would continue to be labeled "foreign" and "immigrant-based" well into the twentieth century. But by 1910 its leadership was largely Argentine.

Although recruitment continued unabated, the overall number of affiliates grew but little at this time. Membership fluctuated between 1,300 and 2,000 in the course of the decade, perhaps with as much as

20 percent of the total withdrawing in 1906 over the syndicalist struggle.[43] A 1905 general vote for members of the executive committee recorded 972 affiliates representing thirty-four groups, attesting to a significant increase in participation in party matters when compared with the 100-to-200 general vote totals for the 1890s.[44]

New members were prominent in electoral activity. Despite the continuance of fraud, corruption, and a restricted electorate, complicated by repressive legislation and general strikes, the party entered candidates in every election for the Chamber of Deputies from the federal capital between 1902 and 1910. Although the Socialists succeeded only once in actually electing a candidate to office (Alfredo L. Palacios in 1904), their organization for political activity continued to grow and gather experience, as did the percentage of voters in the city who cast ballots in their favor.

Socialist centers bore the main responsibility for campaigning, particularly during the 1904–1906 period when the *circunscripción* system of deputy election remained in effect. The overall direction of campaigns rested at first with the executive committee, and *La Vanguardia* played an important role in the dissemination of electoral information. In 1906 the executive committee created a special auxiliary to direct political campaigns, to coordinate electoral activities in the centers, and to serve as liaison between the party hierarchy and local units. The duties of the Comité Electoral Central (Central Electoral Committee) included the organization of lectures, the editing and printing of manifestoes, the distribution of ballots, and the appointment of observers at the polling places.[45]

Pre-electoral activity made special appeals to the working class. Party platforms emphasized those aspects of the Socialist program dealing with specific proletarian concerns. Party statements sought to convince working men that political action was a necessary concomitant to union organization and the strike, general or partial. However, in these years of anarchist ascendancy, significant working-class support at the polls did not materialize. Socialists were particularly aggrieved by the fact that, despite their pleas to the contrary, many of those working-class members who did go to the polls gave their vote to the highest bidder. A note of bitterness with regard to how slowly the working class was educating itself politically began to manifest itself in some declarations. Reviewing the small number of votes the party received in the 1904 deputy elections (1,254 of a total of 29,134—more than half, 830, gained by Alfredo L. Palacios, one of eight Socialist candidates), the lead post-election editorial in *La Vanguardia* blamed this "most paltry" result on "two factors: first, the political deprivation of the Argentine workers, the consequence of a dreadful ignorance concerning the value of the vote; and, second, the ignorant repugnance of foreign workers for acquiring citizenship."[46] Commenting on the July 1905 vote for deputy in the thirteenth *circunscripción*, *La Vanguardia* observed that "the major part of the vote for our candidate [Francisco Cúneo] was from students, lawyers, solicitors, and law clerks. The workers . . . sold their votes."[47]

Failing to draw much working-class support at the polls in these years, the party began to shift its political attention. Although working-class concerns were by no means abandoned or neglected, the party did attempt to reach a broader sector of the electorate. Platforms in the early part of the decade had placed social legislation prominently at the top of the list. The Socialist platform for the 1910 deputy elections presented a more balanced approach, seeking to attract not only the proletariat but also the growing number of middle-class citizens concerned with political and fiscal reform and liberal elements opposed to repressive legislation and the power of the Church and the military.[48]

Whether because of programmatic adjustment or other factors, Socialist performance at the polls, as table 3 shows, improved significantly during the first decade of the twentieth century. From 1896 to 1902 Socialist tallies in the federal capital represented less than one percent of the total vote. The 1904 *circunscripcional* reform, plus the popularity of candidate Alfredo L. Palacios, increased the Socialist showing in that year to 5 percent of the total. By the end of the decade, even after the abandonment of the 1904 reforms, Socialist deputy candidates received one of every four votes cast in Buenos Aires.

A review of the 1900–1910 period, then, reveals a rather optimistic picture for the Socialist political future in Argentina. In spite of the government-imposed difficulties of these years, the party continued to attract able affiliates, increase electoral support, strengthen internal organization, and spread out from the federal capital into the provinces.

As this decade drew to a close, major problems for the party did not stem so much from external pressures as from the growing importance of several internal theoretical debates. The first of these came from an unexpected source.

In 1908 the Italian Socialist congressman Enrico Ferri toured Argentina for three months, observing conditions in the republic and presenting several lectures on a variety of topics. Invited on October 26 to give a lecture to a Socialist audience to raise funds for *La Vanguardia*, the Italian visitor made a surprising criticism of the party. First, he

TABLE 3

SOCIALIST PARTY VOTES IN NATIONAL DEPUTY
ELECTIONS, FEDERAL CAPITAL, 1902–1908

Date	Socialist Votes	Others	Total
March 9, 1902	204	18,447	18,651
March 13, 1904	1,254	NA	19,977
July 24, 1904	26	439	NA
July 16, 1905	92	1,711	NA
March 11, 1906	1,360	28,456	29,816
November 25, 1906	3,677	11,264	NA
March 8, 1908	7,462	17,821	25,283
October 18, 1908	5,505	NA	30,869
March 13, 1910	7,945	23,789	31,734

Sources: Jacinto Oddone, *Historia del socialismo*, II, 284–312. *La Prensa*,
March 14, 1904, p. 5; March 9, 1908, p. 7; and March 14, 1910, p. 9. *La
Vanguardia*, March 19, 1904, p. 1; July 22, 1905, p. 2; March 9 and 10,
1908, p. 1; and March 14 and 15, 1910, p. 1.

argued that a socialist party should be a "natural product of the country where it is formed." In Argentina, he observed, socialism was a
European import, brought by immigrants, imitated uncritically by
Argentines, and not really suitable for prevailing social-economic conditions. Second, Argentina was predominantly agricultural and its proletariat rural, not industrial. Marx, he noted, could never have written
Das Kapital based on the Argentine example because "the 'proletariat'
is the product of the steam engine." The rural working class in Argentina, he concluded, was mobile, transitory, and almost impossible to
organize, while the workers of Buenos Aires were at the moment too
small and weak to affect the course of the republic and were dominated
by "trade-unionism" rather than socialism. In sum, the objective conditions in Argentina were not yet propitious for the "natural development" of a socialist party. The Argentine party was, as Ferri and many
native conservatives claimed, an "artificial flower," an "exotic plant,"
transferred to unsuitable soil.

Ferri's remarks, which anti-Socialist forces in Argentina readily repeated, shocked the party. Not only had the attack come from an unexpected source but it also pointed out major contradictions with which
party theoreticians had not adequately dealt.

Juan B. Justo soon responded. He asserted that the party had ma-
tured from the 1890s, when it pretended to be an exclusively working-
class movement. By 1908, in Justo's words, the party "presents itself
above all as the political organization of the most numerous class of the

population, the wage-earning workers." In other words, party success did not depend simply upon an industrial proletariat, admittedly not yet as large a group for socialist support as in Europe, but upon the mobilization of all wage-earners, urban or rural, lower or middle class.

The development of the Argentine economy, Justo continued, if not characterized by native industrialization, was nevertheless the result of "systematic capitalist colonization" by European industrial nations. This colonial capitalist development produced a numerous proletarian class, not only in the agricultural sector, but also in shops and factories. And this proletariat grew every year with the arrival of between 200,000 and 250,000 immigrants. Argentina, therefore, if seen in a larger perspective than Ferri suggested, that is, as part of a global system of capitalist development, undoubtedly possessed a proletariat exploited and oppressed not only by Argentine capitalism but by world-wide capitalism. The local socialist party, therefore, as part of an international socialist movement, had as valid a role to play in organizing the working class as any similar party anywhere in the world.

The principal problem for the party, as Justo saw it, was to arouse the consciousness and promote the solidarity of the republic's heterogeneous working-class elements. In this regard, Justo admitted, the party had not done as well as it might have. But it would never do well if it stayed within the restricted theoretical boundaries imposed by men like Ferri. Only by dealing with the situation as it existed, be it objectively optimal or not, could the party succeed. Only through action and a pragmatic appreciation of Argentine realities could the party mobilize sufficient support to achieve socialist goals in the republic. Although much remained to be done, Justo continued, a significant amount had already been accomplished, contradicting Ferri's pessimistic assessment.[49]

Ferri's comments, particularly his statement that socialism was an "exotic flower" in Argentina, blended smoothly with a growing nationalist reaction directed in part against the Socialists. In many ways the development of Argentine nationalism during this period represented a twentieth-century re-evaluation of the dominant trends and values of the republic's late-nineteenth-century history. As immigrants came to dominate the work force and control urban real estate, commerce, and industry, spokesmen for native interests expressed concern that Argentina might become a virtual European colony.

Immigrants brought with them new skills, new capital, new ideas, new values. Although many Argentines appreciated the skills and capital, they had doubts about the ideas and values. Immigration might be a mixed blessing, bringing prosperity on the one hand and introducing philosophies that would undermine the economic and political system on the other. While little was done actively to restrict immigration in these years, legislation such as the Residence and Social Defense laws sought to limit the entrance of "undesirable aliens" and forecast future restrictive policies.

Intellectuals articulated Argentine nationalism in these years. Many sought to define and to defend what they considered uniquely Argentine against what they considered foreign, non-Argentine cultural values. The leading figures in the formulation of early twentieth-century nationalism were mainly *provincianos*—Ricardo Rojas, Manuel Gálvez, Leopoldo Lugones—who reacted strongly against the Europeanized, cosmopolitan, and, as they saw it, materialistic values prevalent in Buenos Aires. The true essence of Argentine national character, they argued, could be found in the interior, not in the capital. In the provinces, Spanish traditions prevailed—nobility, honor, idealism, a concern for the spiritual. These traditions, much deprecated by nineteenth-century liberals, were now preferable, they concluded, to the materialism and positivism so influential in the recent past.[50]

Nationalists viewed socialism as a materialistic European philosophy brought to America by immigrants and directly antithetical to the so-called Hispanic tradition. Nationalists tended to overlook various areas where their interests and those of the Socialists nearly coincided. For example, few groups in Argentina were as anxious for immigrants to become naturalized citizens and to integrate themselves fully into national life. Moreover, the party itself sought to serve as an example of nationalization and adaptation to Argentine conditions. Begun in part by foreigners, the party by the turn of the century was led primarily by native-born members, and its rank and file and voting support, by statutory and legal necessity, possessed Argentine citizenship.

The Socialists themselves, however, rarely stressed areas of convergence. Generally, the party and its leadership responded to the nationalist challenge by stressing socialism's internationalism. Juan B. Justo often propounded the internationalist position. The course of history, he argued, was not leading to narrow nationalism but rather to a broader concept without national distinctions. Industrialization, international trade, improved and increased transportation and communication, immigration, all were contributing to the bridging of national boundaries and would eventually render the concept of "nation" or "national" obsolete. Socialism was part of an international movement, representative of working-class interests that cut across all geographic boundaries. When it came to making a choice of final adherence, Justo stated that "I prefer the red [flag] because it means that the blue and white [flag of Argentina] does not hypnotize me, and it presages a free and intelligent humankind, without flags."[51]

Internationalism, however, according to Justo, was not necessarily incompatible with nationalism. "There is no conflict," he stated, "between love for the people of whom we form a part and love for humanity." The major points at issue were how nationalism was defined and employed. For the Socialists, the ruling class used nationalism as an excuse to restrict legitimate social, political agitation, to create anti-foreign and anti-socialist sentiment, and to impose an artificial and dangerous conformity on the Argentine people. Nationalism, they argued, served as a façade behind which the bourgeoisie and its government allies pursued their own selfish class interests.[52] What most Socialist leaders often failed to appreciate, however, was the potent and growing strength of Argentine nationalism generally and its wide appeal to many groups within the country.

Although the internationalist position generally prevailed among Argentine Socialists, serious differences of opinion over this issue arose among important members of the party. At this time these differences resulted only in a clash of opposing ideas. Eventually, however, they led to profound schisms and the loss to the party of some of its most eloquent and effective spokesmen.

Aspects of this intra-party debate surfaced in mid-1909 when the *Revista Socialista Internacional* (International Socialist Review) circulated a questionnaire that asked the respondent to define international socialism and patriotism and to determine if the two concepts could "logically co-exist." Two respondents took the nationalist position. Antonio de Tomaso and Alfredo L. Palacios both agreed that they saw no serious incompatibilities between socialism, internationalism, and patriotism. The nation-state, they asserted, was the basic center for the growth of socialism. Moreover, Palacios sought carefully to define exactly what he meant by patriotism, "in part a natural sentiment determined by impressions and memories . . . [that] aspires to the destruction of caudillismo, of illiteracy, and we struggle, in its name, for the appearance of a vigorous nationality, proposing laws of social well-being . . . that elevate the condition of the workers, that provide them positive advantages, rooting them in this manner more in the country. Socialism does not reject the ideal of the fatherland, it purifies it."

These arguments did not convince the internationalists who answered the questionnaire. Martín Casaretto, for example, active in the labor movement, asserted that the working class should struggle tenaciously against all forms of nationalist sentiment and deny all nationalist symbols that inhibit the internationalist ideal and prevent human solidarity. "How is it possible," he asked, "for there not to be an antagonism between the national flag, which shelters the recognized and legalized preponderance of an oppressive minority, and the red flag, an international emblem that symbolizes the struggle against working-class oppression?"[53]

Few problems posed as many difficulties for members of the party as the nationalism question. For many born in Argentina or for those immigrants anxious to become citizens and to assimilate quickly, the complete rejection of nation and flag for the red banner was impossible and they therefore sought a compromise position. Like many taking halfway positions, the compromisers often found their status uncomfortable and untenable. The mixing of internationalism and nationalism, in the eyes of certain Socialists, produced a theoretical gray area that many could not accept or reconcile. Eventually they left the party, some forming or joining more nationalistic organizations, others rallying to a more internationalist position.

Another and related intra-party dispute also began to emerge at the end of the decade. Generally, those who supported the nationalist position recognized its political potential in any electoral campaign. If the party hoped to win at the polls, they reasoned, it had to convince Argentine voters of the party's commitment to improving national conditions and had to respond successfully to charges of socialism's foreign nature. The internationalists, on the other hand, believed that the party followed an erroneous course in pursuing with such emphasis the political and electoral path. Despite past rebuffs and the anarchist and syndicalist control of most labor organization, they continued to urge the party to focus on working-class unionization rather than parliamentary action. Build at the grass roots, they argued, to construct a solid base of proletarian support first and then worry about ballots and legislative action. The Socialists had ignored working-class organization in the latter part of the decade and had lost the initiative to other radical groups. But a renewed effort, the unionizers concluded, especially at a time of general labor disorientation and disillusionment, would reap important rewards.

By 1910, therefore, lines within the Socialist Party were being drawn with increasing clarity. On one side were those who favored political action to labor organization and some sort of socialist-nationalist response to official and conservative attacks on the party's "right to be" in the republic. On the other side were those who preferred an emphasis on labor organization, doubted that much could be accomplished through parliamentary action, and responded to the nationalist challenge with a proud declaration of their commitment to internationalism. Generally those associated with the nationalist-political group were middle class in origin, those opposed of working-class background. These divisions within the party, along class and theoretical lines, would, in the long run, do more to weaken Socialist effectiveness than any of the repressive measures of the government between 1900 and 1910.

4. Palacios: 1904–1908

Now La Boca has teeth.

Florencio Sánchez on the election of
Alfredo L. Palacios to Congress in 1904

Few conservatives objected to the repressive measures of the 1900–1910 period. Most agreed on the basic need to maintain civil order to preserve existing institutions. Some, however, believed that, within the negative framework of states of siege and restrictive legislation, positive steps had to be taken to accommodate new groups and new forces. Only through reform, they argued, could the structure of Argentine society be maintained and the accomplishments of peaceful political change and progressive economic growth preserved.

Julio A. Roca, president from 1898 to 1904, was not insensitive to the need for change. Known as "El.Zorro" (The Fox) for his political astuteness, he proved willing to initiate the most significant electoral reform of the period. In 1902 Roca's Minister of the Interior, Joaquín V. González, introduced legislation, approved on December 29 as law 4,161, that divided the nation's electoral districts into 120 separate *circunscripciones*, corresponding in number to total seats in the national Chamber of Deputies. Each new unit, or *circunscripción*, elected a single representative, eliminating for the time being the *lista completa*.

The first application of the new law came with the congressional elections of 1904. The Ministry of the Interior directed preparation for these contests. According to a ministry report, as of December 31, 1902, there were 747,968 male citizens over the age of eighteen in the republic. Of these, 695,956 were eligible to vote, and during the period between the promulgation of the law and the 1904 elections the ministry managed to register 596,880 potential voters.[1]

In his report to Congress following the 1904 elections, González ex-

73

pressed his general satisfaction with the electoral reform.[2] The actual results of the 1904 balloting, however, were disappointing. Even though, as the minister claimed, more citizens than ever before in the history of the republic had registered and voted, the continued refusal of the UCR to participate in elections, and widespread public distrust of the political system, remained serious obstacles to the achievement of meaningful suffrage. Of 592,062 persons registered, only about one third, or 205,563, went to the polls. In only two districts, the province of Tucumán and the federal capital, did more than 50 percent of those enrolled cast their ballots. As one official observed, "the Argentine people still do not find themselves accustomed to the strict exercise of their right of suffrage."[3]

The 1904 reform did not succeed in placating the political opposition because it did not solve the essential problem—the lack of honesty and regularity in electoral procedures. Despite government efforts to insure fair voting, fraud remained the dominant mechanism in selecting candidates and electing deputies. In 1904 local political bosses simply concentrated their corrupt practices in a smaller area.[4]

Conservatives swept all but one of the congressional seats contested in 1904. The González reform, however, did produce one surprise. In the March 13, 1904, congressional election in the city of Buenos Aires, *circunscripción* four, San Juan Evangelista, including the Italian waterfront district known as "La Boca" (The Mouth), elected to the Chamber of Deputies Latin America's first Socialist congressman. The victory of Alfredo L. Palacios gave the Socialist Party its first major political triumph in a national election, vindicating in part the party's commitment to political action.

The entrance of Palacios into the Argentine Chamber of Deputies in 1904 initiated a parliamentary career that would span six decades. Born in Buenos Aires on August 10, 1880, his father an Argentine, his mother a Uruguayan, he was from a sufficiently comfortable background to attend the prestigious Colegio Nacional and the law school of the University of Buenos Aires. It was as a law student that Palacios became interested in socialism. His concern with social conditions in the republic led him in 1900 to write his law thesis on *La miseria en la República Argentina* (Poverty in the Argentine Republic), a thesis the conservative law faculty refused to accept. Palacios quickly wrote another thesis on a less controversial subject to attain his degree. *La miseria*, however, was soon published and reflected clearly the young lawyer's concern with social issues.

Palacios based the information in *La miseria* on first-hand observation of working-class conditions in the republic. Visiting *conventillos* and factories, he mixed personal investigation with official statistics and quoted from the studies of various Socialists to describe the misery of long hours, low wages, lack of proper food and clothing, and the crowded and unhealthy homes that were the lot of many Argentines. This misery he traced to the capitalist economic system with its concentration of ownership of the means of production. The government, which served and protected capitalist interests, contributed to increasing poverty and social inequality. The "parasitism" of capitalism must be replaced, he argued, with socialization of the means of production and "equality among men."

Although not yet a member of the Socialist Party, Palacios agreed with party leaders that evolution from a capitalist society to a socialist order was inevitable. For the workers he urged unification and solidarity as the first stage in their emancipation. The means of change, he believed, should come peaceably through political action and legislation. Evolutionary progress would produce revolutionary change.[5]

Although Palacios generally agreed with socialism's principal spokesmen in Argentina, he nevertheless held to certain aspects and emphases different from the mainstream. Although he agreed on the importance of material and economic factors in analyzing and determining historical development, for example, he preferred to credit the force of human will, idealism, and individual personality as the major motivating forces producing change. He rejected a strictly scientific, strictly economic, strictly positivistic approach. As he later wrote, "I do not consider the social movement as a natural process governed by laws, independent of the will, of consciousness, and of intention, but, on the contrary, determined in great part by will, consciousness, and intention."[6]

Nationalism was another area where Palacios set himself apart from other Argentine Socialists. His association with idealism, spiritual values, and individualism placed him philosophically close to the Argentine nationalists of the turn of the century. While he drew inspiration from Jaurès, Marx, Karl Kautsky, and other European figures, he argued that the basic precepts for Argentine socialism were found in the republic's own illustrious political and intellectual personalities. Independence leader Mariano Moreno, he argued, was an incipient socialist. The Socialist Party and its program were not "exotic flowers," but rather were completely within the liberal tradition of nineteenth-century thinkers and statesmen like Esteban Echeverría and Bernardino Rivadavia, the latter, in Palacios's words, "the most elevated figure of our history."[7]

The differences between the Palacios brand of socialism and that of

Socialist Party leadership should not be exaggerated. These differences were real but they were differences of degree and emphasis. Even Juan B. Justo, with whom Palacios was often contrasted, shared to some extent the young lawyer's belief in the strength of subjective forces to change objective conditions. While not a staunch admirer of nineteenth-century Argentine liberals, Justo nevertheless often tried to orient the party in that tradition. Moreover, there was a general tolerance, if not the claimed encouragement, for divergent views within the party. Palacios's agreement with basic tenets and methods probably compensated for the special characteristics of his own brand of socialism.

However, another aspect of Palacios's personality and philosophy caused more serious problems—his reluctance to submit his own individuality to the rules and regulations of Socialist organization. This reluctance marked his initial contacts with the Socialist Party and characterized what proved throughout to be an uneasy relationship. Soon after Palacios received his law degree and news of his rejected first thesis became public, Socialist Adrián Patroni approached the young graduate and asked him to present a lecture based on the material in *La miseria*. Palacios agreed and on August 19, 1900, spoke to a gathering that included Juan B. Justo and Enrique Dickmann. At the end of the talk Dickmann approached the speaker and invited him to affiliate with the Socialist Party. Palacios's reply, as later reported, was at the same time typical and revealing: "I am a socialist," he proclaimed, "but I am not disposed to submit myself to any discipline."[8] This statement reflected more of an attitude than a firm position, for soon thereafter Palacios did join the party. But he affiliated with the center at La Plata rather than becoming a member of any group in the federal capital, and he avoided direct contacts with leaders and "disciplinarians" like Justo, Dickmann, and Repetto.

From 1900 to 1904 Palacios apparently held no important positions within the party. Nevertheless, he began to build his reputation as one concerned with social problems. The small plaque on his law offices in downtown Buenos Aires read "Alfredo L. Palacios, abogado, atiende gratis a los pobres" (Alfredo L. Palacios, lawyer, free legal service for the poor). In addition to his professional duties as a "people's lawyer," he gave numerous speeches in the company of other Socialists before working-class audiences. In these meetings he gained valuable experience as a public speaker and potential political figure.

In late 1903 Palacios became the Socialist Party candidate for national deputy from *circunscripción* four of the federal capital. In the contest he faced stiff opposition from better-known, older candidates with strong oligarchical connections and backing. Nevertheless, he went into the campaign with certain advantages.

First, a strong Socialist center of several years' standing was firmly established in the fourth *circunscripción*. The *barrio* had a large working-class base from which the Socialists could draw electoral strength. Labor militancy to improve living and working conditions in the area was commonplace, and workers from the district were prominent in the growing strike activity of the period.

Second, the *circunscripción* was a microcosm of the social-economic problems to which the Socialists spoke directly. For example, with regard to housing a 1904 municipal census showed section four to have one of the highest concentrations of *conventillos* in the city and the greatest number of dwellings made of wood as opposed to more solid structures of stone and brick.[9]

Third, although he was not actually a resident of the district, lectures and professional activity had made Palacios a well-known and popular personality in the section. His opponents, though formidable in terms of wealth, name, and political influence, were not so well established in the *circunscripción*. *La Luz*, the Socialist center's journal in section four, described the principal PAN candidate, Marco M. Avellaneda, son of former president Nicolás Avellaneda, as an ultraconservative Catholic, a supporter of the 1902 Residence Law, and so ignorant of the large Italian component in the district that he even voted against a congressional appropriation to build a statue of Garibaldi![10]

Campaign techniques were by now familiar and well practiced. Palacios gave speeches in halls, theaters, and the open street. Socialist publications like *La Vanguardia* and *La Luz* urged their readers to vote for the Socialist Party candidate. And on March 13 several months of active campaigning in section four ended in a Socialist victory. Palacios gained 830 votes (of 2,566 cast), besting five rivals and benefiting directly from the electoral reform and the conservative division of the remaining votes.[11]

As Alfredo L. Palacios prepared to enter the Chamber of Deputies he had already laid the foundation for a reputation as one of the republic's most flamboyant, unconventional, and outspoken political personalities. Often called affectionately by the diminutive "Alfredito," he was short of stature, for which he compensated by wearing high-heeled boots. Slim, always well-dressed, usually in black, he made a jaunty broad-brimmed hat his personal trademark. The hat covered a mane of generous black hair that earned him another nickname, "El Melenudo" (loosely, the Long-Haired One). The most prominent feature of Palacios's physiognomy, however, was a magnificent moustache, which grew thicker and blacker with age while retaining its basic upward sweep, looking much like the letter "W" somewhat flattened out. A final nickname, "El Mosquetero" (The Musketeer), was applied to Palacios in later years. This appellation referred not only to his romantic championship of the poor and the underdog but also to his willingness to wield a saber when he believed his own or the Socialist Party's honor was challenged. During his political career he fought half a dozen duels, claiming victory in each.

Palacios cherished both his independence and his individuality. A handsome and dashing figure, he was known as a lady's man but never married. Deeply committed to socialism and with a genuine concern for the poor, he nevertheless had wide contacts with men of other political persuasions and other interests. He counted among his friends archconservative and ultra-nationalist Manuel Carlés, sportsman-aviator Jorge Newberry, and anarchist playwright Florencio Sánchez.

The more colorful aspects of Palacios's personality often obscured his very real talents and abilities as a legislator. A fine orator, he presented his arguments in eloquent language, often laced with quotations from illustrious figures in Argentine history. Quick on his feet, he responded to intellectual debate without hesitation and was a master of irony and wit. His speeches were usually carefully researched, often with the help of Socialist colleagues, and displayed considerable thought and preparation. He read widely, wrote prolifically, and was well versed in a broad range of subjects.

Entering the Chamber of Deputies on May 2, 1904, the only Socialist among 119 other deputies of various conservative affiliations, Palacios set the tone of his four years in office by refusing to be sworn into his seat with the usual oath to God. Such an oath, as he rightly pointed out, was not mentioned in the Constitution and represented an attack on the freedom of religion. After some debate, the president of the chamber sustained this objection and allowed the twenty-five-year-old congressman to take his seat with a simple affirmation that he would serve in accordance with the Constitution.[12]

Palacios's first major presentation was on a subject that occupied much of his first term—defense of the socialist and labor movement in the face of increased government repression. On May 9, 1904, Palacios rose to discuss the police attack on labor gatherings during recent May Day celebrations. The police, according to the speaker, had exceeded their express functions by assaulting the demonstrators and then closing union halls. For Palacios, this action was "simply another link in an interminable chain of police assaults . . . in this capital, and especially through the intervention of a mounted squadron that the people have named 'Cossacks.' " The young Socialist concluded with a motion that the Minister of the Interior, Joaquín V. González, be called to the chamber to explain police activities.[13]

Belisario Roldán, deputy from the capital, immediately responded to Palacios's charge. Roldán argued that a larger proportion of police than demonstrators had been wounded and challenged the Socialist's patriotism with the observation that "under the uniform of those *criollos* charged with public security beats the heart of old Argentine soldiers, accustomed to face all, in accord with a tradition of honor that inspires equally all the sons of this land who carry arms at their side." Palacios countered with the claim that "those poor [wounded] guards are as worthy of pity as the workers shot in the back: more worthy perhaps, because they have been unconscious instruments who went to fight against their brothers when they ought to join with them in the demands they pursue." Those who gave the orders, he concluded, should be those held accountable.[14]

Two days later, on May 11, Minister of the Interior González appeared in the chamber to explain police action. He began by stressing the government's concern for social problems. These could be solved, the minister argued, only through legal procedures and in a climate of public order. The police, charged with maintaining order, acted, he believed, with moderation and respect for legal rights. The major thrust of government-police action, he concluded, was directed against anarchists, not Socialists.

Palacios answered his former professor in the law school with strong language. No matter what the intent to discriminate between anarchists and Socialists, repression ultimately included both. During the May 1 disturbances, Palacios related, he and fellow Socialists Manuel Ugarte and Enrique del Valle Iberlucea were jailed without cause. Instead of responding to questions posed, he continued, González merely told the legislators what they already knew: that the Socialist Party acted legally and non-violently. Palacios concluded by vowing to continue "to protest with all the energies of my convictions against the attempts that have been committed on the first of May in the capital of the republic. . . . I affirm also that, by this road, we are going *inevitably*—underline this, señor stenographer [he did]—we are heading inevitably toward a police dictatorship!"[15]

The Socialist deputy followed his debate with a May 27 motion to overturn the Residence Law. His initial speech, touching off a two-month discussion in the chamber, noted that law 4,144 originally had been approved hastily, with little debate, and under the stress of special circumstances. Those who supported the Residence Law, he argued, failed to take into account the profundity of social problems emerging from a historical class struggle. Legislation seeking to expel foreigners active in labor agitation dealt only with surface manifestations of a much more profound and complex problem.

In his conclusion Palacios presented arguments that were typical of his actions in Congress. He attempted to show that the Residence Law not only was morally repugnant but in the long run contravened the real legal and economic interests of the republic, a concern for conservatives and Socialists alike. Addressing the many lawyers in the chamber, Palacios pointed out the features of the 1902 legislation that violated the letter and the spirit of the Constitution—"because it expresses exceptions hateful for the foreigner; because it gives judicial faculties to the executive branch; and because it allows an individual to be expelled without previous judgement." Moreover, the Residence Law would eventually discourage immigration to the republic, halting the much-needed flow of persons to populate Argentina. "The people as a whole," he concluded, "urge the legislature to suppress this law, because it is a constant threat against foreigners, against our brothers the foreigners, who are the principal factor in the civilization of our people."[16] These concluding remarks were punctuated with loud cheers and the singing of the "Internationale." For the first time in memory the public galleries of the chamber contained groups of working-class representatives, many from La Boca, who had come to see their newly-elected spokesman in action.

Conservative deputies defended the Residence Law. The exchanges that ensued were long, lively, often impassioned, with frequent interruptions by all parties concerned. Conservative arguments presented a vision and interpretation of Argentine reality completely different from that of the Socialists. They rejected the whole notion of class division and struggle in the republic and argued, with some validity, the presence of opportunities for considerable social mobility. Conservative spokesmen opposed foreign ideologies, particularly anarchism, and to a lesser degree socialism, not only because they were disruptive and threatened revolution, but also because, as they saw it, they were simply not applicable to a basically free and prosperous Argentina. Turning to the question of the constitutionality of the 1902 law, and tacitly admitting it might violate the fundamental charter in some respects, they reasoned that special measures had to be devised to deal with those who did not respect the law in the first place. As one defender put it, the freedoms of the majority had to be protected, even at the expense of suppressing the rights of a dissenting minority.

Palacios countered by defending socialism as applicable to Argentina. "I know perfectly well," he said, "that the same essential conditions that exist in Old Europe also exist in the Argentine Republic." Freely quoting Jean Jaurès, he argued on behalf of the socialist credo and its "right to be" in Argentina. Returning to the question at hand, he accused his conservative critics of failing adequately to defend the Residence Law or to justify its non-constitutional nature. Two other deputies, Pedro J. Coronado of Entre Ríos and Emilio Gouchon of the capital, supported Palacios, but to no avail. On July 29 an overwhelming majority of the chamber defeated the Socialist's motion to rescind the law.[17]

In the second year of his term Palacios continued his opposition to government repression. Two states of siege, one in February as a result of the Radical revolt, the other in September in response to labor agitation, bracketed 1905. Palacios objected to both, condemning the first, invoked before Congress was called to session, and voting against approval of the second. Debate generally followed the lines of discussion already established when Palacios challenged the Residence Law. Conservatives defended the state of siege as essential for the restoration of public order. The Socialist deputy asserted that such measures were not constitutional and were applied to include non-violent groups like the Socialist Party, which in the case of the February revolt was not only completely removed from the anti-government action but strongly opposed. Most important, states of siege, like the Residence Law, dealt only with the surface manifestations of a deeper problem—the need to attack the root causes of dissent: low wages, long hours, miserable living and working conditions. As usual, Palacios's arguments made little impact, and the second state of siege was approved by a vote of 57 to 7.[18]

Argentina's first Socialist deputy spent much of his time opposing existing government policies. Eventually, however, he came to be recognized most for his initiation, guidance, and achievement of the republic's first important social legislation. That one Socialist was able to gain the approval of such legislation in a parliament overwhelmingly conservative was testimony not only to Palacios's personal political skill but also to the impact of certain social-economic changes and cultural-intellectual currents on Argentina's political leadership.

Increased attention to social problems in the nation's university curricula was an important factor in laying the groundwork for acceptance of social legislation. Particularly important was the introduction of sociology as a discipline for study in the late nineteenth century. Professors and students, many of whom were active in politics and held government positions, were exposed to sociological literature in the universities of Buenos Aires and La Plata. While not all accepted the critical conclusions that social theories and analyses produced, many were convinced that changes and adaptations had to be made in Argentine society to adjust to new conditions caused by social and economic growth.[19]

Another factor was the increased visibility of social problems. The spread of industrialization and urbanization and the growth of a militant labor movement increased general public awareness of social ills. Artistic works made an additional contribution. By the 1890s and the first years of the new century, young writers connected with militant movements—Roberto J. Payró, Florencio Sánchez, Alberto Ghiraldo— were producing poems, novels, essays, short stories, and plays that depicted the effects of new and changed social-economic conditions in the republic.[20]

These conditions were also the subject of one of Buenos Aires's most popular art forms, the theater. A growing number of plays in these years focused on social ills such as prostitution, alcoholism, gambling, and brutalities within the family, all stemming from the pressures of crowded living conditions and the tensions of urban life. The lives of immigrants and working classes in *conventillos* and factories were popular themes. *La pobre gente* (The poor people), opening in 1904, described the trials and tribulations of a working-class family in La Boca. Roberto J. Payró's *Marco Severi*, a 1905 production, traced the effects of the Residence Law on a hard-working and honest Italian immigrant accused by an employer of falsifying his entrance documents. *Nuestros hijos* (Our children) (1907) depicted the growing social problem of illegitimate children in the tightly-packed and promiscuous urban setting. *La fábrica* (The factory) by journalist Tito L. Foppa, shown to *porteño* audiences first in 1910, detailed the personalities involved in a strike for increased wages and shorter hours. Socialists were sometimes mentioned in these works. *Mano santo* (Blessed hand), staged in 1905, used a set depicting the interior of a *conventillo*, its walls adorned with a large portrait of Karl Marx surrounded by smaller photographs of other socialist luminaries. Nicolás Repetto and José Ingenieros were included in the dialogue as men of science who supported socialism in opposition to more mystical remedies for the ills of the poor.[21]

By 1904 the government itself began to reflect a genuine concern with the emerging "social question." In January of that year Minister of the Interior González appointed a Córdoba engineer, Juan Bialet-Massé, to collect information on the conditions of the working classes in the interior provinces. Bialet-Massé responded with a 400-page report, replete with statistics on wages, salaries, and production in addition to eyewitness descriptions of working conditions in the major industries of each province. The picture he drew corresponded closely to Socialist and other accounts of proletarian life in the federal capital: low wages, long hours, alcoholism, crime, inhuman treatment from employers, a situation that could only be escaped through death or violence and one badly in need of reform. The author urged a series of legislative measures to ameliorate these conditions, measures that echoed much of the Socialist Party's minimum program: the eight-hour day, a minimum wage, on-the-job accident compensation, an end to exploitative and unfair employment contracts, and regulative legislation to protect child and female laborers.[22]

At the same time that González appointed Bialet-Massé to collect provincial information, he requested other specialists to prepare suggestions for a comprehensive national labor code that would cover all aspects of labor-management relations in the republic. Those who were principal collaborators, in addition to Bialet-Massé, included men who either were or recently had been members of the Socialist Party— Augusto Bunge, Enrique del Valle Iberlucea, José Ingenieros, Leopoldo Lugones, and Manuel Ugarte.

The project that emerged and was presented to Congress in May 1904 was the most comprehensive proposal for social legislation yet presented to any Argentine legislative body. Known popularly as the "González Law," it encompassed 270 pages and was divided into 416 articles. The project dealt with a wide range of social matters and concluded with recommendations that, like the suggestions of Bialet-Massé, repeated many parts of the minimum program of the Socialist Party.[23]

However, if the 1904 code seemed like the Socialist Party program in form, it was nevertheless clear that the intent of the conservative government in proposing such social legislation was quite different from the goals of the opposition. Julio A. Roca, in his preface to the legislation, presented in a speech to Congress, admitted that the proposal had been inspired by the general strike of 1902, "which occasioned the announcement of a state of siege to reestablish altered order and the free circulation of national and foreign commerce."[24] González, commenting to Congress on the labor code, noted that it had been "concluded in the first days of May of this year, and presented for your consideration with the idea of anticipating the period in which strikes occur to affect national production in its moment of greatest activity."[25] Not to discount the Roca administration's possibly sincere desire for social betterment, the thrust of their argument to Congress indicated more of a commitment to preserve existing societal institutions through reform and to avoid revolutionary change. Social legislation, coupled with political reform, was seen as a necessary adjunct to repressive legislation to maintain order, increase productivity, and assure continued prosperity.

The presentation of the González proposal meant serious problems for the Socialist Party. Socialist spokesmen like Alfredo L. Palacios and Juan B. Justo admitted that many aspects of the labor code were synonymous with the Socialist minimum program. Party affiliates Augusto Bunge, Enrique del Valle Iberlucea, and Manuel Ugarte had participated in the formulation of the legislation. Therefore, initial Socialist response was favorable. In time, however, other problems arose. One was political. Approval of the 1904 proposal, government-inspired and promoted, would undercut the strength of the party and obviate some of its best issues. The mere presentation of the legislation weakened the Socialist argument that the government acted only to represent and protect the interests of the capitalist class. Another consideration, however, did much to alleviate Socialist worries on this first point. A closer examination of the extensive code revealed articles and clauses that, if enacted, would severely limit and restrict the freedom of labor association and activity.

Party member Juan Schaeffer rallied the Socialist opposition to the González law. Arguing that a comprehensive labor code should emanate from the workers themselves, Schaeffer managed, at the sixth party congress (July 2 and 3, 1904) in Rosario, to make his position official with the following resolution: "The Sixth Congress of the Argentine Socialist Party declares that protective labor legislation is a desire of the working class, which hopes to achieve such legislation with the conscious effort of the workers and repudiates the present Draconian labor law of the executive branch of the nation, without prejudicing the Socialist deputy to combat the law in general and to present amendments in accord with the aspirations of the Argentine Socialist Party."[26]

After the sixth congress Schaeffer continued his opposition to the 1904 project in a two-part La Vanguardia article. One of the proposal's principal supporters, José Ingenieros, admitted that the code represented a kind of "state socialism," had as one of its main purposes the prevention of strikes "ruinous for the country," and contained restrictive provisions on the formation of unions and the nature and duration of labor protests.[27] Schaeffer focused on each of these points, analyzing specific articles that forbade strikes or boycotts in state enterprises and limited the protest powers of workers in areas crucial to the export economy, particularly railroads and ports.[28]

In its opposition to the González code the Socialist Party found itself allied with a strange bedfellow. The Unión Industrial Argentina (UIA) (Argentine Industrial Union) had been formed in 1887. Composed of leading industrialists in food processing and metallurgy as well as small-businessmen, some landowners, financiers, professional men, and bankers, the Unión promoted the growth of native industries and sought higher protective tariffs for Argentine manufacturers. It was, by the turn of the century, the principal spokesman for the republic's industrialists.

In 1899 the Unión clearly expressed its removal from the partisan political arena with the following statement: "That the entity [UIA] cannot and should not mix in politics under any concept; that the mission of the entity is only that of promoting and defending the country's industrial interests; and that it will concentrate on fulfilling these aims in the best form possible, but dispensing with all participation in militant politics."[29] This statement meant that the UIA would not endorse or campaign for particular candidates and parties. But it did not mean that the Unión would refrain from acting politically to present its interests before the government.

Although industrialists were not well represented in Congress, by the turn of the century a few men affiliated with the UIA did serve in the lower house. Capital Deputy Carlos Delcasse, as well as Francisco Seguí and Francisco Uriburu of Buenos Aires province, all founding members of the UIA, entered the Chamber of Deputies in the same year as Alfredo L. Palacios. Seguí had served recently as president of the UIA. In 1906 they were joined by Ernesto Tornquist, a prominent banker and UIA member, elected to a capital seat. Small in number, but influential, they constituted a significant Unión presence in the Chamber.

Another way in which the Unión made its wishes known was through direct petition to the legislative and executive branches of government. During the first decade of the century these petitions often concentrated on growing radical-labor activity, which was aimed for the most part against the employers and owners who directed or supported the UIA. On December 15, 1904, following a rash of strikes, the directive council of the organization sent a note to the Minister of the Interior stating its position on labor disturbances and summarizing Unión attitudes on such problems.

First, the note argued, the major demand of striking workers—the eight-hour day—could not be met without reducing productivity (from the usual nine or ten hour day) by 20 percent. Moreover, Argentine industries could not take up the slack with higher prices because of continued European competition in manufactured goods and a lack of government protection. Second, a demand for higher wages could not be met for the same reasons. Decreased production without an increase in prices for goods would reduce profits and make wage increases impossible. Third, echoing a general conservative position, the UIA argued that workers in Argentina enjoyed higher salaries and better working conditions than elsewhere. The major cause of labor discontent, the note contended, stemmed from professional agitators who promoted philosophies inapplicable to Argentine conditions and from irresponsible labor associations that, according to the UIA, tyrannized and intimidated most workers, forcing them into unwanted and unnecessary walkouts and boycotts.[30]

The Socialist Party, representing workers, and the Unión Industrial, representing owners and employers, clashed frequently. Tariff policy was a principal area of contention. The Socialists advocated free and unencumbered trade, arguing that high customs duties increased consumer costs on food, clothing, and shelter. The UIA countered that most basic necessities were produced at home and were little affected by import duties and that higher costs resulted more from higher rents than from the price of manufactured articles. Moreover, the Unión argued, government protection of domestic producers would lead to industrial expansion, increased production, more jobs, higher salaries, and generally improved conditions overall.[31] In debates over the tariff the UIA and its supporters often accused the Socialists of adopting an anti-nationalist position on this issue. Higher tariffs, they argued, would serve to protect and to encourage the growth of national manufactures, thereby decreasing Argentine dependence on foreign-made goods.

In 1904–1905 the UIA and the Socialist Party both opposed the González law, albeit for different reasons. The industrial representatives remained silent about articles restricting labor activity, articles that presumably met with their approval. Their major objection, as stated in a 1905 document directed to legislators, centered on what they perceived as untoward state intervention in the private sector. Government regulation of labor-management relations, hours, wages, and working conditions would hinder private capitalist development and discourage individual initiative. Argentina was pictured as at a stage of industrial growth in which undue obstacles, such as the application of progressive labor legislation, would make competition with European manufacturers impossible. This kind of legislation was all right for England, France, and Germany, the UIA implied, but a certain amount of labor exploitation was necessary for Argentine industrialists to catch up and compete with more developed rivals. The article concluded with a warning that, if the labor code was passed, many industrialists might move to neighboring countries where public support would be greater and official obstacles fewer.[32]

The impact of these arguments on legislation cannot be measured, but the opposition of labor and management, the Socialist Party and the UIA, undoubtedly contributed to the ultimate congressional failure to report the González bill out of committee for full consideration. Nevertheless, the fact of the code's formulation and presentation, and the ensuing debate, indicated a climate somewhat more conducive to social reform than a period dominated by states of siege and repressive laws might suggest. Although Congress refused to accept a sweeping, encompassing labor code, legislators were willing to consider and finally pass piecemeal measures that fulfilled certain parts of the González proposal, and the most significant of these bore the signature of the first Socialist deputy, Alfredo L. Palacios.

Palacios's first major legislative victory came at the end of his first year in office. On September 22, 1904, as the regular congressional session came to a close (Congress met in ordinary session from the first of May to the end of September and frequently in extraordinary session from September through January and sometimes beyond into April) without yet considering the González law, still in committee, Palacios proposed that the chamber approve the part of the code providing for an obligatory one-day's rest a week for workers. Palacios argued that while the González law remained in committee the legislators should demonstrate to the people of the republic a proof of their concern for and commitment to social justice. The so-called "Sunday rest law," he noted, was a basic need, widely supported. In this instance, Palacios added, the interests of Socialists and the Catholic workers movement coincided, and Deputy Santiago O'Farrell from the federal capital, a spokesman for the Catholic movement, supported Palacios in his efforts to pass this legislation.

Debate centered on whether the regulation should be expressly for Sundays or any day of the week, whether it was constitutional, and, most important, whether if passed it should apply only to the federal capital or to the republic as a whole. Opponents tried to delay consideration until adjournment, but Palacios's constant insistence and skillful maneuvering led to the formation of a five-man committee, composed of those most active in debate, to produce a compromise measure for approval. The committee (Palacios, O'Farrell, Juan Argerich of the capital, Amador Lucero of Tucumán, and Mariano de Vedia of the capital) presented their six-point project on September 30. Article one stated that "In the federal capital all employers will be obligated to concede rest with salary or one day's wages to his workers and clerks the day of Sunday." Other articles included exceptions, a clause seemingly Socialist-Catholic inspired, prohibiting "the sale of alcoholic beverages, with the exception of beer, on Sunday," and provisions for fines of 100 pesos for first offenders and fifteen days in prison for repeated violation. The chamber removed the words "In the federal capital" from article one, implying thereby a national scope, and then approved the proposal.[33]

Passage in the Chamber of Deputies, however, represented only the first step. The legislation was next sent to the Senate for further debate and possible amendment. The Unión Industrial Argentina, increasingly active as a lobbying group, sent a note to the upper house urging the modification of article one to delete the employer's responsibility to compensate employees for Sunday salaries, claiming this represented an unacceptable financial burden in conjunction with lost productivity.[34] The Senate agreed and the final amended law, promulgated on September 6, 1905, provided for Sunday rest but with no compensation. Other changes included the restoration of the federal capital limitation in response to those who argued that a national extension of the legislation would violate constitutional provisions, the reduction of penalties to a fine ranging from 10 to 50 pesos, and the elimination of jail terms for infringement.

Even with this somewhat weakened and limited version, Palacios later noted, Argentina was in the forefront of western nations in enacting Sunday rest legislation. "Only Belgium," he noted, "had sanctioned such legislation in the same year as ours; Denmark, France, and Canada, in 1906; Italy, Portugal, and Chile, in 1907 . . . other nations much later."[35] For the Socialist deputy "the law of Sunday rest was the beginning, the difficult beginning, of a new legal structure that would transform the social aspect of the country."[36]

Palacios's second major legislative achievement experienced greater difficulties before final passage. The Socialist deputy, responding to a basic plank in the Socialist Party program and referring to similar provisions in the González code, on June 22, 1906, introduced a nineteen-point projected law intended to regulate child and female labor. On September 7, 1906, the legislation was reported out of committee with unanimously favorable support. The entire chamber, on that same day, gave general approval to the project.[37]

Opposition came from expected quarters. The Unión Industrial Argentina made its objections known, arguing again that social legislation would reduce production.[38] Within the Congress, UIA representatives Francisco Seguí and Ernesto Tornquist tried to prevent passage of the Palacios initiative. Their principal tactic was to delay consideration of the specific articles of the legislation, thereby avoiding a direct confrontation that would place them squarely in opposition. And for the rest of the 1906 session and into the special sessions of 1907 this tactic worked, as consideration of the legislation was postponed a total of eight different times.

Palacios fought delay at every turn, rising to challenge each opposition assertion. Throughout his speeches he stressed certain themes. Referring to official statistics, personal observation, and verified medical reports, Palacios drew a grim picture of labor conditions for minors and women in Argentina. Technological growth, the development of machines, the replacement of physical effort with mechanical devices had stimulated the increasing entrance of women and children into factories and shops. However, long hours without rest in front of often dangerous equipment, together with closed and choked atmospheric surroundings, made these workers old before their time. Many working conditions, he continued, were particularly injurious to the female organism and produced high rates of infant mortality.

Palacios's arguments, as usual, sought to mix a plea to the heart with a corresponding appeal to the practical considerations at hand. Social legislation, he argued, would get at the real causes of labor dissent and slow the steady spiral of strikes and violence. Responding directly to the assertions of the UIA, Palacios, drawing on British examples, claimed that shorter workdays and improved working conditions served to increase rather than decrease production.[39]

Finally, Palacios sought to touch the legislators' sense of national pride. Much of the impetus for the republic's nineteenth-century development had stemmed from a comparison of the country's status vis-à-vis Europe and the United States and a corresponding desire to catch up with what were perceived to be more progressive and advanced nations. Now Palacios and other Socialists adapted this argument to labor legislation. Although the republic had modernized economically, he maintained, it had failed to develop socially. The approval of the Sunday rest law had been a step in the right direction, but procrastination over regulation of child-female working conditions and other proposals kept Argentina in a secondary position. Palacios summarized these points in the following statement: "In those countries where labor laws exist, like New Zealand, Australia, the United States, England, etcetera, the struggles of the workers develop normally, the war of classes evolves pacifically, many rough edges are smoothed. On the other hand, in those backward countries that lack social legislation, where the government does not concern itself with worker problems, there . . . agitations are profound and are produced with true fiery explosions. Why deny it? We are on the list of backward nations."[40]

On July 12, 1907, the chamber finally voted its approval of Palacios's proposal. Passage came more than a year after the bill originally had been introduced and after hard and long debate, during which time the issue dominated the attention of the legislators. The law, number 5,291, promulgated on October 14, 1907, and put into effect on April 14, 1908, contained provisions of national jurisdiction that forbade contracted work for minors under ten years of age, prohibited those under sixteen from working at night or in occupations "that damage their health, their education, or their morality," and obligated "owners and administrators of shops and factories . . . to maintain their locales, installations, machines, and equipment and to organize labor in such a way that women and children do not run any danger."[41]

Alfredo L. Palacios ran on the Socialist Party ticket for reelection to the Chamber of Deputies in March of 1908. Once again Socialists defeated conservatives in *circunscripción* four, this time by a vote of 853 to 631. However, the *circunscripción* reform had been replaced with a return to the *lista completa*, and PAN candidates defeated the Socialist Party slate city-wide 15,651 to 7,576.[42]

From 1908 to 1912 no Socialist sat in the national Congress. Nevertheless, the four-year term of the party's first deputy had set the pattern for later and larger Socialist Party participation in Congress. Palacios had introduced many new issues, issues that became integral parts of congressional debate and consideration. His arguments in support of reform measures, particularly appeals to nationalist pride and conservative self-interest, were repeated often and effectively by subsequent Socialist deputies.

The lone Socialist also displayed an ability to carve out a substantial slice of the chamber's time and attention, reflecting an influence out of proportion to numerical representation. This, too, proved a characteristic of later Socialist Party action in the chamber, as did the techniques employed by Palacios to gain this time and attention: the dogged, repetitive introduction of Socialist-supported measures, despite consistent setbacks and the frequent resort to interpellation of executive officials.

Another striking characteristic of Palacios's first term, also seen in later Socialist Party representatives, was the care and research that went into preparations for debate. Legislative proposals were backed with foreign references and examples and specific information on particular Argentine conditions, usually supplemented with expert testimony, and, when available, voluminous statistics. Palacios continued the practice, begun with the writing of his law thesis *La miseria*, of investigating areas of concern first-hand. For example, in July 1907, when maritime police attacked a group of workers in Bahía Blanca, Palacios immediately traveled to the site and interrogated those involved. When he confronted the Minister of the Interior and the head of the Navy Department in a congressional interpellation on the incident, his personal research allowed him to ask penetrating questions and to refute official second-hand accounts with his own version gathered from personal interviews.[43]

Palacios's election and actions gave a considerable boost to the Socialist Party. Its first deputy, with his legislative successes such as the Sunday rest law and the regulation of child and female labor, strengthened the party's claim that major, concrete achievements for the working class could be gained through participation in the political and parliamentary process. The party, largely through *La Vanguardia*, publicized Palacios's activity with full-page reprints of his speeches and urged their readers to subscribe to the *Diario de Sesiones* (Congressional Record) to follow even more closely the activities of the man who in Congress echoed "the desires, yearnings, and necessities of the working class."[44]

Finally, Palacios in Congress represented for the Socialist Party a growing respectability and effectiveness, setting them clearly apart from their anarchist rivals. Men at the highest levels of government recognized the acceptability of much of the party's program and commended the party on its pacific tactics. Although eventually opposing the González labor code, Socialists obviously inspired much of the form and substance of the executive proposal. Socialist activity in favor of greater government attention to social matters probably played some part in the establishment of a national Labor Department in 1907. An adjunct of the Ministry of the Interior, the Labor Department was to collect information on labor matters, suggest social legislation, enforce existing labor statutes, and arbitrate labor-management disputes.

In sum, party strategy had succeeded in a trial run. Political organization had helped elect a Socialist deputy, who in turn promoted social legislation. The Palacios experience augured well for the party if future reforms should open the political system to broader participation.

5. Reform: 1910–1913

"It is not sufficient to guarantee the vote: we need to
create and to move the voter."

President Roque Sáenz Peña in his
inaugural address, October 12, 1910

For most of the 1910–1915 period Argentine economic growth followed the pattern set in the late nineteenth century. Exports of agricultural products grew, trade balances were favorable, railway mileage increased, and immigration continued. By 1914 the impact of World War I began to affect and to reverse these trends, at least temporarily. However, the major features of change during these years were not economic but political.

On February 10, 1912, a conservative Argentine Congress approved electoral reform legislation introduced by a conservative chief executive, Roque Sáenz Peña, and profoundly altered the course of Argentine politics. The elections that followed passage of this legislation terminated more than half a century of conservative control of the Argentine political process. From 1912 to 1930, active enforcement of the new law served to enlarge the electorate, increase political awareness and participation, promote the development of stable parties, bring new social-economic groups into the political life of the country, and instill in much of the citizenry a faith in democratic procedures. Moreover, by creating new channels of access to political power for emerging opposition groups, conservatives managed, at least for the short term, to avoid violent revolution and to end periodic internal strife over political issues.

The man who introduced and oversaw the passage of the 1912 reform, President Roque Sáenz Peña, was born into a noted *porteño* fam-

93

ily in 1851. He graduated from the University of Buenos Aires law school in 1875 and soon embarked on a distinguished political and diplomatic career, during which he associated with the more moderate and reform-minded elements of the conservative establishment.[1] In 1909 these elements formed a new party, the Unión Nacional (National Union), and chose Sáenz Peña as their presidential candidate. Running virtually unopposed, the Unión standard-bearer promised political reform as a means of avoiding revolution and of integrating foreign-born sectors into national life.[2]

The election that placed Sáenz Peña in the presidency differed little from those which had preceded it. The turnout in the capital on March 13, 1910, produced only 24,732 votes for the Unión Nacional candidate. In deputy contests in the city of Buenos Aires the Unión list handily defeated the Socialist Party slate by a margin of three to one.[3]

Once elected, Sáenz Peña proceeded quickly to insure that his own managed election would be the last of its kind in Argentina. Two months after his inauguration the new president sent to Congress the legislative projects of his intended electoral reform. On July 4, 1911, the Congress approved the law of "General Enrollment," which based voting qualifications and enrollment on the obligatory registration for military service, required since 1901 of all males who were over eighteen years of age and Argentine citizens. Two weeks later, legislation with regard to the electoral census and registration was sanctioned (law 8,130), the most important feature of which was to assign to the federal judiciary the responsibility for preparing national elections.[4]

These two measures passed with little resistance. The third proposal, however, containing provisions for minority representation and obligatory voting, aroused several months of controversial debate. Proponents argued that the changes were necessary to avoid violent revolution, to incorporate new groups into the governmental process, and to accomplish political development that would match social and economic growth. Opponents argued that the Argentine population was not yet fully prepared to exercise suffrage and that substantial peace and prosperity had been achieved under existing political procedures and institutions.[5] In the end, however, the proponents of change prevailed. On February 10, 1912, Congress approved by an ample margin law 8,871, which established provisions for obligatory voting and the guaranteed representation in parliament of more than one party.

The law that emerged in 1912 was an extensive and thorough set of rules. It displayed in its 107 articles the painstaking care its authors had taken to cover all aspects of the electoral process and to remedy as many past faults as possible. The key provisions established obligatory and universal suffrage for all males over eighteen who were either native or naturalized citizens. Excluded from the vote were those physically or mentally incapacitated, members of the regular clergy, members of the armed forces below the rank of lieutenant, convicted criminals, deserters from military service, and "the owners and directors of brothels." There were no property or literacy qualifications for voting. Penalties for not voting included a ten-peso fine and publication of the names of delinquent voters in public print. The *lista incompleta* (incomplete list), meaning citizens voted for only two-thirds of the candidates for deputies, assured minority representation. A step-by-step formula to cover the transaction of elections sought to assure the secrecy of the vote. Voters cast their ballots directly for deputies and indirectly for electors for president and vice president and senator from the federal capital. Provincial legislators chose the national senators from their districts.[6]

Comprehensive and elaborate provisions notwithstanding, the crucial test of the law would come during actual elections. In a country where legal and legislative forms had represented ideals to be attained rather than practices to be followed, many interested citizens waited to see the response of the executive and the conservative apparatus to the reform's initial application. The first proof that the law would be effective and that Sáenz Peña himself was committed to enforcing its provisions was provided on March 31, 1912, with the holding of gubernatorial elections in the province of Santa Fe. When all three parties in the contest claimed fraud in its preparation, Sáenz Peña appointed a special federal representative to oversee the election. The final result was a victory for the Radical Party, which defeated two conservative groups. All agreed as to the election's eventual honesty, and its successful outcome marked the beginning of the end for the UCR policy of abstention and non-participation.[7]

Although the Socialist Party objected to certain aspects of the Sáenz Peña law, it appreciated the opportunities offered by more honest and more open electoral procedures and responded rapidly and enthusiastically to these. Drawing on fifteen years of practice, Socialists prepared for the April 1912 congressional elections in the capital, the second major test of the Sáenz Peña law, with confidence and skill.

The six-man central electoral committee directed the campaign. On February 17, seven weeks before the election, the committee began its preparations, notifying centers and other affiliated groups to prepare lists of nominees for a March 4 meeting at the Club Vorwarts. According to the committee, the March meeting would determine whether the party was to participate in the deputy contest and, if so, would draw up the electoral platform and select candidates. All could vote on the platform. Women affiliated with citizen members were allowed to attend and to vote in the selection of candidates.

From the meeting emerged a straightforward five-point platform: 1) abrogation of the Residence and Social Defense laws; 2) enactment of an on-the-job accident compensation law; 3) suppression of taxes that increase the cost of consumables and implementation of a progressive tax on income from land; 4) an electoral system based on proportional representation in parliamentary and local elections; and 5) separation of Church and state and establishment of an absolute divorce law.

Men of prominence in positions of party leadership composed the candidate list. The eight chosen were Juan B. Justo, Alfredo L. Palacios, Mario Bravo, Francisco Cúneo, Enrique Dickmann, Nicolás Repetto, Enrique del Valle Iberlucea, and Alejandro Mantecón. The list included three doctors (Justo, Dickmann, and Repetto) and four lawyers (Palacios, Bravo, del Valle Iberlucea, and Mantecón). These middle-class professions were not noted in campaign material, as had been the case previously when working-class representation was stronger.

La Vanguardia, which in March and April devoted almost all its space to electoral matters (pushing labor news to the back pages), noted after the March 4 meeting that the task now was "to interest the people in the civic struggle; it is necessary to attract the mass of new voters, teaching them the practical use that can be made of their votes."[8] To this end a special committee, the Comité Pro Fondo Electoral (Committee for Electoral Funding), was organized to raise finances for the campaign. Party members were urged to make special contributions, their names thereby appearing regularly as contributors in *La Vanguardia*. Social events were planned to augment other areas of funding. One such, organized by the Socialist center of section four, was an all day *fiesta campestre*, or picnic, including games and dances. Nightly lectures were arranged in each *circunscripción*, usually featuring a candidate speaking on some aspect of the party platform. The electoral committee ordered the printing of 200,000 ballots, which, according to the new reform law, were to be supplied by the competing parties themselves, 100,000 copies of the party manifesto to the public, and 100,000 leaflets with the declaration of party principles and program. The committee made constant appeals to members to perform the basic work of campaigning—to stuff and seal envelopes, affix posters, and distribute leaflets. By all accounts the affiliates responded enthusiastically.

The 1912 Socialist campaign reached its peak with two large public rallies. One, held indoors on March 21, attracted a crowd of 6,000 persons. The second, an outdoor rally, was held on March 31, one week before the election. Gathering at the Plaza Constitución, on the near south side of the city, a crowd filling ten blocks heard speeches from the candidates and words of encouragement from Uruguayan Socialist Emilio Frugoni, invited to cross the Río de la Plata to lend his presence to the proceedings. Despite some difficulties in receiving police permission to assemble, both these rallies took place peaceably, without untoward interruption or incident.[9]

In sum, the Socialist campaign was impressively well prepared and well organized. Socialist candidates were chosen and a platform composed a full month prior to the election. The principal competing parties delayed selection of their slates until the end of March, and failed at any time to present comprehensive programs. As compared with their major opposition in the capital, the UCR, the Socialists enjoyed a fifteen-year edge in the techniques of campaigning.

On April 7 *La Vanguardia* published a special edition that contained general voting information and facsimiles of the party's lists of deputy candidates and electors for senator. Candidates and officials toured the various *circunscripciones* of the city as the voting took place. They encouraged their co-workers and used automobiles to transport supporters to polling locations. The day passed without report of any of the kind of vote-buying or voter intimidation that had characterized previous elections.[10]

In 1912, more voters than ever before went to the polls throughout the republic. The final tally showed 640,852 voters of 935,001 registered that year.[11] This compared with a turnout of only one in every three in 1904. Moreover, the voting in the capital, where more than four out of five eligible voters participated, was another impressive indicator of the reform's success.

It should be noted, however, that the effectiveness of the Sáenz Peña law in enlarging the electorate was relative. Two important groups remained excluded from voting: foreigners and women, the latter not gaining the right to suffrage until 1949. While the 640,852 voters in 1912 represented a significant increase over past turnouts, they were still less than 10 percent of the total estimated population of 6,870,608. Between 1912 and 1928 the number of voters in the republic steadily increased, but the percentage of voters to total population never exceeded 15 percent.[12]

On April 7, as on every election day following the Sáenz Peña reform, the polls closed at 6 p.m. The official in charge of each *mesa*, or table, where voting took place sealed the ballot boxes and placed election information and other material in an envelope, all of which was sent first to the nearest post office and from there to the national Chamber of Deputies for elections in the capital or to provincial legislatures for elections outside of Buenos Aires. On the day following the election, the counting of ballots began under the direction of a committee appointed by the Ministry of the Interior. Participating parties were permitted to send representatives to observe the tally and to note discrepancies or challenge irregularities. The ballot boxes were opened and the results read aloud for each vote and then recorded. After the final count, which usually lasted about two weeks in capital elections, the written ballots were burned.

According to Enrique Dickmann, the first two votes read out in the chamber on April 8 were in favor of Radical and Socialist candidates, setting a tone of confrontation between the two parties in the capital that continued for two decades.[13] The final results came as a rude surprise for the conservatives, who previously had swept all Buenos Aires elections with overwhelming margins. The Radicals captured eight of the twelve deputy seats contested. Of the remaining four, two went to Socialist candidates and one each to the Unión Cívica and the Unión Nacional. In the senatorial contest, the UCR's José Camilo Crotto, with 27,440 votes, defeated the Unión Cívica's Francisco J. Beazley (24,319), Benito Villanueva of the Unión Nacional (19,417), and Manuel Ugarte of the Socialist Party (14,314).[14]

The Socialist totals in 1912 showed a four-fold increase in their votes from 1910. Alfredo L. Palacios led the ticket, placing third in the overall balloting. Juan B. Justo was a precarious twelfth, just nosing out a conservative rival.[15]

The distribution of votes in 1912, noted in table 4, suggests strong Socialist support in working-class districts. Palacios carried sections three, four, and six, all, as Appendix A shows, with a significant proportion of worker, artisan, and small merchant voters. He also made a respectable showing in sections two, eight, and eighteen, all with large working-class voting blocs. The party's most serious weaknesses were in those areas with a high percentage of employees, owners, and professionals (five, eleven, twelve, thirteen, fourteen, and twenty), where Radicals and conservatives enjoyed the edge.[16]

These results, then, implied a two-pronged policy for the Socialists. First, to continue to build working-class support, particularly through urging the naturalization of immigrant workers. Second, to pursue the difficult course of strengthening their position with middle- and upper-middle-class voters in competition with the UCR and the conservative parties.

TABLE 4
DEPUTY ELECTIONS, FEDERAL CAPITAL, ABSOLUTE AND PROPORTIONATE VOTES BY CIRCUNSCRIPCIÓN, APRIL 7, 1912

Circun-scripción	UCR	%	PS	%	UC	%	UN	%	Voted	Enrolled	Turnout %
1	1,201	(25.9)	1,047	(22.5)	1,127	(24.3)	1,600	(34.5)	4,644	5,493	84.54
2	1,264	(32.2)	1,159	(29.5)	719	(18.3)	1,037	(26.4)	3,931	4,684	83.92
3	2,888	(36.4)	2,994	(37.7)	1,745	(22.0)	1,599	(20.1)	7,941	9,124	87.03
4	1,990	(28.1)	2,605	(36.8)	935	(13.2)	1,041	(14.7)	7,070	9,380	75.37
5	1,517	(31.2)	1,141	(23.5)	1,462	(30.1)	1,718	(35.4)	4,859	5,594	86.86
6	1,699	(34.8)	1,747	(35.8)	1,439	(29.5)	1,407	(28.8)	4,877	5,536	88.09
7	1,346	(28.2)	884	(18.5)	1,340	(28.1)	975	(20.4)	4,768	5,469	87.18
8	2,155	(35.7)	2,051	(34.0)	1,589	(26.4)	1,606	(26.6)	6,028	7,021	85.85
9	2,185	(37.8)	1,920	(33.3)	1,787	(30.9)	1,663	(28.8)	5,774	6,872	84.02
10	1,117	(35.7)	1,075	(34.4)	1,092	(34.9)	971	(31.1)	3,125	3,681	84.89
11	1,172	(35.0)	1,112	(33.2)	1,425	(42.6)	1,056	(31.6)	3,346	3,875	86.34
12	2,463	(43.8)	1,688	(30.0)	1,906	(33.9)	1,505	(26.7)	5,628	6,427	87.56
13	2,283	(38.3)	1,849	(31.0)	2,648	(44.4)	2,044	(34.3)	5,965	7,273	82.01
14	1,768	(34.1)	1,515	(29.2)	2,330	(44.9)	1,858	(35.8)	5,186	6,256	82.89
15	982	(29.7)	758	(22.9)	701	(21.2)	1,009	(30.5)	3,309	4,136	80.00
16	1,681	(35.9)	1,337	(28.6)	1,553	(33.2)	1,440	(30.8)	4,680	5,432	86.15
17	1,478	(34.7)	1,187	(27.8)	1,322	(31.0)	1,186	(27.8)	4,264	5,359	79.56
18	2,656	(35.4)	2,410	(32.1)	2,355	(31.4)	2,254	(30.1)	7,497	8,882	84.40
19	2,609	(34.1)	2,832	(37.0)	3,346	(43.7)	2,473	(32.3)	7,662	8,915	85.94
20	1,442	(37.0)	1,140	(29.3)	1,918	(49.2)	1,372	(35.2)	3,896	4,527	86.06
Totals	35,896	(34.4)	32,451	(31.1)	32,739	(31.3)	29,814	(28.5)	104,450	123,936	84.27

a. Source: Darío Cantón, *Materiales para el estudio de la sociología política en la Argentina*, II, 3. Totals and percentage calculations are mine.
b. The four parties in competition were the Unión Cívica Radical (UCR), Partido Socialista (PS), Unión Cívica (UC), and Unión Nacional (UN).
c. The party figures for each *circunscripción* represent the total for the leading vote-getter on each ticket, explaining percentages that sometimes total over 100.

The Sáenz Peña law made the Argentine political system more competitive, stimulated the growth of political parties, and changed the nature of one of the principal arenas of political combat—the national Congress. In 1912 two Socialists and eleven Radicals took seats in the 120-man Chamber of Deputies and one Radical sat in the 30-man Senate. The congressional representation of these two parties, particularly the Radicals, grew significantly in the following decades, breaking the former conservative monopoly over the legislative process. As a result there was an increase in congressional activity, a consideration of more issues, and debates reflecting a broader gamut of opinion than previously had been the case. Also, there was a change in the tone, style, and content of congressional discussion. Visiting the new Congressional Palace, inaugurated in 1906, with its beautiful pink marble columns, ornate brass and woodwork, leather chairs, and velvet curtains, Jean Jaurès noted in 1911 that congressional debate seemed "a meeting of well-educated people who do not wish to contradict one another."[17] The man to whom that remark was directed, Juan B. Justo, did much to change that situation.

When Justo entered the Congress he was a relatively unknown quantity. Founder and leader of what was still a small and "exotic" political group, he lacked the flamboyance and the legislative antecedents of his colleague Palacios. With his walking stick, bowler hat, and dark, conservative dress he looked more the prosperous businessman than a champion of the proletariat. Although he was bearded, his hair was of conventional length and he exhibited none of the fashionable flair of his younger associate. Appearance, however, was deceiving. When Justo rose to introduce legislation, challenge a fellow legislator, or interrogate an administrative official, his language and the tenor of his remarks often surpassed the revolutionary and outspoken manner of his Socialist predecessor. In many ways, Justo was the best representative of the new spirit that invaded the staid halls of Congress after 1912.

The two Socialist deputies, Justo and Palacios, began their term with a refusal to take the oath of office in the name of God, instead swearing only to serve the nation and the Constitution. Justo gave his first major speech on May 31 during a discussion of the approval of deputy elections in San Juan province.[18] His language and his interpretation of the facts previewed the parliamentary course he would take in the future. Using the charge of election fraud in San Juan as an opening wedge, Justo described the social injustices of the province, blaming them on the parasitic land-owning classes, who lived abroad "from the profits that they draw from the Argentine land and from the working class that peoples this country." He then proceeded to make a broader

attack on the entire political system, claiming that fraud still dominated the electoral process despite new regulations. When conservatives
responded with a defense of the Sáenz Peña law as a product of the
very class Justo attacked, the deputy replied that "if there is a new
political era in the country, it is precisely because of the appearance of
new social forces and materials, and not because new virtues have appeared: it is because there is a new popular class, numerous and vigorous, that imposes itself on the attention of public powers, and because
it is easier to form a new election law than to repress a general strike
each six months."[19]

In his speeches Justo combined a bluntness of language with an iron-
ic and biting sarcasm that often enraged his fellow deputies and led to
personal insults and shouting matches that often had to be stricken
from the official record. And the effectiveness of Justo's speech and
manner is difficult to measure. Many times he employed a verbal sledge
hammer when a scalpel would have better served his purpose. However, there were more aspects to Justo's parliamentary activity than his
irritating language. He was intelligent, well-educated, able to read six
foreign languages, at ease with arcane economic subjects, and the bene-
ficiary of two decades of political experience. He offered carefully-con-
sidered and clearly-presented projects that gradually won the admiration and respect of many of his fellow congressmen. Justo worked hard
at his job; he attended nearly every session, traveled on weekends or
after hours to investigate matters of legislative concern, and generally
played a role in Congress that belied the small numerical representation of the Socialist Party.

During his first year in office Justo made his mark in a number of
areas, many of them jointly with Palacios. He co-sponsored legislation
to abrogate the Residence and Social Defense laws, to provide legal
protection for unions, to provide compensation for on-the-job accidents, to raise the fees for liquor licenses, to raise salaries and supply
retirement benefits for school teachers, and to assure secular education
and the removal of Church influences from public schools. These measures did not proceed far in the chamber, but they did set precedents
for future Socialist action.

Economics, particularly the correlation between government expenditures and the rising cost of living, captured much of Justo's parliamentary attention during his first term. On June 19, 1912, he spoke
against a proposal to subsidize an Argentine student group for a trip to
Lima, Peru, to attend an international student meeting, arguing that
the time of the chamber and the money of the government could be
better spent on working-class concerns. His objection was overruled

and the subsidy voted.[20] Two days later, June 21, Congress considered another special subsidy, this time for the city of Tucumán to celebrate July 9, the date of the signing of Argentina's Declaration of Independence in 1816. Justo claimed the payment to be no more than a special allowance for the President to visit Tucumán. He went on to warn the chamber that "we are embarked on the most expensive forms of patriotism. . . . If we are going to misspend public money in this manner, voting these 250,000 pesos for an ordinarily celebrated anniversary in Tucumán and in all the other parts of the territory, we are going to produce truly disastrous results for the national treasury. We would have to establish a Ministry of Patriotism, charged with the fiestas and anniversaries of the year, that would mark beforehand the expenses made for these celebrations." Considerable applause from the galleries punctuated these remarks, and with Palacios and Justo voting in the negative the chamber defeated the Tucumán subsidy proposal 45 to 26.[21]

Justo had a further opportunity to discuss governmental fiscal policy when Minister of the Interior José M. Rosa appeared on July 22 to report on continued increases in the cost of living in Argentina. Rosa stated that higher prices resulted inevitably from the economic growth of a rich country. Justo disagreed. Beginning his presentation with the assertion that in the past economic matters and fiscal policy had been discussed secretly and out of public view (here he brought cries of objection from the floor but shouts of encouragement from the public galleries), Justo traced higher prices for the consumer directly to specific government policies. He singled out the monetary law of 1899 and the overproduction of paper money as principal culprits in lowering the real value of wages and raising prices. Government expenditures, particularly to create unnecessary bureaucratic positions and special subsidies for non-productive purposes, were another source of economic malaise. But the major fault, Justo contended, could be found in the methods used to gather revenue: tariffs and taxes. High duties on essential goods, especially foodstuffs, he labeled as a prime cause of higher prices. These tariffs, he continued, were not intended to increase revenues so much as to protect "aristocratic industries, those that have been defended in government by influential members of the oligarchy. . . ." Tariffs should be raised, the Socialist deputy suggested, on such items as alcohol, lead-based paints, automobiles, and revolvers, which, he added "play a certain role in Argentine politics." But the basic source of government income should be a tax on land, the revenue from which should be distributed by the government in a way to close the gap between rich and poor. The result he envisioned would be a situation in which "the salary of the worker comprises that which he needs to live—healthfully and decently—that which he needs to raise and to educate his offspring, that which is necessary to develop his political and societal capacity, that which is necessary, finally, to assure his old age and to cultivate his highest faculties. In this way the Argentine parliament can contribute so that this country will not be a region of rich and ignorant bosses and of an oppressed, exploited, and miserable working class, but rather the seat of a modern, healthy, vigorous nation, worthy of a prominent place in the concert of other nations."[22]

As the first year of Justo's first congressional term neared an end, the self-proclaimed "peoples' deputy" focused his attention on a final matter of fiscal concern, the annual national budget. The executive branch formulated the budget and submitted it to Congress at the end of each yearly session. A lengthy and complicated balance sheet, it was usually approved with little discussion. Justo radically changed this routine, examining and questioning nearly every expenditure. In his first challenge he concentrated on three major areas of criticism. First, he argued, the budget included too many unnecessary bureaucratic positions, filled usually by relatives of influential politicians who were given make-work jobs. "There is," he noted, "a superabundance of useless employees, employees doubly pernicious, for what they cost and for what they hinder." Most high officials, Justo continued, were overpaid and underworked, while the reverse was true of lower officials. He suggested a cutting of the fat at the top and a beefing up of salaries for those at the bottom. Second, he attacked the federal system under which national funds were distributed to the provinces to rectify local budgetary deficits but without any national control. Waste and corruption resulted, indicating a need for greater centralization in the disbursement of these resources and greater federal jurisdiction over how they were used. Third, he questioned money earmarked for various public works projects, which, he asserted, usually implied a project to benefit powerful private interests rather than the general population.[23]

Justo's initial critique produced little immediate action. Much of what he said was true. The Argentine executive budget, like most such spending proposals, contained many provisions that were wasteful and many projects beneficial to groups tied closely to politicians. The Socialists enjoyed a major advantage in Congress: they were not tied to any special interests. Their financial support came from party dues, voluntary contributions, and professional and congressional salaries. When they spoke of serving the public without compromise or the need to pay off political debts they spoke with considerable authority.

Such was not the case, however, for most men in public life, particularly in Congress. They did have debts to pay and interests to support. Therefore, rarely were Justo's or the other Socialists' objections to the budget heeded. Nevertheless, by focusing parliamentary and eventually public attention on previously neglected aspects of governmental fiscal policy, the Socialists contributed to a growing national awareness of and concern with such matters and undoubtedly strengthened their own political position in an area with considerable popular appeal.

Alfredo L. Palacios supported his Socialist colleague in a number of ways. He jointly sponsored with Justo legislative projects stemming from the party's minimum program, joined him in ministerial interpellations, and rose to his defense when conservatives—sometimes Palacios's personal friends—made strident attacks against the party founder. In addition to working closely with Justo, Palacios also amplified those proposals and achievements that had marked his first four years in the chamber. By 1912 the problem of enforcing the provisions of his 1905 Sunday rest and 1907 child-female protection laws came to his attention. Regulation of these measures fell to the police and the recently-created national Department of Labor, which was generally understaffed and insufficiently funded. In an August 12, 1912, interpellation of Indalecio Gómez, Minister of the Interior, Palacios noted various violations of the 1905 and 1907 laws, particularly with regard to the sale of alcoholic beverages on Sunday, which continued unabated, and the failure to respect age and hour limitations for women and children employees. "The national Department of Labor," he observed, "has disconnected itself completely from its principal function [regulation], delegating it to other administrative branches and thus converting itself into a subaltern office, vegetating and useless." To remedy this situation Palacios proposed on September 18, 1912, a reform of the statutes of the Labor Department, providing the office with greater scope, independence, and authority. Working in conjunction with Radicals and conservatives, Palacios helped promote final passage of law 9,040, an eleven-article piece of legislation reforming the department and including Palacios's principal contribution, article three, which read: "The department will establish a service of direct and permanent inspection and vigilance in industrial and commercial establishments, with the purpose of watching over the fulfillment of laws relative to labor."[24]

The enforcement of existing regulations of working conditions underscored a major dilemma for Palacios and his party. The Socialists based much of their political appeal to the working classes on the importance of introducing and enacting social legislation. This, they argued, was the solidest, surest, indeed the only practical method of improving the lot of the working man and woman. This, too, was the major Socialist premise when competing with anarchists for proletarian support. But, as the Palacios discussion in late 1912 showed, it was one thing to pass legislation, difficult enough in itself for a minority party, and quite another to ensure that such legislation was enforced or made effective. In Argentina a gap between theory and practice, between law and administration, was a tradition dating back to colonial times. To overcome this tradition, to make legislation effective, the party had to do more than elect congressmen. It also had to capture national administration. Until the Socialists could influence both ends of the reform process their arguments for the efficacy of peaceful political change through participation and legislation would have a hollow ring for those who saw little change in actual conditions in spite of the passage of Socialist-sponsored measures.

The March 30, 1913, off-year elections in the capital to fill three deputy seats and one Senate post gave the Socialist Party an imposing victory. Socialists Nicolás Repetto, with 48,593 votes, and Mario Bravo, with 48,453 votes, topped all deputy candidates. Radical Lauro Lagos also captured a seat, running third with 30,612. Most surprising, however, was the victory of Socialist candidate Enrique del Valle Iberlucea in the senatorial contest. Little known outside of party circles, his 41,484 votes helped him to defeat Leopoldo Melo of the UCR (30,748), Francisco J. Beazley of the Unión Cívica (22,880), and independent Estanislao S. Zeballos (8,899).[25]

Generally, press reaction to the Socialist victory was favorable. *La Prensa*, for example, credited the party's organization and "disciplined action" for the triumph.[26] Unfavorable reaction came primarily from conservatives, who saw Radical and Socialist election victories as the conquest of revolutionary parties. Conservatives, also, especially attacked the Socialists as representing the low-born, the illiterate, and the foreigner. Socialist votes, some claimed, came from mobilization of the immigrant masses who threatened Argentine traditions and stability.

President Sáenz Peña himself sought to counterbalance unfavorable conservative reaction to the two capital elections. In a May 6, 1913, speech to a joint session of Congress he pointed out, in answer to those who viewed recent Radical and Socialist gains as the harbinger of foreign immigrant influence, that of the 109,000 citizens who voted in 1913, only 13,300 were naturalized citizens, the rest native-born. Even with the highly unlikely possibility that all 13,300 new citizens voted

Socialist, the party's 48,000 votes included an ample Argentine-born margin over Radical and conservative totals.[27]

The Radical Party, soundly defeated by the Socialists in 1913, joined the alarmist conservative chorus Sáenz Peña sought to calm. Radical arguments focused on a supposed conservative-Socialist alliance to thwart the UCR and echoed nationalist sentiment that the Socialist Party was a foreign, non-Argentine party composed of the "amoral scum of European civilization." [28]

A Radical-Socialist confrontation in the Senate highlighted this debate. When Enrique del Valle Iberlucea entered the Senate as the only Socialist among the thirty members, José Camilo Crotto, the only Radical, rose to challenge the new member's right to assume his seat. Unfurling the nationalist banner, Crotto questioned the credentials of a man who belonged to a party that "has perverted completely the national soul and has proscribed the Argentine Hymn in all its meetings, substituting for it one that is completely foreign." Referring to del Valle Iberlucea's editorship of the *Revista Socialista Internacional,* Crotto implied that the anti-national comments expressed in the *Revista*'s questionnaire on the issue of internationalism versus nationalism were the editor's responsibility. Moreover, the Radical concluded, "he [del Valle Iberlucea] is of foreign birth [and] should not enter this chamber. He does not love the country [Spain] where he was born, nor this one where he has been nationalized." [29]

The Socialist answered eloquently and effectively. He noted that his election resulted from the votes of Argentine citizens, fully aware of where he stood as compared with the vague and non-programmatic UCR. These votes, he added, came mostly from native-born Argentines. Admitting his role in the *International Socialist Review*'s questionnaire, del Valle Iberlucea pointed out that the thrust of Socialist thinking indicated a conciliation of national and international elements. Socialists, he continued, advocated a "healthy" nationalism, concerned not so much with symbols as with working for the well-being of the nation and all the people who were its inhabitants. They also advocated the incorporation of the immigrant working class into national life through naturalization and in the past twenty years had worked to that end through peaceful participation in the political process, while the intransigent Radicals conspired and revolted against established national authority. "The Socialist Party," he concluded, "is not a party of foreigners, no; in its majority it is formed of native citizens, and if there are foreign elements in it, these have the sentiment of nationality, in the true sense of the word, as deeply rooted as does the senator from the capital." With only two votes against him, one of which was

Crotto's, del Valle Iberlucea took his seat on April 29, 1913, as Latin America's first Socialist senator.[30]

Radical and conservative objections notwithstanding, the 1913 elections more than doubled the Socialist representation in Congress and injected new vigor into the party's already energetic representation. Meeting soon after the final tabulation of votes, the five Socialist representatives resolved to convene regularly to plan strategy and to carve out special areas of interest. The first legislative concern, it was decided, should be the budget for the coming year. Each deputy took a part of the proposal to investigate, criticize, and bring to the attention of the chamber.

At the opening of Congress only 62 of the 120 elected representatives appeared at the first session. The initial Socialist attack on the budget dealt specifically with absenteeism. In discussing congressional salaries, which were 1,500 pesos a month, Palacios proposed that they be pegged to attendance. Justo added that even so pegged the allotted salaries were too high, ironically warning the conservatives that since half of every Socialist deputy's salary went to the party for propaganda and campaigning it was in their own best interests to keep compensation low. Nevertheless, the Palacios amendment was easily defeated.

Nothing daunted, the four Socialist deputies continued their attack. Justo led the Socialist charge, arguing that the budget was too important to be treated as a "closed book" without careful congressional study. He repeated his objections to what he considered superfluous public employees and "exorbitant taxes for public works that have as their principal object the enrichment of the landowning class."[31]

Justo's three Socialist allies supported him throughout the budgetary debate. Palacios and Bravo concentrated on what they considered unnecessary expenses to subsidize Catholic educational institutions and the diplomatic corps. Nicolás Repetto made his first speech on May 14, using the occasion to criticize the superfluity of employees in the Senate, mostly hired as political favors, and further suggested that public monies could be saved with the elimination of the congressional buffet that provided snacks of tea and crackers for deputies and senators. Three days later, on May 17, Repetto made a more extensive attack, criticizing in particular expenses of the national Department of Health, which, he charged, wasted money on useless experiments instead of improving the health of the general public. He also proposed that special government subsidies for aristocratic private yachting, rowing, and touring clubs be eliminated. He urged, however, that the subsidy for "football," or soccer, which was becoming a great favorite among the working classes, be retained.[32]

The immediate impact of the Socialist campaign against excessive expenditures again was slight. Despite their energetic denunciations, most of the budgetary provisions were approved. Once more, special interests prevailed. However, by 1913 the party representatives had succeeded through their joint action in concentrating more congressional attention on budgetary matters than ever before. The Socialist-inspired debate occupied the first three weeks of the session. Ministers were called in to defend and explain past, present, and future expenses for their departments. Enough congressmen agreed with the Socialists on the need at least to discuss these matters to vote with them against motions to close debate on May 15 and 16. Although some, like conservative deputies Arturo M. Bas of Córdoba and José M. Penna of Buenos Aires, accused the Socialists of playing politics with the issue and delaying consideration of more important items, others voted with them. Rogelio Araya, Radical deputy from Santa Fe, agreed on the need for more careful scrutiny of national expenses. Araya, along with six of his Radical colleagues, joined the four Socialists and eleven others to oppose final closing of debate on the budget on May 29, 1913. However, forty-four conservatives voted in favor of shutting off discussion and sent the budget to the Senate for final approval.[33]

Within the context of the budgetary debate, spirited and impassioned Socialist-conservative confrontations frequently occurred. These often had little to do with the matters at hand. One, during a May 19 discussion of government expenditures for the University of Córdoba, ended with Justo calling conservative Arturo Bas a "Jesuit deputy" and Bas labeling Justo a "wretch." Another conservative claimed that Justo "sits in parliament by an aberration!"[34]

Socialist activities throughout the 1913 sessions provided ample opportunity to provoke many such exchanges. Nicolás Repetto and Alfredo L. Palacios, in June 1913, called the Minister of Public Works to account for an explosion in a government-owned gasworks that resulted in the deaths of fourteen workers. The Socialists accused the government of negligence; the minister and his conservative allies responded with nationalist attacks on their accusers.[35] On August 6 Repetto called for official action to improve the conditions of military barracks in the federal capital. José F. Uriburu, conservative deputy from Salta, objected to Socialists acting as personal inspectors of military installations. He concluded that a first-hand investigation, which Repetto had made of the barracks, was not part of a deputy's responsibilities.[36]

Mario Bravo, like Repetto a freshman deputy, initiated his congressional career with a proposed amnesty for those who had violated the law of obligatory military service. The bill would give such infractors a second chance to enroll without punishment.[37] Bravo also spoke for a party proposal to ease the acquisition of citizenship for foreigners, arguing that a once simple procedure had become time-consuming and complicated. Because of recent restrictive legislation, according to Bravo, a foreigner seeking naturalization was forced to obtain a police clearance that certified his "good conduct," that is, his non-participation in strike activities. Such barriers should be removed, the Socialists proposed, and a special administrative department created to attend exclusively to the granting of citizenship.[38] This measure, like the suggested amnesty, languished in committee for the duration of the session.

Bravo, like his colleagues, focused on legislative issues of particular personal concern. One of these was reform in the election of municipal government—basically, to extend the Sáenz Peña law from the national to the local level.[39] Another was protection of and improved conditions for sugar workers. On September 26, the Socialist deputies introduced legislation providing for the eight-hour day normally, ten hours during the harvests, twenty-four continuous hours of rest a week, overtime pay, and regulation of child-female workers for those employed in the sugar industry. Bravo, from the sugar-producing center of Tucumán, gave the principal supporting speech. In his comments he noted that conservative objections would center as usual on some nationalistic counterargument. His response in advance was: "If a patriotic color has to be given to the defense of the material and moral interests in question, I shall say, to conclude, that I aspire with the presentation of this project to extend the blue and white banner of industrial protectionism, which only waves over the chimneys of the sugar mills, out to the fields of cultivation, to the poor dwellings, so that one hundred thousand Argentines can share in this way in the defensive legal action that only pertains today exclusively to the *caudillos* of the industry."[40] The measure, however, was not considered.

Government protection of sugar and other industries became a prominent Socialist issue. While the Unión Industrial Argentina struggled with scant success to gain official support and protection for new manufacturing industries, certain interests—meat, sugar, wine, and railroads—enjoyed considerable influence. Their representatives had political power and their workers were among the most exploited in Argentine society. In 1913 Juan B. Justo first spoke against what he considered the excessive concentration of wealth and power of these economic sectors. The Socialist position on trusts and monopolies, as developed by Justo, was that such concentrations were an inevitable and not altogether undesirable aspect of capitalist evolution. Such concentrations provided more efficient means of production and cut down on competition, thereby allowing, in theory, for lower prices for goods. "We consider them [monopolies and trusts]," Justo stated, "simply as the last superior stage that immediately precedes the absorption by the collectivity of the technical-economic directive functions." But in Argentina the growth of monopolies had produced higher rather than lower prices. Until the socialization of these sectors occurred, Justo continued, they must be regulated and their abuses checked.

Justo mentioned two monopolies in particular. One was sugar, a "nutritional article of prime importance and general consumption, and whose price, in our country, has been raised in an exorbitant manner by the constant favors of Argentine law to a capitalist syndicate, a syndicate that is formed by the great mills of Tucumán and by the great refinery of Rosario, which completely dominate that branch of production and the commerce of our country." The second area was the meat producing and packing industry, by this time the primary base of the Argentine economy, and, like sugar, strongly represented politically as well as protected by the government.

The thrust of Justo's argument was that trusts should be regulated. The state had the responsibility to regulate, but so far had not met this responsibility. Indeed, Justo pointed out, historically the state had encouraged rather than controlled such concentrations. The Socialist role, he averred, would be to press for regulation and to counter protection with free trade policies.[41] On August 20, 1913, Justo, Bravo, and Repetto, with the additional signatures of Radicals Miguel M. Laurencena of Entre Ríos and Francisco G. Valdez of Santa Fe and conservative Víctor R. Pesenti, also of Santa Fe, presented legislation to lower the tariff on sugar. Justo, who provided the principal supporting statement, argued that a lower tariff for sugar would lower prices and force the domestic producers, for the last thirty years "the spoiled child of Argentine commercial policy," to improve working and living conditions for their employees, "to moderate the sugar trust monopoly," and "to create a new source of fiscal resources."[42]

Socialist action in this area produced few concrete results. The interests involved were too entrenched, too powerful, and too well represented. As with its budgetary fight, however, the party delegation brought to congressional and public view the connection between government policy and concentrations of private economic power and made them part of public political dialogue.

The key Socialist-inspired legislative achievements of the 1913 session stemmed primarily from the work of Alfredo L. Palacios. Largely through his efforts, law 9,104 extended the principle of obligatory weekly rest for workers to the national territories (areas in the north and south of the republic not yet given provincial status and under the control of the national administration). Law 9,114 provided government funds to shelter orphans, and law 9,143, entitled the "Ley Palacios," imposed severe penalties on those engaged in white slavery and prostitution. These three measures all received some support from Radicals and conservatives. Conservatives Juan F. Cafferata and Arturo M. Bas, for example, who clashed bitterly with the Socialists on other matters, praised Palacios for his initiatives against prostitution, which Bas labeled "a malign cancer of civilization."[43]

In August 1914 President Roque Sáenz Peña died in office and was succeeded by his vice-president, Victorino de la Plaza. Juan B. Justo, speaking in the Chamber of Deputies, paid homage to the statesman who "acted in a moment of Argentine history in which the fundamental problem was that of the reality of suffrage, that of the truth of popular suffrage. He understood this problem, he translated the conviction into a new law, and he applied that law with loyalty and energy, seeking to make our parliament a truly modern parliament. . . . He has realized, without resort to force, in this continent of bloody and sterile revolts, a truly bloodless and fruitful revolution."[44] A revolution, Justo might have added, that justified the tactics of his own party and provided the Socialists a national forum from which to promote their own program.

6. Elections, Congress, and the 'Palacios Affair': 1914–1915

> The candidates of the Socialist Party represent a new orientation in Argentine politics and a great human ideal.
>
> *La Vanguardia* prior to the 1914 congressional elections

Following their successes of 1912 and 1913 the Socialists looked forward to the March 22, 1914, capital deputy elections with confidence. On February 13 the party chose its list of candidates, once again selecting men of considerable experience in the party and generally of professional, middle-class backgrounds.[1]

The Socialists placed their 1914 campaign within the framework of past and future parliamentary activity. The March editions of *La Vanguardia*, devoted almost exclusively to the upcoming elections, explained in detail how present Socialist congressmen had worked for social and economic reforms and how, if elected, future Socialist representatives would continue and strengthen this work.

On election day, after another energetic and well-managed effort, *La Vanguardia* predicted that "today social democracy will triumph in the capital of the republic, marching toward the conquest of more liberty and more justice."[2] The partisan *La Vanguardia* was not always an accurate prophet, but in this case the prediction was correct. With President de la Plaza issuing special orders to assure compliance with the electoral reform laws, the party recorded its second straight victory in a federal capital deputy contest. The Socialists captured seven seats, top vote-getter Nicolás Repetto receiving 44,335 votes. The Radicals took three seats, their leading candidate getting 38,722 votes. The leading conservative vote-getter, Francisco J. Beazley of the Unión Cívica,

113

with a little over 20,000 votes, lagged far behind Socialist and UCR candidates.[3]

The distribution of votes, as noted in table 5, showed the party with continued comfortable margins in working-class *circunscripciones* one through four, six through eight, fifteen and eighteen. The edge in more middle-class districts like nine and ten was narrower, and Radicals bested the party in sections five, eleven through fourteen, and nineteen, all with high percentages of employees, owners, and professionals. The Unión Cívica managed to carry only the conservative bailiwick of *circunscripción* twenty. In the battle for the middle-class voter the UCR was beginning to reveal its strength, improving its overall showing from 1913 in *circunscripciones* eleven through fourteen and nineteen by almost 3,000 votes, while the Socialists dropped some 1,416 votes in these same districts.

The 1914 elections augmented congressional representation for the Socialists and the UCR. The Socialists more than doubled their numbers, from four deputies to nine. The Radicals, winning seats in several provinces, had a total of twenty-eight deputies in 1914.

The addition of five new Socialists helped to spread the responsibility within the party's delegation and bring new expertise to a variety of subjects. Each deputy was assigned to a committee, usually one related to an area of personal interest. In committees and from the floor the Socialists promoted legislation reflective of their minimum program, building on the base Justo and Palacios had established.

On June 3, the day on which committee assignments were announced, the Socialists re-introduced a proposal permitting divorce and presented for the first time a project to institute the so-called *semana inglesa* (English week), whereby on Saturdays employees working until noon would receive a full day's pay. Enrique Dickmann, making his debut in what would be a long and productive parliamentary career, provided the supportive comments for this proposal. He gave a detailed exposition, producing facts and figures from other countries where the *semana inglesa* had been implemented, and argued that such legislation would improve employee performance and increase production.[4]

On June 5, young Antonio de Tomaso rose to question the Minister of Defense as to recent army maneuvers in which several conscripts had been killed. He extended his talk to present the Socialist position on the military, in which he claimed that the party was not an enemy of the army but rather was concerned with "correcting abuses or serious errors of the directors of the army, in order that it not be separated from the country, . . . in order that it not cost as much money as it costs

TABLE 5
DEPUTY ELECTIONS, FEDERAL CAPITAL, ABSOLUTE
AND PROPORTIONATE VOTES BY CIRCUNSCRIPCIÓN,
MARCH 22, 1914

Circun- scripción	UCR	%	PS	%	UC	%	PC	%	Voted	Regis- tered	Turn- out %
1	1,683	(36.0)	1,896	(40.5)	679	(14.5)	700	(15.0)	4,677	6,571	71.2
2	1,219	(29.4)	2,067	(49.8)	394	(09.5)	474	(11.4)	4,149	6,027	68.8
3	2,636	(32.3)	3,860	(47.3)	831	(10.1)	869	(10.6)	8,154	11,192	72.9
4	2,401	(30.8)	4,314	(55.4)	705	(09.0)	505	(06.5)	7,794	11,288	69.0
5	1,745	(33.0)	1,483	(28.1)	1,116	(21.1)	806	(15.3)	5,283	7,446	71.0
6	1,714	(31.9)	2,300	(42.8)	720	(13.4)	862	(16.0)	5,375	7,149	75.2
7	1,578	(32.0)	1,888	(38.2)	947	(19.2)	613	(12.4)	4,936	6,819	72.4
8	2,064	(32.5)	2,909	(45.8)	887	(14.0)	852	(13.4)	6,347	8,536	74.4
9	2,211	(36.5)	2,357	(39.0)	1,069	(17.7)	750	(12.4)	6,050	8,187	73.9
10	1,149	(36.7)	1,247	(39.8)	602	(19.2)	423	(13.5)	3,135	4,237	74.0
11	1,237	(36.1)	1,099	(32.1)	729	(21.3)	564	(16.4)	3,429	4,725	72.6
12	2,617	(44.0)	2,054	(34.5)	1,086	(18.2)	701	(11.8)	5,954	8,343	71.4
13	2,468	(42.4)	1,808	(31.1)	1,389	(23.9)	822	(14.1)	5,820	8,675	67.1
14	1,976	(38.2)	1,579	(30.5)	1,473	(28.5)	862	(16.7)	5,177	7,538	68.7
15	1,069	(28.2)	1,586	(41.9)	564	(14.9)	642	(17.0)	3,786	5,745	65.9
16	1,737	(33.2)	1,755	(33.6)	1,257	(24.0)	847	(16.2)	5,226	7,216	72.4
17	1,463	(32.0)	1,825	(39.9)	856	(18.7)	723	(15.8)	4,570	6,839	66.8
18	2,446	(30.4)	3,396	(42.3)	1,529	(19.0)	1,311	(16.3)	8,037	11,223	71.6
19	2,721	(35.5)	2,665	(34.8)	1,998	(26.1)	1,330	(17.3)	7,669	10,537	72.8
20	1,383	(33.5)	1,179	(28.5)	2,300	(55.7)	628	(15.2)	4,130	5,710	72.3
Totals	37,517	(34.2)	43,267	(39.4)	21,131	(19.3)	15,284	(13.9)	109,698	154,003	71.2

a. Source: Darío Cantón, *Materiales*, II, 7.
b. The major parties in competition were the Unión Cívica Radical (UCR), Unión Cívica (UC), Partido Socialista (PS), Unión Cívica (UC), and Partido Constitucional (PC) (Constitutional Party).
c. The use of different sources to review total votes for candidates and for parties sometimes produces slight variations be- tween the totals noted in *circunscripcional* tables and the totals for individuals in the text.

today, in order that it be, for the ends of national defense, a more secure and efficacious safeguard [and] not be a cause of alarm in the concert of our international relations."[5] On June 10 de Tomaso concluded his interpellation with a proposal that the families of those
conscripts recently killed on maneuvers receive financial compensation
from the government.[6]

World War I's economic consequences for Argentina were of immediate concern to the Socialist deputies. Disruption of the export trade
led to unemployment and rising prices for imported goods. The unemployment problem was relieved somewhat when many immigrants
returned to Europe to fight for their original homelands. A constantly
rising cost of living, however, persisted.

The Socialists attacked these war-influenced problems by adapting
long-standing principles and positions to current necessities. A major
concern was beef, in increasingly short supply as European demands
for meat grew and the export market expanded, and increasingly more
expensive. Beef was the staple of the Argentine diet, and its rising cost
contributed significantly to the high cost of living. In response, the
party suggested first that exports be discouraged by applying a 15 percent ad valorem tax to beef shipped abroad. "It is a true monstrosity,"
Enrique Dickmann claimed, ". . . that we export annually millions and
millions of heads of cattle abroad, and permit the sale of horsemeat to
the Argentine people!" An export tax, he contended, would increase
national revenues and provide better meat at lower prices for the Argentine consumer.[7] A related measure introduced by the Socialist
delegation, with a supporting statement from Francisco Cúneo, suggested abolishing duties on imported fresh meat, compensating for the
decline in Argentine cattle production and creating another source of
cheaper beef.[8] Both these measures, however, received little attention
in the chamber at this time.

Another economic consequence of the war found the Socialists in
opposition to government policy on the gold standard and the value of
the paper peso, an additional issue of long-standing debate. The exi-
gencies of the war and the trade disruption, the government argued,
required that executive authority suspend payments in gold for paper
issue to prevent a drain on the nation's supply of that precious metal.
On August 5, 1914, the congressional committee on emergency legislation to grant the administration this authority reported favorably.
Committee member Juan B. Justo objected. Such legislation, he argued, was unnecessary and would contribute to inflation. Other Socialists joined in, de Tomaso noting that "we shall vote against whatever other measure that tends to alter or to touch the system of the

Caja de Conversión. We do not want any further diminution of already scant real wages; we want people to be able to buy with the paper peso, tomorrow or the next day, the same quantity of coffee, of sugar, of liters of kerosene, of bread, and of meat that they were buying before the decree."[9] In September the executive requested further authority to close the *Caja* completely for a thirty-day period. Once again the Socialists objected, but to no avail. Permission was granted and later extended indefinitely, despite continued Socialist opposition and legislative attempts to reopen the institution whose very establishment they had questioned in 1899.[10]

Another important effect of the war on the Argentine economy was to slow the rate of foreign investment and to force a cutback in foreign controlled and operated services. On September 4, 1914, Minister of Public Works Manuel Moyano reported to Congress on recent slowdowns and economies in the British-owned railroads, which prompted a response from Enrique Dickmann to the effect that these railroads had been built primarily for British profit and only incidentally to benefit Argentina. The Socialist Party, he continued, often accused of being "sin patria," or without patriotism, nevertheless "defends the sources of wealth of the nation . . . against the snares of foreign capital, we defend the Argentine producers against the voracity of foreign railroad enterprises." In conclusion, Dickmann pleaded that "to assure and to consolidate our political independence, it is necessary to conquer true economic independence."[11]

But it was one thing to proclaim the need for economic independence, quite another to achieve it. For the Socialists the question of the role of foreign investment in Argentina posed serious theoretical problems. The party stand that emerged from these theoretical difficulties was complicated and sometimes contradictory. Once again, Juan B. Justo traced the major lines of Socialist thinking on the subject. In an 1895 article Justo had stated that "in reality the entrance of great masses of foreign capital is necessary and inevitable." It was "necessary and inevitable," he argued, because "the great enterprises of construction that are necessary to complete the development of the country for the working people who inhabit it cannot be done by the inept and dissipated *criollo* bourgeoisie." Moreover, "foreign capital is going to accelerate the economic evolution of the country, and with still greater force is going to accelerate its political and social evolution."[12] In other words, foreign capital, emanating from more technically advanced, "civilized" nations, would efficiently and productively develop the Argentine economic infrastructure. Like the growth of monopolies, foreign investment accelerated the evolutionary process, laying the groundwork for the eventual socialization of production. Except for this last analysis, Justo's position on the role of foreign capital in Argentina in 1895 differed little from that of the "inept and dissipated *criollo* bourgeoisie."

By 1910 Justo was more critical. In that year he wrote, "We understand as never before that foreign capital is already for us a great political power, against whose extortionate and corrupt action it is especially urgent to struggle."[13] The wording was important. Justo did not condemn foreign capital *per se*, but rather its "extortionate and corrupt action." As with monopolies, the necessity and inevitability of foreign investment was respected; it was against its more flagrant abuses that the Socialists must struggle. These abuses included the inequitable remittance of profits abroad, the increasing concentration of foreign control in the transportation sector and port facilities, the location of management in European cities rather than in the field, the slowing of all attempts at meaningful and peaceful settlement of labor disputes and the hindering of employer accountability, and the close alliance between foreign and domestic capitalists facilitating continued exploitation of public interests.

The next question was how to counter these abuses. One answer was to reject foreign capital altogether, a step that few Argentines or the Socialists were willing to take at this time. Another answer was for the government to nationalize important sectors of the economy, preempting areas not yet dominated by foreign concerns and taking over those areas so controlled. This solution had broader backing and a growing public appeal. For the Socialists, however, so long as the state reflected the interests of the native capitalist class it was preferable to retain the more efficient foreign investor and manager. Once the state came under Socialist control, then nationalization might occur, but not before. Therefore, the Socialist answer was to take a middle-of-the-road position. The education of the public and the introduction of regulatory legislation would be the party's instruments to combat the abuses of foreign capital. Consistent with the entire historical orientation of the party, these instruments in the long run proved of dubious political value.

For the Socialists, the congressional sessions of 1915 followed the pattern set the previous year. With one year's experience as a nine-man unit, they spent the recess period organizing the details of interpellations and projected legislation. Each delegate could prepare and initiate a proposal of particular personal concern. However, the deputies met regularly in caucus to discuss and to approve individual initiatives and to plan strategy for the most effective manner of presentation.[14] Delegates sought to aid one another in the arduous and often complicated task of formulating these proposals, lending professional expertise whenever possible. In these years congressmen had no staffs and little extra help. Most research was an individual responsibility, with the assistance of party personnel and the growing party library. All deputies had to undergo a constant process of education on unfamiliar and difficult subjects, whether in behalf of their own proposals or in making ready to comment on and to criticize those of the opposition.

One of the major issues debated in the 1915 Congress dealt with pensions and other benefits for workers in the crucial transportation sector. In 1912 a two-month railroad strike stimulated the chamber to propose a pension and retirement benefit plan for rail workers. Approved by the lower house, it was significantly modified in the Senate, which appended a restrictive clause reminiscent of the 1904 González proposal. When the legislation returned to the chamber on June 9, 1915, debate centered on article 11, which read, in part: "The employees or workers who voluntarily abandon their services, or who lend them in any way to the interruption or disruption of the continuity and regularity of the running of the railroads, will be considered as separated from their service and should be substituted for, losing all rights that they might have acquired to retirement benefits and pensions to which this law refers."

The Socialist deputies, led by Alfredo L. Palacios, spoke against the article as unfairly limiting the workers' right to protest. "The strike," Palacios noted, "such as has been carried out by the railroad workers of La Fraternidad [the principal rail workers' union], constitutes the normal and regular exercise of a right; it is a legitimate means of defense of the worker to better his working conditions." Radical Rogelio Araya of Santa Fe supported article 11, questioning Socialist interpretations of the legal right of labor to organize and to strike. Railroad companies were entities, he argued, "that fulfill public functions and services and consequently are obligated to guarantee to society the continuity of their services; the companies cannot allow the strike to detain their trains: they must make them run always and respond to all the clauses of their contracts."[15] Voting on article 11 took place June 21, 1915. Thirty-five delegates, including seventeen Radicals, voted on its behalf. The nine Socialist deputies voted against, but only twenty-one others supported them and the restrictive clause remained in law 9,653, promulgated by the chief executive on June 30.[16]

Soon after their unsuccessful attempt to block article 11, the Socialists introduced legislation to improve the working conditions of another group in the transport sector—those employed in the expanding streetcar and subway lines of the republic, concentrated particularly in the federal capital and representing a source of potential electoral strength. Nicolás Repetto introduced and gave the supporting speech for the measure, which provided an eight-hour day and four-peso daily minimum wage for streetcar employees; a seven-hour day and four-peso daily minimum wage for subway employees; and an employer-sponsored pension plan. Repetto devoted the substance of his remarks to defining the differences between the party proposal and a similar project introduced a few days earlier by Tomás de Veyga, UCR deputy from the capital.[17] Both projects were sent to committee, but neither was approved in these sessions.

Although the Socialists were the most consistent champions of social legislation within the chamber, they were not the only proponents of measures seeking to improve the working and living conditions of the general populace. Within conservative ranks deputies connected with the Catholic social movement sought to outflank the Socialists with projects of their own. Moreover, although the Radicals had no clear-cut legislative platform, their representatives, particularly from the capital, increasingly sponsored measures that seemed to echo aspects of the Socialist minimum program. In September 1915 conservatives Juan Cafferata, Arturo M. Bas, and Julio A. Roca, all of Córdoba, along with Radical Tomás de Veyga, co-sponsored legislation to establish a government agency—Comisión Nacional de Casas Baratas (National Commission for Low-Cost Housing) —that would build low-cost public housing.[18] The Socialist delegation, led by Dickmann, Repetto, and Justo, agreed with the aim of the proposal but disagreed with the means proposed. The creation of one more bureaucratic instrument, they argued, would perpetuate budgetary problems and not get at the main difficulties involved in the construction and availability of public housing. They suggested, instead, special credits and loans to stimulate housing cooperatives, a lowering of taxes and import duties on construction materials, and taxation on unused lands to finance "the construction of hygienic, comfortable, attractive, and inexpensive houses."[19] Socialist objections notwithstanding, Congress approved the conservative-Radical measure, and it became law on September 27, 1915.

The Socialists did not, however, object to all social legislation that bore conservative signatures. On September 25, 1915, the chamber discussed and approved the republic's first comprehensive accident compensation law, placing the responsibility for accidents and compensation on employers. The bill had many antecedents, including two with Socialist sponsorship. But the major architect of the 1915 legislation was conservative Arturo M. Bas of Córdoba, who was connected with the Catholic social movement and had often crossed verbal swords with the Socialist delegation. Nevertheless, in this instance the party representatives gave full support to the measure, urging its prompt adoption and enactment.[20]

A notable feature of the 1915 sessions was an increasing hostility between Socialist and Radical deputies that paralleled a growing antagonism between the two parties in the larger political arena. From the 1890s the two parties had been at odds over philosophy, organization, and methods of achieving power. But for most of the 1895-to-1915 period the Socialists had concentrated the bulk of their criticism on those in power, the conservatives. However, with the Sáenz Peña reform of 1912, the end of UCR abstention, electoral contests in which Socialist and Radical candidates were principal contenders, and the real possibility that the Radicals would gain control of national administration in 1916, the Socialists increasingly ignored conservatives and drew sharp lines between themselves and their new opponents.

Socialist criticism of the UCR, often greatest during the weeks immediately preceding elections, was basically an intensification of historic differences. A 1912 *La Vanguardia* editorial, commenting on recent Radical victories in Santa Fe province, indicted the UCR's lack of a program and predicted that the heterogeneity of the movement would produce inaction and eventual dissolution: "The Radical Party lacks the cohesion of a common ideal and a concrete program accepted by all as banner and guide in propaganda and action. . . . Unity among such divergent interests will be impossible. Soon difficulties and disagreements will cause the disintegration of the party, which will not be able to continue governing, or which, weakened internally and attacked externally, will degenerate into the most absolute impotence and sterility."[21]

Another argument centered on the few differences the party perceived between Radicals and conservatives. Referring in 1914 to the failure of UCR deputies to join the Socialists in scrutinizing the national budget, despite the claimed Radical emphasis on administrative honesty and fiscal responsibility in government, *La Vanguardia* wrote that such action proved what "we have always believed, that the Radical Party was an unattached branch of the oligarchic trunk."[22] In the election campaign of that same year the Socialists noted that among the UCR deputy candidates from Buenos Aires province were a president of Argentina's principal landowners' association, the Sociedad Rural Argentina (José de Apellániz), an ex-president of the Unión

Industrial Argentina (Alfredo Demarchi), a well-known *latifundista* (Leonardo Pereyra Iraola), and others either large landowners themselves or closely connected with these interests (Federico Alvárez de Toledo, Horacio Oyhanarte, Domingo E. Salaberry, Horacio C. Varela, and Carlos M. Pradere). "What deep difference is there between Radicals and conservatives in the province?" *La Vanguardia* asked rhetorically. "Both plan to win the election with the unconscious vote of the herd that the *estancieros* will send to the polls."[23]

In 1915 the *Revista Argentina de Ciencias Políticas* (Argentine Review of Political Sciences) invited Socialists and Radicals to contribute a series of articles that would more clearly define their respective positions. The Socialists described their organization and platform and presented the views of several prominent members on a variety of issues.[24] The Radicals used the occasion to respond directly to opposition criticism and to issue countercharges of their own. Vicente C. Gallo noted that the Radicals, with their committees established throughout the republic, were every bit as organized as the Socialists. Other spokesmen argued that the heterogeneity of radicalism, appealing to all social-economic groups in all parts of the nation, was an asset rather than a drawback. Moreover, they defended the Radical emphasis on political change, observing that political power had to be gained first before social and economic reforms could be considered or accomplished. Finally, UCR contributors remarked with pride that their movement had arisen spontaneously from a particular Argentine situation and with particular Argentine characteristics, making it a truly unique, *criollo* party. Where the Socialists saw this as another failing, the Radicals saw it as an important strength. As one put it, "It is not French Radicalism, nor Spanish, nor Italian: it is Argentine."[25]

While Radicals and Socialists were defining their differences in these years, another political party, the Democratic Progressive, competed for local and national office. Based in Santa Fe province, the Partido Demócrata Progresista (PDP) began as a local party that aimed to shift provincial power from the capital city of Santa Fe to the expanding port city of Rosario. It drew on federalist strains and argued strongly for decentralization of governmental authority in the province and in the republic. Led by ex-Radical Lisandro de la Torre, the PDP also advocated the ballot for non-Argentines who owned real estate or had Argentine-born offspring. In 1912 and 1914 PDP representatives were elected to the national Congress. In 1914 and 1915 various conservatives were drawn to the party as an alternative to what appeared a certain Radical victory in the presidential elections of 1916. Eventually, these conservative elements abandoned the PDP, leaving it essentially a local organization under the influence of de la Torre. Nevertheless, that influence was considerable, and the PDP became a permanent and lasting participant in Argentina's emerging multiparty system.[26]

As the 1916 presidential elections approached, four main groups vied for electoral success: Conservatives, Democratic Progressives, Radicals, and Socialists. The third national census, taken in 1914 and published in 1916, offered these competing parties some statistical indications as to the nature and size of the potential electorate.

The story the census told was of Argentina's most dramatic demographic growth to date. From 1895, the time of the second national census, to 1914, the total population of the republic almost doubled in size, from 3,954,911 inhabitants to 7,885,237. A large percentage of this increase resulted from foreign immigration. The new population total included 5,527,285 Argentines and 2,357,952 foreigners.

Three other trends noted in the second census were reinforced in the third. By 1914 the republic's population had become more urban-based than rural-based, 4,525,500 living in cities over 2,500 inhabitants, 3,359,737 in rural areas. Moreover, the population had become more literate than illiterate, 3,915,949 Argentines over seven years of age being classified as literate, 2,213,916 as illiterate, and 172,096 as semi-literate. Finally, information with regard to occupations marked significant continuing increases in commerce, transportation, industry, public administration, and education (see table 6).

TABLE 6
OCCUPATIONAL GROUPS IN THE ARGENTINE
REPUBLIC, 1895–1914

Classification	1895	1914	Increase
Agricultural and stockraising	393,948	529,866	135,918
Industries and manual arts	366,087	841,237	475,150
Commerce	143,363	293,646	150,283
Transportation	63,006	110,774	47,768
Services	222,774	218,619	−4,155
Public administration	23,934	108,852	84,918
Jurisprudence	5,661	9,078	3,417
Medicine	4,946	14,763	9,817
Education	18,358	83,184	64,826

Source: República Argentina, *Tercer censo nacional*, I, p. 254.

As marked as increases were for the republic as a whole, they were even more conspicuous for the federal capital. From 663,854 persons in 1895, the population of Buenos Aires had more than doubled by 1914 to 1,576,597, an addition of almost one million persons in the span of two decades, giving the city almost 20 percent of the republic's total population. The foreign element represented almost half the city's total, though by 1914 there were slightly more Argentines (798,553) than non-Argentines (778,044). Moreover, the rate of literacy in the capital when compared with the rest of the republic was also considerably higher. According to the third census, 1,063,491 *porteños* above the age of seven were literate, with 237,126 illiterate and 30,168 listed as semiliterate.

Most significant for those in competition for the capital's votes were the figures for persons employed in particular occupations. (See table 7.) The results for 1914 showed an almost three-fold increase in total numbers of persons counted from the time of the second census. In comparison with 1895, the proportions of persons in each occupational category remained about the same except for a 4 percent decrease in category B and a 6 percent increase in category C. The proportion of foreign born in working-class categories A and B remained a high 78 percent.[27] In specific occupational groups potentially sympathetic to the Socialist Party, the percentage of foreign born was about the same as the overall total or even greater. Of the capital's 25,986 masons and bricklayers, for example, 22,050 or 85 percent were foreign-born males. About the same proportions were found for carpenters (14,067 foreigners or 81 percent out of 17,370), longshoremen (1,466 of 1,631 or 90 percent), mechanics (7,198 of 10,741 or 67 percent), tailors (10,377 of 11,891 or 87 percent), and shoemakers (10,281 of 13,523 or 76 percent). These sectors all indicated considerable voter potential in the capital, but figures on naturalization forecast that this potential would not soon be realized. The 1895 census had recorded only 1,638 foreign-born persons as having obtained Argentine citizenship. By 1914 this number had grown to 33,219 for the republic, but still represented only 0.4 percent of the total population. More than half of those who had received citizenship certificates, 18,450, resided in the federal capital.

In addition to describing potential working-class voters, the occupational data for Buenos Aires revealed the growing importance of two key groups: public officials and those in education. With regard to the whole republic, personnel in these two occupational groups had shown the greatest expansion of any category, each increasing more than four times between 1895 and 1914. In Buenos Aires, by 1914,

TABLE 7
ARGENTINE AND FOREIGN MALES OVER 14 YEARS OF AGE BY OCCUPATIONAL CATEGORY, FEDERAL CAPITAL, 1914

Category	Argentine	Percent Total	Percent Category	Foreign	Percent Total	Percent Category	Total	Percent
(A) Manual worker	33,864	17.1	17.3	161,495	37.7	82.7	195,359	31.2
(B) Artisan and small merchant	57,871	29.2	25.9	165,491	38.6	74.1	223,362	35.6
(C) Employee	57,669	29.1	51.5	54,294	12.7	48.5	111,963	17.9
(D) Owner	6,641	3.4	38.2	10,747	2.5	61.8	17,388	2.8
(E) Professional	28,220	14.3	69.1	12,600	2.9	30.9	40,820	6.5
(F) Various and without profession	13,725	6.9	36.2	24,244	5.7	63.9	37,969	6.1
TOTAL	197,990			428,871			626,861	

Source: República Argentina, *Tercer censo nacional*, IV, pp. 201–212.
For information on the specific occupations included in each category, see Appendix A.

Argentine males employed by the government numbered 33,775 (of a total 53,388) and the same group in education, including students, numbered 14,229 (of a total 30,422). Generally middle class, their combined strength of over 50,000 gave them one-quarter of the total Argentine male professional population (197,990) and made their support crucial for any political party hoping to capture the capital.

A final important piece of electoral information from the third census was the extraordinarily high rate of literacy for those from the capital who were registered for the 1916 elections. The literacy rate for voters in the capital was just over 96 percent. In the republic the next highest percentage of literate voters was in the province of Buenos Aires (La Plata section), with 72.82 percent.

For Argentine labor, the years of the Sáenz Peña–de la Plaza presidencies were quiet ones. Organizations remained divided between anarchists (FORA), syndicalists (CORA), and autonomous unions. Socialist influence was almost non-existent. Gradually, however, central federations began to plan and support strikes and to meet to discuss the possibility of fusion. In June 1914 the leadership of the CORA decided to dissolve that organization and to join in a united FORA. This "unity" did not last long. At the ninth congress of the FORA, held in Buenos Aires in April 1915, the syndicalists captured control of the federation. The anarchists left what was now the main organization, the FORA of the ninth congress, and formed an independent federation that also bore the name FORA, but with the appendage of the original founding date of 1901 to distinguish it from the syndicalist group.[28]

Statistics on the number of strikes in the federal capital reflect the general quiescence of these years. Reviewing nearly a decade of labor agitation (1907–1916) in Buenos Aires, the national Labor Department determined that a total of 315,363 workers participated in strikes over that period, but only 44,437, or 14 percent, took part in walkouts that produced favorable results for the strikers.[29]

The Socialist Party, eliminated from any major role in central organizations, sought to support the labor movement through legislation and sympathy with major strike movements. In January and February 1912, when the railroad workers' union, La Fraternidad, called a mass walkout, the party publicized all developments and lent editorial backing to the cause. At the end of January the party's executive committee bitterly criticized the government for using the Social Defense Law against workers engaged in a peaceful strike and also for threatening to import foreign workers to replace the strikers.[30] Other Socialist statements accused the government of being more concerned with the interests of the British stockholders than the welfare of the nation.[31]

Following the formation of the syndicalist FORA in 1915, the Socialist Party joined the new federation (and the anarchists) in its first major action. In May of that year a group of workers in a meat-packing plant in Berisso, a suburb of La Plata, struck to protest, among other things, the elimination of overtime pay. In the ensuing confrontation nine of the strikers were jailed and sentenced to lengthy prison terms. The party appointed a committee (Senator Enrique del Valle Iberlucea, Deputy Antonio Zaccagnini, and Provincial Deputy José P. Baliño) to investigate the incident and joined with the Federación to organize public rallies to demand the release of the imprisoned strikers.[32] After an arduous campaign the workers were freed in mid-1917.

The party's most important support of a strike during this period, however, concerned not the urban proletariat but tenant farmers. Following a year of bad harvests, falling prices, and foreclosures, a tenants' strike to lower rents and secure more stable contracts began in June 1912 in Santa Fe province. The movement soon spread to neighboring Buenos Aires and Córdoba provinces and produced the formation of a national confederation to promote and protect the interests of small farmers, the Federación Agraria Argentina (Argentine Agrarian Federation).[33]

The Socialist Party supported this rural movement in much the same manner it supported urban strikes. *La Vanguardia* reported developments in Santa Fe in detail. In July, Juan B. Justo, who had initiated party interest in rural problems, traveled to Rosario to consult with strike leaders and to give a speech delineating the party's program for tenant farmers.[34] Returning to Buenos Aires, Justo questioned the Minister of Agriculture, Adolfo Múgica, about the Santa Fe strike. Justo challenged the government to consider progressive taxation on the value of land as one measure to reach the bases of agrarian unrest. Officialdom, he noted, had blamed "outside agitators" (presumably Socialists) for the recent disturbances. This was a typical conservative response, the Socialist deputy observed, that overlooked the spontaneous reaction of the strikers to an ever-worsening economic situation and obscured the real cause of such unrest—the inequitable concentration of land ownership. Justo heralded the strike as "a transcendental event in Argentine politics" and viewed it as the beginning of a linkage between the proletariats of countryside and city (with the Socialist Party forging the chain) that would transform national politics. The minister replied with a witty and sarcastic attack on Justo, but without responding to the substance of the Socialist's charges.[35] The minister's attitude reflected that of the Sáenz Peña and de la Plaza administrations, heavily influenced by *estanciero* interests and little concerned with the plight of tenants and small farmers.

The Socialist congressional contingent continued to push for government action that would improve the renters' lot. Tenants were responsible for transporting the landowner's part of the harvest from farm to railway at their own expense. This meant placing grain in burlap bags, purchased by the renter, and storing the bags at cost at the railhead. The Socialists proposed that burlap be allowed into the country duty free (December 16, 1912) and that storage facilities be provided without cost by the government (September 10, 1913). Other actions included continuous legislative proposals for taxation on land ownership, more equitable contracts, and compensation to renters who improved their properties.

For the most part these efforts produced few results. The *estanciero*-controlled congresses and administrations of these years refused to approve these Socialist-sponsored measures. Moreover, the hoped-for alliance between rural and urban working classes did not develop. Despite its efforts, the party realized few political benefits from championing farmer interests. The Federación Agraria, while welcoming Socialist support and encouraging Socialist legislative initiatives, remained as independent from partisan political control as urban unions. In addition, as with the working classes in the cities, the overwhelming number of farmers (72,995 of 102,881 in 1914) in the agricultural provinces of Buenos Aires, Santa Fe, Entre Ríos, and Córdoba and the territory of La Pampa were foreigners without political rights.[36] These provinces either remained conservative or, if shifting, went to the Radical or Democratic Progressive column after 1912. The Socialist interest in the interior was a healthy sign for the future of the party, but ultimate success at the polls remained a remote possibility unless further organization and activity could sway the foreign farmer first to accept naturalization and second to vote for the party.

The Sáenz Peña reforms, increased Socialist electoral participation and victories, and the growth of the congressional delegation greatly stimulated overall party growth. Between 1911 and 1914 the number of affiliated centers in the party rose from 35 (15 in the capital, 20 in the provinces) to 133 (30 in the capital, 103 in the provinces).[37] While the number of centers in the capital doubled during these years, those in the interior increased five times in the same period. Interior growth corresponded with increased electoral activity by the party in the provinces and some minor electoral successes in two areas, Buenos Aires and Mendoza.

In Buenos Aires province, where Socialist centers were established in most major cities during the first decade of the century, the party ran candidates for national deputy in 1912. The results were not encouraging. Socialists received only 4,354 votes as compared with the victorious conservative total of 75,010 and the UCR's 27,818. In the 1914 deputy elections the party ran a slate of nine candidates on a fifteen-point program that included the ten-hour day and hygienic lodgings for agricultural workers, protective legislation for land renters, and a progressive tax on the value of land. The outcome showed improvement: the Socialists gained over 8,000 votes, which was double their previous total. However, they still lagged far behind conservatives (62,000) and Radicals (58,000), and even a one-third minority position appeared unlikely for the immediate future.[38]

Party appeals to the countryside produced little support. The party generally fared best in coastal cities and performed poorly at the polls in agricultural centers. Thanks to a system of proportional representation in provincial elections, this coastal strength, particularly in the working-class city of Avellaneda, permitted the party in 1914 to elect two deputies to the provincial legislature, Adolfo Dickmann and Jacinto Oddone. Their election augured future victories at the local level, though the overall control of Argentina's most populous province and its national representation remained basically a contest between conservatives and Radicals.

In Mendoza province, an active and well-run Socialist center began to register some significant local electoral victories. In April 1914 they managed to elect lawyer Ramón Morey to the provincial legislature. In October of that same year they captured two-thirds of the seats on the city of Mendoza's governing council. Also in that year the Socialists elected delegates to an assembly to revise the provincial constitution, and there managed to push through an eight-hour day for provincial employees.[39] However, most of their strength remained limited to the capital city. In the province as a whole, conservatives and Radicals dominated.[40]

In other provinces, the pattern was much the same. In Santa Fe, for example, a Socialist committee was formed in September 1913. A provincial Socialist federation, with its seat in Rosario, helped found seven other centers in smaller cities between 1913 and 1915. These centers initiated normal Socialist activities: lectures, libraries, labor organization, and political campaigns.[41] In the national deputy elections of

1914 the party candidates in Santa Fe province won 2,222 votes, but as in other interior districts badly trailed Radicals (36,747), conservatives (17,857), and, in this particular province, the forerunner of the PDP, the Liga del Sur (16,609).[42]

In sum, while Socialist organization in the provinces grew significantly between 1910 and 1915, and certain local election victories were won, interior affiliates enjoyed much less success at the polls when compared with their capital colleagues. What strength the Socialists did enjoy was restricted to urban areas. Despite efforts to reach the rural voter, the party was unable to tap this potentially rich source. Expanded organization and the formation of a larger structural base in the provinces, however, did provide the national party leadership with a more solid foundation from which to enlarge Socialist influence in areas removed from the capital.

Party congresses continued to reflect the party's growth. The tenth and eleventh congresses met in the city of Buenos Aires and dealt principally with routine matters. The twelfth party congress, held in Rosario from May 23 to 25, 1914, considered a major issue of internal discipline involving a single individual. The issue was the practice of dueling and the individual was Alfredo L. Palacios. Party statutes prohibited any member from accepting "the judgment of arms to resolve personal questions of any kind, being in contrary case separated from the party." The independent-minded Palacios, however, made it clear that he did not subscribe to this regulation. In 1911 he said that dueling was a personal and not a party matter and that fighting a duel "is, sometimes, unavoidable and even *simpático*."[43] Most of the party leadership, including Juan B. Justo, did not agree.

In 1912 the dueling issue came to the fore when Palacios accepted challenges from two conservative deputies. At the eleventh congress the matter was introduced for general discussion, with the executive committee announcing its decision not to discipline Palacios for this first transgression.[44] In 1913 the same matter arose again. Manuel Ugarte, Socialist candidate for senator in 1912, left the party in late 1913, at the same time issuing several severe blasts against the party's leaders and orientation.[45] Palacios, in response, invited his former friend and supporter to a duel. Although the combat never took place, the challenge again came up for party discussion. At the twelfth congress, debate over the "Palacios affair" became so heated that the assembly itself almost degenerated into violence.[46] At this meeting Palacios momentarily prevailed. An amendment to the article on dueling—"The affiliates who fight a duel or accept seconds will be separated from the party, whatever their situation"—was rejected by a vote of 2,050 to 1,770 with 77 abstentions. Then the total suppression of the disciplinary provision was passed by a vote of 1,891 to 1,396 with 40 abstentions. The victory was only temporary, however, as a general vote following the congress reestablished the prohibitive statute with the aforementioned amendment.[47]

The matter finally came to a head in 1915. On June 2, in the Chamber of Deputies, during debate on government distribution of grain seeds to farmers, Radical Horacio Oyhanarte made a sharp personal attack on the various members of the Socialist delegation. Palacios rose to defend his colleagues, engaging in a boisterous exchange with Oyhanarte that resulted in a mutual challenge to duel, eventually accepted by both.

Following this third transgression the executive committee and the parliamentary delegation determined to expel Palacios from the party. This action became the principal item of business at the second extraordinary congress, held on July 9 and 10, 1915, in the Teatro Verdi, located ironically where Palacios's political career had begun, La Boca. The meeting, presided over by Enrique del Valle Iberlucea, opened with packed public galleries and the representatives of 129 groups. The "asunto Palacios" was resolved quickly, with the representatives of 4,203 members supporting the leadership decision, 983 opposed, and 273 abstentions.[48] Latin America's first Socialist congressman was no longer a member of the Socialist Party.

On July 12 Palacios offered his resignation from the Chamber of Deputies. In his emotional farewell speech he noted his fifteen years of service to the cause of social justice and reaffirmed his "profound socialist faith, despite the gentlemanly prejudice, which I have not been able to root out from my soul, because it is part of me, because I have in me *criolla* and Spanish blood!" With regard to his former colleagues, he concluded, "even outside of the party, which was for me a school of democracy and against which I shall never raise my voice, my action and my thought will always be at the service of the workers, for whom I am proud to have been their first representative in this chamber."[49]

The Palacios separation, however, was not as amicable as these farewell remarks might suggest. One Socialist journalist accused Palacios of excessive vanity and of attempting to create a "cult of personality" within the party.[50] Enrique Dickmann characterized Palacios as an incurably rebellious personality who hoped to use the party for his own ends, "a rude guest in the breast of Argentine socialism."[51] Socialist José Baliño argued that Palacios was irresponsible, removed from working-class concerns, and a believer in certain principles, particularly *nacionalismo criollo* (native nationalism), antithetical to the best interests of the party. Socialist principles and the Socialist Party, he concluded, remained, while men passed on: Ingenieros, Payró, Lugones, Ugarte, and finally Palacios.[52] What Baliño did not mention was the fact that the men named who had "passed on" were individuals of outstanding intelligence and ability. Moreover, in Palacios the party had lost a man who represented qualities of idealism, individualism, and machismo that, though little appreciated within the party, were widely accepted and admired among the general populace. The continued presence of the men Baliño read out of the party—men committed, to oné degree or another, to *nacionalismo criollo*—might well have helped the party bridge the gap between international socialism and the nationalist sentiments of many Argentine voters.

The consequences of Palacios's departure were significant. Not only did the party lose its most experienced deputy and leading vote-getter, but several other party members left with him to form a rival organization, the Partido Socialista Argentino (PSA) (Argentine Socialist Party). The principles and program of the new group paralleled that of the old party in most particulars. The major difference was the PSA's attempt to inject more of a nationalist sentiment into Argentine socialism. Spokesmen for the new party claimed that, in contradistinction to the Socialist Party's stand, "internationalism, for us, does not annul the fatherland. In accord with Juarès, we maintain that socialism supposes the existence of strong and cultured nations."[53]

In the journal of the PSA, *La Acción*, considerable attention was given to other complaints. One major theme emerged: the belief that the older party was increasingly under the control of a small, elite group that monopolized positions of leadership. As one article put it, despite the party's claim to be a democratic entity, "a handful of men convert themselves in fact and by right into directors of that democratic party, eternalize themselves on the executive committee . . . [and] occupy simultaneously all the posts from which they can exercise considerable influence on the opinion of the affiliates."[54] Not only did this monopoly mean non-democratic control, it also implied that positions of influence and prestige were effectively closed to ambitious younger members. This, in turn, contributed to internal differences and, under certain circumstances, schisms such as that which had occurred in 1915 and would most likely occur again.

By the end of 1915 the Partido Socialista Argentino claimed to have established branches in most of the capital's twenty *circunscripciones* and to have formed thirteen centers in Buenos Aires Province, three in

Córdoba, and one each in Santa Fe and Entre Ríos. The Socialist Party did not take the new rival very seriously, considering it no more than a personal vehicle for Alfredo L. Palacios. Nevertheless, Palacios was still Argentina's best known and most popular Socialist. His name on any party's ticket would draw votes, and, as the elections of 1916 approached, the potential effects of the separation threatened to damage the older party's chances at the polls.[55]

7. Yrigoyen, War, and Labor: 1916–1919

> . . . a terrible enemy of all that is modern. As the head of a party he has never expressed a concrete, a clear, political idea, and never have the people seen his face except in the mediocre drawings of Radical cartoonists. Thus, without ideas, without thoughts, he himself must be the Radical Party, its highest expression, its symbol, its human and tangible representation.
>
> *La Vanguardia* on Hipólito Yrigoyen, March 24, 1916

The presidential and congressional elections of April 2, 1916, provided the severest test yet for the Sáenz Peña reform laws. Contests in 1912, 1913, and 1914 had produced opposition triumphs in the capital and some provinces and had sent Radical, Socialist, and Democratic Progressive representatives to the national Congress. But an opposition victory in 1916—and a Radical win was generally expected—would mean for the conservative oligarchy a loss of control over the all-important administrative branch of government.

The Socialist Party prepared for 1916 with customary and practiced thoroughness. Having decided at the July 1915 second extraordinary party congress to enter the presidential race, it selected its ticket of Juan B. Justo and Nicolás Repetto well in advance of other competing parties. In early 1916 Justo and Repetto embarked on a speaking tour of the interior, planned by the executive committee to reach every province. The party had no realistic hopes of capturing the presidency but used the campaign to bolster provincial organizations and to edu-

135

cate. the interior population with regard to the party program and philosophy.

A contest in which the party did have a realistic chance to win was the election of national deputies from the federal capital. On February 6, 1916, the capital representatives met to choose their candidates. Past successes and the growth of the party produced a more complicated selection procedure. To participate, members had to have belonged to the party for six months instead of the previously required three, be fully paid in their dues, and possess national voting rights. Voting for candidates took place at five different locations before the final tally.

The February 6 meeting registered 1,003 voting affiliates. The candidates selected were Juan B. Justo, Enrique Dickmann, José M. Lemos, Augusto Bunge, José F. Grosso, Fernando de Andreis, Basilio Vidal, and José F. Penelón. Justo, Dickmann, and Bunge were doctors, de Andreis a lawyer. Lemos, Grosso, Vidal, and Penelón were of working-class occupational backgrounds originally, but probably had improved their status since joining the party through positions of leadership in the Socialist hierarchy.[1]

The Socialists directed the bulk of their campaign against the Radicals, who represented the major opposition. Criticisms echoed long-standing complaints: the UCR's lack of a program, its frequent recourse to violence, its closeness to conservatism, its twenty years of intransigence. The bitterest attacks were leveled against the *personalismo* of the Radicals and their "caudillo," Hipólito Yrigoyen. Socialist cartoons depicted Yrigoyen as a cleric, a mystic, or a gaucho, somber, unsmiling, mysterious, and conniving. The UCR, party editorials stated, would last only as long as Yrigoyen lived and directed the party.[2]

The Radicals, for their part, met on March 5 to select capital deputy candidates. The eight men who composed their ticket—Benjamín Bonifacio, José Luis Cantilo, Vicente C. Gallo, Arturo Goyeneche, Lauro Lagos, Carlos Melo, Víctor M. Molina, Fernando Saguier—included key figures in Argentine Radicalism, men who had been in the UCR since the 1890s and who would provide much of the movement's leadership in Congress during the 1916–1930 period. Of the seven about whom biographical information is available (Lagos being the exception), all were native-born Argentines, four (Gallo, Melo, Molina, and Saguier) had law degrees from the University of Buenos Aires, and one (Bonifacio) had a medical degree from the same university. Unlike the Socialist list, it offered no working-class representatives. Indeed, three Radical candidates, Goyeneche, Molina, and Saguier, were members of the Sociedad Rural Argentina.[3]

Following their selection, these candidates initiated a campaign based on the work of Radical committees in the various *circunscripciones* of the capital. Techniques paralleled those of the Socialists: lectures, written propaganda, and street rallies. The major difference between the two competing parties remained the UCR failure to produce a program other than the call for political change and national regeneration.

The national convention of the UCR met March 20 to 22 in Buenos Aires to select a presidential candidate. On the 22nd, less than two weeks before the national election, the Radicals chose Hipólito Yrigoyen to head their ticket. In the days between his nomination and the April 2 election Yrigoyen himself did not appear in public, nor did he campaign. This he left to others, and in terms of electoral success it worked. To the credit of the conservative administration, the election itself passed without major incident. Headlines in *La Prensa* labeled the balloting "the best accomplished up to now in the republic" with "active and free action of the parties in the federal capital and all the provinces." [4]

The presidential contest brought 745,852 voters to the polls, or 62.7 percent of the 1,189,254 registered. The Radical ticket, with something over 340,000 votes, won a plurality of the popular vote. After several months of maneuvering, Yrigoyen gained the needed majority of electoral votes (152) to claim the presidency. The Socialist candidates won only 66,397 popular votes and 14 electoral votes, 52,895 popular votes and all the electoral tallies coming from the federal capital. [5]

The results of the presidential contest for the Socialist Party were as expected. What was unexpected was the UCR victory in the capital deputy election. In that contest the Radicals gained the eight majority seats, the Socialists the three minority positions.

The total for the party's top vote-getter, 42,745 for Justo, indicated a drop from the 48,778 for Repetto in 1913 and the 44,335 for the same candidate in 1914. The Radical increase was spectacular, from 30,712 (Lagos) in 1913 to 38,722 (Joaquín Castellanos) in 1914 to 59,009 (Gallo) in 1916. The conservatives were the biggest losers, declining from between 15,000 to 20,000 votes in 1912–1914 to around 11,000 for the Democratic Progressive candidates in 1916. [6]

The UCR carried all *circunscripciones* except two and four, strong working-class districts still in the Socialist column. The Radicals swamped the party in middle-class areas like five, ten through fourteen, nineteen, and twenty. But most disappointing for the Socialists were the substantial opposition victories registered in largely proletarian *circunscripciones* one, three, six through eight, and fifteen through eighteen. These gains forecast future Radical support among the working-class voters, so long cultivated by the Socialist Party. (See table 8.)

The relative stability of the Socialist vote between 1913 and 1916 and the impressive growth of Radical strength during the same period suggest greater UCR success in drawing conservative and independent support. Moreover, the entrance of the Palacios-led Partido Socialista Argentino into the deputy contest clearly hurt the Socialists. Palacios himself collected 33,683 votes and other PSA candidates drew between 7,000 and 9,000.[7]

Hipólito Yrigoyen was inaugurated as President on October 12, 1916. Popular reaction was the most enthusiastic in memory. A general aura of expectation that the UCR would enact significant change in the republic surrounded the proceedings. But with expectation came a certain unease. Aside from a general commitment to do things differently, the Radicals had no program. Left, right, and center awaited the first days and weeks of the new administration to gauge the exact direction of the new government.

President Yrigoyen during his inauguration offered little enlightenment. Other than appearing quite uncomfortable amidst the mass public emotion heralding the new Radical government, he revealed no glimpse of what the next six years might bring. His first cabinet consisted of men little known to the general populace and without much administrative experience.

Although the Radicals now controlled the administrative branch of government, opposition representatives still outnumbered the UCR handily in Congress and the Radicals governed only three of Argentina's fourteen provinces. In the Chamber of Deputies in 1916 the UCR had forty-four congressmen, the largest single bloc. The conservatives, representing mainly the Conservative Party of Buenos Aires province, were next with twenty-eight. The Socialists followed with nine and the Democratic Progressives with eight. The rest were divided among several conservative groups and four Dissident Radicals from Santa Fe. Although the conservatives, Democratic Progressives, and Socialists often disagreed with one another, their shared dislike of Yrigoyen and the Radical government just as often produced coalitions to block administration-sponsored legislation. And if a Radical measure passed the lower house, its chances in the Senate, with only four Radicals in a body of thirty, were even more remote.

Within the chamber the nine-member Socialist delegation continued to perform much as it had in previous years. Juan B. Justo again led

TABLE 8

DEPUTY ELECTIONS, FEDERAL CAPITAL, ABSOLUTE AND PROPORTIONATE VOTES BY CIRCUNSCRIPCIÓN, APRIL 2, 1916

Circun-scripción	UCR	%	PS	%	PSA	%	PDP	%	Voted	Regis-tered	Turn-out %
1	2,702	(47.6)	1,893	(33.4)	1,292	(22.8)	506	(08.9)	5,675	7,433	76.3
2	1,898	(38.2)	2,061	(41.5)	1,079	(21.7)	359	(07.2)	4,965	6,782	73.2
3	4,043	(44.1)	3,805	(41.5)	2,194	(24.0)	499	(05.4)	9,159	11,925	76.8
4	3,121	(36.2)	4,030	(46.8)	1,833	(21.3)	484	(05.6)	8,618	12,020	71.7
5	3,453	(54.1)	1,607	(25.2)	1,758	(27.5)	750	(11.7)	6,386	8,191	78.0
6	2,759	(43.1)	2,238	(35.0)	1,860	(29.0)	477	(07.4)	6,403	8,123	78.8
7	2,490	(43.9)	2,060	(36.3)	1,381	(24.3)	679	(12.0)	5,674	7,377	76.9
8	3,073	(42.7)	2,775	(38.5)	1,979	(27.5)	641	(08.9)	7,201	9,177	78.5
9	3,242	(47.7)	1,370	(20.2)	1,867	(27.5)	626	(09.2)	6,791	8,614	78.8
10	1,616	(47.8)	1,141	(33.8)	1,014	(30.0)	323	(09.6)	3,380	4,346	77.8
11	1,913	(68.1)	1,138	(40.5)	1,128	(40.2)	587	(20.9)	2,809	4,870	57.7
12	3,607	(54.0)	1,993	(29.8)	1,828	(27.4)	616	(09.2)	6,677	8,543	78.2
13	3,538	(55.1)	1,827	(28.4)	1,980	(30.8)	865	(13.5)	6,423	8,869	72.4
14	3,061	(53.0)	1,595	(27.7)	1,832	(31.8)	927	(16.1)	5,766	7,861	73.3
15	2,187	(44.1)	1,734	(35.0)	1,136	(22.9)	521	(10.5)	4,958	6,786	73.1
16	3,128	(50.4)	1,635	(26.3)	1,537	(24.8)	729	(11.7)	6,209	8,179	75.9
17	2,622	(46.7)	1,843	(32.8)	1,277	(22.8)	538	(09.6)	5,613	7,640	73.5
18	4,103	(43.6)	3,100	(32.9)	2,661	(28.2)	1,323	(14.0)	9,420	12,261	76.8
19	4,164	(47.7)	2,682	(30.7)	2,612	(29.9)	1,294	(14.8)	8,724	11,098	78.6
20	2,341	(51.2)	1,224	(26.8)	1,435	(31.4)	888	(19.4)	4,573	5,828	78.5
Totals	59,061	(47.1)	41,751	(33.3)	33,683	(26.9)	13,632	(10.9)	125,424	165,923	75.6

a. Source: Darío Cantón, *Materiales*, II, 17.
b. The main parties in competition were the Unión Cívica Radical (UCR), Partido Socialista (PS), Partido Socialista Argentino (PSA), and the Partido Demócrata Progresista (PDP).

the delegation. Briefly crippled by a June 7, 1916, attempt on his life, Justo resumed his congressional duties on December 15.[8] The issue that drew him back to the chamber was discussion of the budget for 1917, the first budget submitted by the new administration.

Justo began his presentation with an expression of disappointment that a new administration and new deputies continued to perpetuate the same old budgetary abuses. Despite Radical claims of administrative honesty and efficiency, new proposals provided for additional and, as Justo saw them, unnecessary bureaucratic positions. Instead of focusing on national concerns, proposed allocations catered to special interests.[9]

Following Justo's lead, other Socialists attacked each section of the budget, criticizing especially military, diplomatic, and clerical appropriations. The first major struggle between the Socialists and the new Radical regime had begun on the battleground of governmental fiscal policy.

The Yrigoyen administration took office at a time when World War I seriously affected the country's export-import economy. While the quantity and value of exports, particularly frozen beef, remained relatively high during this period, European-manufactured imports declined by almost 200 million pesos, from a high of 496,227,094 in 1913 to 305,488,006 in 1915. Government revenues from import duties fell correspondingly.[10]

The demands of the export economy, plus the scarcity of imported goods, contributed to a constant rise in the cost of living. Beef for the Argentine consumer increased from an index price of 100 in 1910 to 148 in 1918. During the same period bread grew from 100 to 139, potatoes from 100 to 155, and sugar from 100 to 169.[11] The overall cost of food, housing, and clothing expanded from an index of 108 in 1914 (from the same base of 100 for 1910) to 146 in 1917. Real salaries for the same years declined by one-third.[12]

Yrigoyen and the Radicals responded to the crisis with a call for higher customs duties, taxes on exports, and a proposal to institute Argentina's first income tax. The Socialists, though agreeing with the latter two expedients (export taxes were ultimately approved, with the income tax not considered), opposed higher tariffs included in the budgetary discussions. Basing their objections on advocacy of free trade and defense of the consumer, they particularly opposed the Radicals' continued protection of the domestic wine and sugar industries. Willing to back Radical proposals to place heavy taxes on imported alcohol, the Socialists refused to go along with heavier duties on basic necessities, which were nevertheless approved over their opposition.[13]

As the budgetary debates drew to a close, Justo used Socialist disagreement over fiscal policy to issue a series of challenges to the Radicals. In a lengthy speech on February 5, 1917, he noted that the Socialists voting *en bloc* with the Radicals could pass most administration proposals through the chamber. And if these proposals were
sound they would receive Socialist support. But the Radical performance so far had been disappointing. The budget included the same fat,
tariff policy continued to benefit the same monopolies, and fiscal measures were hastily conceived in a state of panic. All seemed the natural
result of a party come to power without a program. To gain Socialist
support, Justo implied, these policies had to be reversed and measures
delineated in the party program adopted and proposed. He called on
the Radicals specifically to rescind the Social Defense Law, formulate
an agrarian program to aid the small landowner and renter and to
encourage further rural colonization, and to present fiscal policies that
would tax the wealthy rather than place undue burdens on the consumer.[14]

The possibility of collaboration between Radicals and Socialists that
Justo suggested was never realized. The philosophical divisions of the
two movements, grounded in twenty years of antagonism, were irre-
concilable. Also, both parties sought to appeal basically to the same
group of voters, the competition for this support producing alternative
routes to the solution of national problems. Finally, Yrigoyen's manner
of dealing with Congress made administration collaboration with any
segment of the non-Radical sector difficult. Consistently intransigent,
even in office, he insulted the Congress by refusing ever to appear before it, sending the presidential message that opened each session to be
read by his vice-president or a cabinet member. He fought with the
opposition at every turn, instructing his deputies not to appear at sessions in which legislation he objected to was to be voted on, thus denying a quorum, and having his cabinet members delay interminably
their appearance for interpellations. He sought not to work with Congress but rather to frustrate it, hoping that popular pressures eventually would defeat Socialists, conservatives, and Democratic Progressives
at the polls and give him a workable Radical majority.

To shift the legislative balance in his favor, both at the local and the
national level, Yrigoyen resorted to the device of executive intervention to suspend and reform provincial government. One of the few
clear goals of the Radical movement from the 1890s had been to restore respect for local autonomy, a stance that attracted many federalists to support the UCR. Yet the first Radical administration inter-
vened in the provinces twenty different times during the 1916–1922

term. All provinces, with the exception of Radical-controlled Santa Fe, suffered intervention at least once. Yrigoyen used this executive power with greater frequency than had any previous Argentine president. The new executive sought to justify his interventionism with the argument that "real" provincial autonomy could only be achieved through genuine popular suffrage guaranteed by the new regime. Most local contests before 1916, he argued, had been little affected by the Sáenz Peña reforms. It was his duty and the duty of the government, he concluded, to spread to the interior the reforms enacted on the national level.[15]

Fifteen of Yrigoyen's twenty interventions were enacted through presidential decree. The five discussed in Congress occupied an inordinate amount of legislative time and concern. Although the Socialists generally favored centralized government, they believed that such a system should evolve naturally through basic reforms and not unnaturally through forced intervention. Therefore, they opposed interventions for political purposes and consistently voted against them, although they did back executive intervention if intended to redress social or economic inequities.[16]

Although Radicals and Socialists occasionally collaborated, the 1917 sessions, like those of the year before, were characterized more by continued antagonism between the two parties. The Socialists again particularly criticized the economic policies of the Radical administration, seeking to compete with Yrigoyen for the votes of wage earners and consumers in a period of rising prices and declining salaries. On June 6, 1917, Repetto spoke in favor of Socialist legislation to allow imported sugar to enter the republic duty free.[17] That same month Francisco Cúneo spoke for a party proposal to allow duty free imports of fresh and on-the-hoof beef, a project later approved (law 10,342).[18] Soon thereafter Enrique Dickmann re-introduced a proposal to tax beef exports.[19] The essence of this measure was ultimately included in a general law to tax exports, passed with Radical support at the end of 1917.[20]

In the presentation of these initiatives the Socialists tried to picture the Radicals and Yrigoyen as captives of the privileged sugar and beef interests tied to the UCR. Generally, however, the Radicals outflanked them, agreeing with and backing Socialist revenue proposals or incorporating them into their own initiatives. The Socialists nevertheless pressed the issue, interpellating the ministers of Agriculture and the Treasury to expose politics as usual under the supposedly "renovating" new regime. The party deputies also made their regular attack on the Yrigoyen budget for 1918, depicting it as no different from the practices of past conservative administrations.

While the Socialist leadership in 1917 confronted the Yrigoyen administration at one level, it faced an internal rebellion within party ranks on another. At issue was Argentina's role in World War I. In some ways the conflict posed as many difficulties for the Argentine party, far removed from the battlefield, as for European socialist parties.

From the beginning of the conflict most leading Argentine Socialists branded Germany the aggressor and hoped for an Allied victory. In the early months of 1917 German submarines began to attack and to sink Argentine ships and vessels of other nations carrying Argentine goods to and from Europe. On April 6 the United States entered the war. In response to these developments, the Socialist congressional delegation met in Justo's home and on April 17 issued a statement urging the Argentine government "to adopt all measures necessary . . . to protect as fully as possible Argentine commerce."[21]

This statement prompted the calling of the third extraordinary congress of the party on April 28 and 29. Two reports were presented at the meeting. The majority report backed the position of the congressional delegation. Party leaders spoke in its behalf. Juan B. Justo argued that it was vital for Argentina to protect commerce and trade, the lifeblood of the country's economy. The use of submarine warfare, he concluded, was unprecedented and demanded unprecedented actions in response.

The minority report argued that the April 17 statement violated Socialist pacifist principles. Spokesmen for this position backed a policy of strict neutrality rather than involvement of any kind in what they saw as a capitalist-imperialist conflict. Some objected strongly to the manner in which the statement of the congressional group had been formulated, in a private home without consulting the total membership of the party. The report itself concluded that Argentina's Socialists should "orient their action in the sense of being resolutely contrary to any intervention of the country in the war."

After two days of near-violent debate the matter finally came to a vote during a turbulent night session on April 29. Despite the best efforts of the leadership, the minority report was approved by a substantial margin, 4,210 in favor, 3,557 opposed. The assembled representatives had clearly rebuked the congressional delegation of the party and had firmly marked a course of strict, non-active neutrality.[22]

In 1917 the Socialist leadership was not the only group caught up in debate over continued Argentine neutrality in the face of German submarine warfare. As more Argentine and allied shipping was sunk, anti-German feeling led to assaults in Buenos Aires on German-owned companies. Conservatives and Radicals implored Yrigoyen to act force-

fully in defense of Argentine trade. Yrigoyen did seek and gain reparations from Germany for lost shipping, but he refused to abandon his
own policy of "positive neutrality." Pressure increased on the president, however, in September 1917 when the United States Department
of State released decoded messages from the German Minister to Argentina, Count Karl von Luxberg, that urged the Kaiser's government
to ignore Argentina's claims for reparations and included insulting
references to the host government. Yrigoyen responded with an order
that the Count be expelled from the republic within forty-eight hours.
Others, however, wanted more drastic action. On September 11, 1917,
Socialist Deputy Antonio de Tomaso introduced a resolution in the
chamber to invite the Minister of Foreign Relations to appear before
Congress to explain what steps the government was taking to assure
the freedom of the seas for vessels flying the Argentine flag and to
describe the details of the Luxberg affair.[23] Ten days later, on September 21, a group of conservative, Radical, and Democratic Progressive
deputies introduced a resolution recommending the suspension of diplomatic relations between Germany and Argentina.[24]

On September 22, the Minister of Foreign Relations, Honorio
Pueyrredón, appeared before the chamber to support Yrigoyen's policy
and to oppose the breaking of diplomatic relations with Germany. The
debate lasted into the early morning hours of the following day. Juan
B. Justo, speaking for the Socialist delegation, was one of the last to
express his views. He reiterated the importance of free trade, claimed
that submarine warfare had caught the Socialists surprised and unaware, and argued that neutrals should take affirmative action to protect themselves against this unforeseen threat. Justo concluded that the
present issue—to break diplomatic relations with Germany—was not
particularly important since the major economic ties between the two
countries already had been severed. Nevertheless, he stated, the Socialists would vote for the break as a "courtesy to those citizens who appear to desire that declaration as a great deed."[25] On September 24
eight Socialists joined nineteen conservatives, six Radicals, and twenty
others (for a total of fifty-three) in favor of the resolution recommending the break in relations with Germany. Only eighteen, including
fourteen Radicals, voted against.[26] A similar resolution, with Enrique
del Valle Iberlucea's support, had been passed by a majority of Argentina's senators on September 19.[27]

The joint resolution had little impact. Yrigoyen simply ignored it,
maintained diplomatic relations with Germany, and continued to adhere to his "positive neutrality." For the Socialists, the parliamentary
group's votes in late September produced a major crisis. Those who

had supported the minority position approved in the April extraordinary congress accused the party leadership of violating the mandate of the membership with their September vote. In response, the Socialist deputies and senator offered their resignations, which were refused by a general vote of the party's affiliates. In late September and early October the dissident "internationalist" members of the executive committee—Juan Ferlini, José F. Penelón, and José F. Grosso—resigned from their positions. They soon left the party in protest over the actions of the leadership and planned to form their own organization.

The separation of the "internationalist" faction was the second major party schism in three years. It may have been that Justo and the leadership purposely planned the division. Certainly Justo must have known that a vote for the break of relations would cause an adverse reaction among those already disaffected. His stated willingness to go along with the majority of congressmen on the issue "out of courtesy" was glaringly out of character. He may have foreseen that the party would not long survive divided between those of the majority and minority position and acted in September to separate the dissidents indirectly, thereby strengthening the leadership and restoring homogeneity of thought and unity of action.

In November 1917 the "internationalists" formed a "Committee in Defense of the Resolution of the Third Congress" as a temporary haven for centers and individuals who abandoned the parent party over the war issue. "Nothing," they claimed, "separates us from the declaration of principles and the program of action of the party, but what does separate us is the ideological interpretation that its dictators try to apply to party principles and program and the methods they employ." If the recent orientation of party and leadership should change, the dissidents stated, then they would consider returning to the fold. Until then "we shall continue struggling for socialist ideas. . . . We have not changed, but rather the party that expels us has changed."[28]

From this temporary base, the "internationalists" determined to form a more permanent organization. On January 5 and 6, some 750 representatives, mostly former Socialist Party members, met in Buenos Aires to organize a new party. From the meeting emerged the Partido Socialista Internacional (PSI) (International Socialist Party), destined to evolve into the Argentine Communist Party. One of the party's first measures was to send a message of solidarity to the Bolshevik leaders of the Russian Revolution. The party's own declaration of principles, however, was considerably less than revolutionary. In essence, its program and tactics differed little from those of the established party, calling for participation in elections, encouragement of unionization, and support for the cooperative movement.[29]

In early 1918 the newly-formed PSI selected seven candidates for the March 3, 1918, capital deputy elections. For the Socialist Party, the competition of the PSI posed few problems. The principal need was to defeat the increasingly powerful Radicals, who again put forward a strong ticket composed primarily of native-born professional men who had been important affiliates of the Radical movement from the turn of the century.[30]

The Socialists also selected men with considerable political experience.[31] Furthermore, their electoral platform indicated that they would direct their main attack against the economic policies of the Radical administration. The first two articles were: "Abolition of taxes that increase the cost of living and burden labor" and "A progressive national contribution on the value of land, and a tax on the greater value of same, in all the republic."[32]

Socialist campaign literature and speeches sought to inform and to stir the electorate regarding what the party considered the anti-consumer fiscal policies of the Yrigoyen government. They focused on official protection of the sugar and wine trusts and the inequities of taxation. A particularly hot issue was an increased tariff on imported shoes, a basic consumer necessity. The Argentine shoe industry had powerful allies, including the Sociedad Rural Argentina. In January 1918 a proposal to double the duty on imported shoes was introduced and approved in Congress, with thirty-four voting in favor and twenty-eight, including nine Socialists, opposed. La Vanguardia underscored the Radical role in the debate with the following editorial comment: "The new protectionism, which will be as strong as the others from which we suffer, is of pura cepa Radical. Deputy [Horacio] Oyhanarte was the initiator and supporter of the project elevating the custom duty . . . on shoes. The chief executive made the project his, including it in the custom law that accompanied the budget, and twenty Radical deputies, in association with fourteen conservatives, produced its passage."[33]

The party continuously emphasized the coincidence in thought and action between conservatives and Radicals. The Yrigoyen government, party candidates charged, differed little from its forerunners. The Radicals had "kicked the rascals out" only to glory in the same spoils of office previously enjoyed by others. The expansion of unnecessary bureaucratic positions to repay political favors, for example, and the inefficiency and waste of public administration continued apace.

Nevertheless, those new employees swelling the ranks of government were a sizeable bloc of the capital's voters, and the Socialists tried the neat trick of attracting them while still attacking Radical corruption. *La Vanguardia* noted that three Radical senators had helped defeat a proposal to establish a minimum wage for state employees.[34] Another Socialist article urged state workers to join in class solidarity with other wage earners to support the party and win "the emancipation of their class."[35]

Socialist campaigning notwithstanding, the Radicals in 1918 chalked up their most impressive victory in the capital to date. The UCR captured seven majority seats, with ticket leader Carlos A. Becú receiving 74,174 votes. The Socialists took the three minority seats, Mario Bravo leading the slate with 49,354 votes. Alfredo L. Palacios, running on the PSA ticket, got 35,277 votes, far ahead of the rest of his party, which averaged around 4,500 tallies. The leading candidate for the PDP polled 9,067 votes, and the top vote-getter for the PSI polled 2,753.[36]

In 1916 the leading Radical had topped the leading Socialist by a vote of 59,008 to 42,745, or by 16,263 votes. By 1918 the difference had grown to 24,820. Also, the UCR carried all *circunscripciones* except four, which remained in the Socialist column, even though the margin of victory was less than two percentage points (see table 9).

The Socialists responded to the defeat in typical fashion. The 1918 election in the capital, they claimed, was merely a temporary setback on the path to inevitable victory. They pointed to increases in party votes in sections one through four as signs of continued strength in working-class areas and accused the PSA and PSI of aiding the Radical triumph.[37]

What the Socialists refused to acknowledge, at least explicitly, was the political astuteness of Yrigoyen as a contributing factor in the Radical sweep. Personally popular, he had helped his party cut significantly into former Socialist strongholds. On issues like the tariff he managed to placate both domestic producers and consumers. In 1917 and 1918 the Socialists rallied opposition to and public awareness of the Radical protection of northern sugar interests. As sugar scarcities and prices increased, the party pressed for free importation of the basic commodity. Yrigoyen reacted by having the government purchase foreign sugar and then distribute these purchases at reduced prices, making clear to the public the role of the UCR in providing this largesse.[38]

Yrigoyen's policy of provincial intervention also produced political benefits. In 1918 the Radicals gained control of provincial governments in Buenos Aires, Catamarca, La Rioja, Mendoza, and San Juan. In

TABLE 9
DEPUTY ELECTIONS, FEDERAL CAPITAL, ABSOLUTE AND PROPORTIONATE VOTES BY CIRCUNSCRIPCIÓN, MARCH 3, 1918

Circun-scripción	UCR	%	PS	%	PSA	%	PSI	%	PDP	%	Voted	Regis-tered	Turn-out %
1	3,881	(54.6)	2,286	(32.1)	1,507	(21.2)	208	(02.9)	235	(03.3)	7,112	9,465	75.1
2	2,609	(44.0)	2,526	(42.6)	1,102	(18.6)	150	(02.5)	206	(03.5)	5,926	8,196	72.3
3	5,338	(50.1)	4,247	(39.9)	2,022	(19.0)	177	(01.7)	370	(03.5)	10,654	14,023	76.0
4	4,113	(43.3)	4,299	(45.3)	1,777	(18.7)	158	(01.7)	175	(01.8)	9,498	13,791	68.9
5	4,486	(60.6)	1,913	(25.8)	2,009	(27.1)	87	(01.2)	435	(05.9)	7,407	9,890	74.9
6	3,684	(49.5)	2,548	(34.3)	2,010	(27.0)	301	(04.0)	334	(04.5)	7,438	9,625	77.3
7	3,196	(49.9)	2,280	(35.6)	1,546	(24.1)	125	(02.0)	465	(07.3)	6,408	8,592	74.6
8	3,734	(46.2)	3,157	(39.1)	2,126	(26.3)	184	(02.3)	508	(06.3)	8,079	10,665	75.8
9	3,801	(50.7)	2,600	(34.7)	1,870	(24.9)	150	(02.0)	501	(06.7)	7,497	9,864	76.0
10	1,914	(50.2)	1,393	(36.6)	1,067	(28.0)	81	(02.1)	277	(07.3)	3,809	5,086	74.9
11	2,055	(49.8)	1,388	(33.6)	1,221	(29.6)	78	(01.9)	456	(11.0)	4,129	5,686	72.6
12	4,340	(58.2)	2,266	(30.4)	1,640	(22.0)	142	(01.9)	405	(05.4)	7,462	10,057	74.2
13	3,962	(57.7)	1,980	(28.8)	1,973	(28.7)	113	(01.6)	613	(08.9)	6,872	10,231	67.2
14	3,453	(55.4)	1,923	(30.8)	2,015	(32.3)	68	(01.1)	695	(11.1)	6,236	9,190	67.9
15	3,217	(50.7)	2,135	(33.7)	1,407	(22.2)	163	(02.6)	329	(05.2)	6,342	8,808	72.0
16	4,348	(60.5)	2,052	(28.5)	1,663	(23.1)	34	(00.5)	515	(07.2)	7,191	9,857	73.0
17	3,611	(55.2)	1,961	(30.0)	1,413	(21.6)	194	(03.0)	360	(05.5)	6,539	9,347	70.0
18	5,382	(51.3)	3,467	(33.1)	2,702	(25.8)	365	(03.5)	617	(05.9)	10,490	14,505	72.3
19	4,738	(49.7)	3,310	(34.7)	2,843	(29.8)	56	(00.6)	903	(09.5)	9,526	12,835	74.2
20	2,318	(48.7)	1,573	(33.0)	1,368	(28.7)	55	(01.2)	631	(13.3)	4,762	6,672	71.4
Totals	74,180	(51.7)	49,304	(34.4)	35,281	(24.6)	2,889	(02.0)	9,030	(06.3)	143,377	196,385	73.0

a. Source: All figures except PSI from Darío Cantón, *Materiales*, II, 35. PSI figures from República Argentina, *Memoria, 1917-1918*, pp. 54-55.
b. The main parties in competition were the Unión Cívica Radical (UCR), the Partido Socialista (PS), the Partido Socialista Argentino (PSA), the Partido Socialista Internacional (PSI), and the Partido Demócrata Progresista (PDP).

Buenos Aires province the UCR captured the majority of ten national deputy seats for the first time, the leading Radical topping the leading conservative 115,607 to 68,195.[39] From 1918 through 1930 the Radicals continued to predominate in Argentina's most populous province, wresting it from decades of conservative control.

When the Chamber of Deputies resumed sessions in April the Radicals had increased their total representation from forty-four in 1916 to fifty-six in 1918. Democratic Progressives increased their total from eight to fourteen in the same period, and the Dissident Radicals grew from four to eight, while conservatives dropped from twenty-eight to nineteen, and the Socialists from nine to six.

Most Socialist congressional work in 1918 was directed toward the re-introduction of social legislation. These included measures for an eight-hour day (May 27, 1918), legal protection of labor unions (June 3, 1918), reform of the work-accident compensation law (June 3, 1918), a new measure to restrict and regulate the labor of women and children (June 21, 1918), and protection of working women before and after childbirth (June 26, 1918), none of which was passed in 1918. The Socialists also urged the national administration to enforce existing social legislation more strictly.

These efforts were rooted in a long struggle to introduce and to pass such initiatives. However, renewed attention in 1918 to laws that would aid the working class also reflected a response to three particular interrelated phenomena of the moment. These were: 1) the impressive growth of organized labor and labor militancy between 1916 and 1919; 2) the seemingly sympathetic attitude of Yrigoyen and his government toward labor and the apparent support labor gave Radicals at the polls; and 3) pressures within the Socialist Party itself to direct more attention and concern to proletarian problems.

Following the 1915 split in the Federación Obrero Regional Argentina, the anarchist faction, or the FORA of the fifth congress, passed through a period of general decline and minimal influence and effectiveness. And in the months immediately after the meeting it appeared that the syndicalist group, the FORA of the ninth congress, would suffer the same fate. However, by 1916 the FORA IX began to gather strength and adherents and to initiate a growth that made it Argentina's most successful central labor organization to date and the first organization with a truly valid claim to be a group of national dimensions. From 1915 to 1920 the number of member syndicates increased from 51 to 734, the number of affiliates from 3,000 to almost 80,000, and the yearly quotient of dues from 20,521 to 700,000.[40] The official organ of the FORA IX, *La Organización Obrera* (The Workers' Organization), first published in May 1915 but appearing irregularly, sometimes at intervals of three months, began to appear as a regular weekly in September 1917 and to record in detail the activities of the increasingly important Federación.

Several factors contributed to this growth. For one, the syndicalists managed to maintain their stated commitment to an apolitical, nonpartisan position. Avoiding much of the factional bickering that had cursed previous efforts, the syndicalists retained firm control of the central organization while allowing Socialists and anarchists to continue to participate in the work of the Federación and its leadership. For another, the FORA IX, while espousing a revolutionary philosophy, in practice took a more pragmatic stand in labor-management disputes. Still willing to back the general strike or the threat of a general strike when necessary, the Federación's leadership nevertheless abandoned the "all or nothing" philosophy of previous years and accepted half a loaf when conditions so dictated. Finally, and perhaps most important, the FORA IX supported major strikes of affiliated members with skill and frequent success. Providing propaganda and coordination, the Federación also collected funds and made financial contributions to compensate workers off the job.[41]

The growth and success of the FORA IX in this period must also be seen within the larger framework of the social policies of the new Radical government. These policies, like all aspects of the first Radical administration, were intimately tied to the complex personality of Hipólito Yrigoyen. The Radical president, in his usual vague manner, had indicated upon inauguration a desire to extend the political equality of the Sáenz Peña reform to the social and economic sphere. Nevertheless, he was slow in making clear just how this would be achieved. His first concrete proposal was a June 1918 project to reform the law of Sunday rest, which Congress did not consider, and a July 1918 project to regulate work in the home, which was approved.

The major changes with regard to Yrigoyen and Argentina's working classes occurred in the areas of image and attitude. Yrigoyen himself adopted much of the form and substance of a "man of the people." Ignoring the luxuries and pleasures of *porteño* society, he dressed simply and lived humbly. Renting a Spartanly-furnished apartment above a pharmacy, he was one of a handful of Argentine political leaders to live in the predominantly working-class southern half of the capital. Reversing the aristocratic and closed traditions of Argentine presidents since the mid-nineteenth century, Yrigoyen opened his doors to persons of all class backgrounds, listened to their complaints, and often provided them with money or employment. Although he did not actively encourage working-class organization and activity, neither did he discourage it. Strikes, for the most part, were settled without the repressive paraphernalia of the state of siege or the expulsion laws of 1902 and 1910. Workers' demonstrations, at least before 1919, were not marred by the police cavalry attacks of earlier years. Finally, Yrigoyen was the first Argentine president personally and actively to intervene as arbitrator in labor-management disputes. And it was here that the lines of Yrigoyen's policies and the activities of the FORA IX most frequently intersected.

The first major strike that the new Federación backed, that of the meatpackers at Berisso in 1915, was not a success. Poorly planned and executed, the strike did not achieve the desired results and nine of its leaders were sentenced to prison. After a lengthy campaign by the FORA IX, and with the collaboration of the Socialist Party, the detained strikers were pardoned and released in June 1917. The man who ordered the release was José Luis Cantilo, the Yrigoyen-appointed interventor in the province of Buenos Aires. The second FORA IX-supported strike, that of the Federación Obrera Marítima (FOM) (Maritime Workers' Federation) for shorter hours and improved working conditions, in November 1916, produced more satisfactory results. After the strike had lasted a month, tying up Buenos Aires, the republic's major port, employers asked Yrigoyen to intervene. The president did so by calling in the workers to get their side of the story. Representatives of the FOM and the FORA IX met with the president and an eventual settlement was reached through the arbitration of the chief of police of the federal capital. The unions claimed to have achieved 75 percent of their goals, in this case a bit more than half a loaf. But of greater significance was the fact that labor had met with government's highest official, initiating a dialogue between two interests that more often had clashed in the streets. Moreover, the successful resolution contributed greatly to the prestige of the FORA IX. The Federación had responded to the FOM strike with full support but not undue interference. The Federación's federal council had sent a representative to consult with the strikers, had raised funds, and had organized backing in other unions. The Federación also had made it clear that it could organize and call a general strike of affiliated unions as an added lever to achieve labor's ends.[42]

Between mid-1917 and mid-1918 the FORA IX concentrated on a continuous series of railroad strikes. By and large these strikes ended favorably for the workers. Once again, as in the maritime strikes, the Yrigoyen government was asked by employers to intercede. The president, concerned with the economic consequences of the rail stoppages, listened personally to both sides and then appointed his Minister of Public Works, Pablo Torello, to arbitrate the disputes. Torello did so in a manner that labor historians seem to agree benefited the workers.[43]

The president's intervention in another major strike of this period, however, led to a different outcome. In late 1917 workers at the Armour and Swift meatpacking plants in Berisso sought to organize and to affiliate with the FORA IX. When management retaliated by laying off workers, the movement spread to plants in Avellaneda and a strike was called for the eight-hour day, overtime pay, the elimination of fines, an increase in salaries, and May 1 as a holiday. The Radical government, both at the national and provincial level, supported the employers. Members of the armed forces were used to man the plants in the absence of striking workers and provincial police protected the plant property in what became a violent strike action. The central Federación again rallied to the workers' cause, coordinating activities among the 18,000 striking employees and raising funds through contributions and a new practice of issuing special bonds to support the strike. In January 1918 representatives of the FORA IX met with Yrigoyen to discuss the Berisso-Avellaneda strike. In a note to the chief executive, the Federación's secretary-general, Sebastián Marotta, called for the removal of troops from the plants, impartial police vigilance, and recognition that "the workers have the right to strike, defending their only property, the force of their labor, as the capitalists have the right to defend their capital." If such an agreement were not reached, Marotta concluded, the Federación would call a general strike.[44] The troops were withdrawn, but the strike failed and the meatpackers returned to work in February. Marotta placed the blame for the failure on "the lack of organization" and "the persecutions of the authorities."[45] In this instance Yrigoyen's actions seemed to favor more the foreign owners of the packing plants, closely tied to the Sociedad Rural Argentina, than those of the proletariat.[46]

The most that can be said for Yrigoyen's labor policy, then, was that it appeared to be a relative improvement over that of past administrations. Supporters pointed to his personal intervention in disputes as evidence of a new concern. However, intervention did not always mean intervention on the side of labor, even when, as in the case of the meatpackers' strike, labor's demands seemed moderate and just. In further support of Yrigoyen, Radical writers pointed to an increase in the number of strikes and strikers and the growth of labor unions in Argentina after 1916. However, it is not clear how much of this growth was due to Yrigoyen's attitudes and policies and how much to the internal organizational skill of unions, general economic conditions, and a growing world-wide labor militancy in the ambiance of World War I and the Russian Revolution.

The seemingly sympathetic attitude of the new Radical government toward labor and the increasing interaction between the Yrigoyen administration and the FORA IX presented obvious difficulties for the Socialist Party. Yrigoyen, with popular appeal and in control of the national executive, was in a position to produce concrete benefits for the working classes or to identify himself closely with coincident improvements. The Socialists, in a minority position and with only small legislative representation, could only contribute to slight improvements and make promises for future betterments as their movement spread. Although the majority of the working class remained apolitical, those who did vote appeared to be giving more and more electoral strength to Yrigoyen and the Radicals.

The party sought in several ways to counter growing Radical influence among labor elements. They pointed to such stands as Radical support for article 11 of the railroad pension law, which hindered strike activity. They accused Yrigoyen's administration of cynically manipulating strikes and arbitration for its own narrow political profit. The party publicized labor-management disputes and gave special prominence to those instances in which the Yrigoyen regime seemed to back capitalists to the detriment of the proletariat. Commenting on the 1918 *frigorífico* strikes in Buenos Aires province, *La Vanguardia* claimed that "the Radical government has formed a shameful alliance, toward which it has always been disposed, placing police and armed forces at the service of an enterprise at whose head are known capitalist sharks as well as illustrious conservative big shots."[47]

The Socialists' uneasy relationship with the FORA IX, however, further complicated the party's position on labor matters vis-à-vis the Radicals. Although the central Federación was syndicalist-controlled, Socialist representatives like Felipe di Tella and Jerónimo Della Latta served on the federal council. Other Socialists sat on the directive bodies of individual unions.

In these years, however, the syndicalists kept a carefully defined distance from the Socialist Party. The FORA IX had been formed on the base of apoliticism and from this position had grown in size and effectiveness. Moreover, the revolutionary philosophy of the FORA IX implicitly rejected the gradualist approach of the Socialists. A 1915 article in *La Organización Obrera*, for example, severely criticized deficiencies in a recently-approved accident compensation law, which, according to the writer, was of more use to employers than employees.

The parliamentary path, he concluded, was not particularly profitable for the working class.[48]

Relations between the Federación and the party were further strained by the activities of certain Socialists who sought on their own to organize working-class groups. The FORA IX saw these activities as direct competition and demanded of the party leadership that they be halted. After some hesitation, the Socialist directors agreed. The end result, however, was to alienate many members who believed that the party concentrated too much on elections and not enough on the needs of the working class. And despite the actions of the party's leaders, relations with the FORA IX did not noticeably improve.[49]

The Socialist Party did have an opportunity to strengthen its position with Argentine labor during the "semana trágica" (tragic week) of January 1919. This important event in twentieth-century Argentine history had its immediate antecedents in a December 1918 strike of workers at the Pedro Vasena and Sons metalworks plant on the outskirts of southern Buenos Aires. The strikers called for the usual higher wages and improved conditions. The employers refused these demands and recruited strike-breakers and scabs. On January 7, 1919, a clash between the strikers and strike-breakers led to police intervention. A number of workers were killed. The central Federación responded two days later, after other incidents, with a call for a general strike on the basis of two demands: "1) The solution of the conflict of the metalworkers at Vasena to the workers' satisfaction. 2) Liberation of all those imprisoned because of labor activity."[50]

As in previous general strikes, anarchists and Socialists joined with the syndicalists to support the protest. Their joint efforts paralyzed the capital. It was not a peaceful paralysis. The police accused strikers of attacking police headquarters and the mails. Strikers, in turn, accused the police of excessive brutality and arbitrary arrests during the course of the week. Two civilian organizations entered into the conflict. One, the Asociación del Trabajo (Work Association), led by conservative Joaquín S. de Anchorena, formed to protect the interests of employers and provided strike-breakers who clashed with protesting labor groups. Another group, the Liga Patriótica Argentina (Argentine Patriotic League), led by conservative Manuel Carlés, gathered together young aristocrats of the stripe who in 1910 had destroyed the offices of *La Vanguardia*.[51] In 1919 they blamed "foreign agitators" for the January disturbances. Spurred by international events, particularly the Bolshevik Revolution of 1917 and more recent left-wing uprisings in Germany, the members of the Liga singled out the Jewish community of

Buenos Aires for persecution, accusing it of Bolshevik sympathies. The young reactionaries invaded the centrally-located Jewish district of the capital, destroyed libraries, religious meeting places, and shops, and physically assaulted persons they found in these surroundings.[52]

During the strike Yrigoyen tried to use both the stick and the carrot. On January 10 he called on the armed forces, under the command of General Luis Dellepiane, to take control of the city. At the same time he offered the executive branch as an instrument to arbitrate the outstanding points of difference between labor, management, and government. Representatives of the FORA IX met with Chief of Police Elpidio González, Minister of the Interior Ramón Gómez, and Yrigoyen himself to work out the details of a settlement. After government consultations with the managers of the Vasena works, the arbitrators agreed to the Federación demands, granted the metalworkers the improvements in wages and conditions they originally had sought, and released those arrested in January and during previous disturbances. The FORA IX, in turn, on the night of January 11, voted to go back to work. After a delay of several days, complicated by continued police and Liga Patriótica attacks against labor and civilians, the strikers returned to their jobs and the city returned to normal activity. Estimates of property damage ran into the millions of pesos. Estimates of those killed and wounded ranged from a minimum of 65 and 300 to a maximum of 800 and 4,000. There could be no disputing the fact, however, that after nine years of relative peace on the Argentine labor front, the "semana trágica" had been the worst outbreak of social violence in the republic since the bloody series of conflicts at the beginning of the century.[53]

The role of the Socialist Party during the January events resembled its participation in earlier general strikes. The party organized protest demonstrations and issued protest manifestoes. Special committees investigated charges of police brutality against those jailed during the strike. But the major contribution of the party to the strike effort came through its representatives in the national Congress. On January 8 the Socialist delegation in the Chamber of Deputies urged that the Minister of the Interior appear before Congress to explain the initial police fusillade against the Vasena strikers. On January 14 Minister Gómez made his appearance, assuring the deputies that the executive was taking all steps necessary to restore order. Sounding much like those ministers whom Alfredo L. Palacios interpellated between 1904 and 1907, Gómez claimed that "the workers' demands have been given consideration as always, with the legitimate desire to satisfy them where possible, but the subversive action of elements foreign to the nation, which have tried to take advantage of these conflicts for their own criminal ends, have been repressed with the necessary energy."[54]

After conservatives Jerónimo del Barco of Córdoba and Luis Agote of Buenos Aires supported the government's hard line, Nicolás Repetto rose to make a blistering attack on the Radical administration. The initial response of the government, he began, had not maintained or restored order, as claimed by the minister, but rather had served to escalate violence and confrontation. The Radicals and their police officials over-reacted "because of an absolute lack of a feel for things on the part of the government, [a lack of] capacity and of a modern concept by which to understand the labor movement." The Yrigoyen administration, he continued, had only paid lip service to social reform; it had failed to enforce social legislation already enacted, failed to introduce comprehensive new measures, and failed to support Socialist initiatives to better the living and working conditions of the masses. To blame "foreign agitators" for social violence was mistaken. What caused outbursts like the "semana trágica" were "the conditions of the Argentine social environment: the conditions created for the urban worker and for the agricultural worker are abominable, deplorable, and these conditions, and their evils, have been aggravated considerably with the increase in the cost of living." To avoid future violence and agitation, Repetto concluded, the government should listen to and resolve workers' demands in particular disputes and then go on to serious consideration of social legislation to demonstrate to the working classes that the government cared about their situation and their needs.[55]

Repetto's remarks made no discernible impression on the Radicals in the chamber. In the same January 14 session ten Radical deputies proposed that Congress vote in favor of declaring a state of siege to restore order. The Socialists objected, observing that the situation in the capital was gradually easing and the principal need was now for basic social legislation. The proposal, however, passed overwhelmingly, with sixty-three in favor and only five (four Socialists and conservative Julio A. Costa) opposed.[56] The Senate, however, refused to approve the project, arguing that by the end of January the crisis had passed.[57] Yrigoyen's record of never having called a state of siege remained intact, even though he and his party recommended such a course in January 1919.

These debates did little more than let off steam and provide Socialists and Radicals a chance to delineate once more their differences. They did, however, underscore the Socialists' continued concern for basic social legislation and, less explicitly, the political advantage that the "semana trágica" afforded. The exact nature of Yrigoyen's role in these events has not yet been determined. But there seemed little question that his pro-labor, "man-of-the-people" image emerged seriously tarnished.

Yrigoyen had offered executive offices to arbitrate the dispute. The precedent he had set of personal intervention in such conflicts undoubtedly made negotiations easier and prevented the situation from becoming much worse. Moreover, these negotiations produced favorable results for labor. However, the police who fired on workers, arrested and beat strikers, and spoke of Bolshevik plots were police under the authority of a man Yrigoyen personally appointed, Elpidio González. The reaction of the president's party in Congress—to blame "foreign agitators" and to urge the state of siege—smacked of the earlier conservative administrations from which Yrigoyen had tried to distinguish himself and lent credence to Nicolás Repetto's observation that "we are today, with respect to the labor movement, as we were ten years ago, [with] the same hostility toward that movement."[58] Whether Yrigoyen, who at the same time incurred the wrath of conservative elements for not acting more firmly, more quickly, in January, could restore his image, and whether the Socialists could exploit this Radical setback, would become apparent in the months to follow.

8. Socialists and Radicals after the 'Semana Trágica': 1919–1921

> We hope to count on the backing of the entire working class and of all really progressive citizens, despite the simulation of working-class concern by the Radical government.
>
> Juan B. Justo during the 1920 deputy campaign in the federal capital

The "semana trágica" provides a convenient chronological dividing point between the two halves of Hipólito Yrigoyen's first administration. Following the events of January 1919 the Radicals appeared to lose, at least for the moment, some of their political momentum and popular support. In the first electoral test following that bloody week, a March 23, 1919, election to fill two deputy positions and one Senate seat in the federal capital, Radical Vicente C. Gallo, with 50,843 votes, barely edged Socialist candidate Juan B. Justo, who collected 48,078 votes for the upper house position. In the deputy contest the UCR's José O. Casás, with 54,749 votes, finished second to Socialist Federico Pinedo with 56,418 votes. The showing by Casás represented a 20,000 vote drop for the UCR from 1918, while the Socialists increased their totals by about 7,000 votes.[1]

In the first congressional sessions of 1919 Yrigoyen attempted to display a continuing concern for social and labor problems in the wake of the "semana trágica." In May his administration introduced three projects providing for conciliation and arbitration of labor disputes, collective labor-management contracts, and definitions for professional association. The government, through the Department of Labor, would play an important role in regulating and managing all of these measures if passed. Another sign of continuing concern was to send an

159

official delegation to an international labor conference held in Washington, D.C., at the end of 1919. The Argentine delegation brought back from the conference suggestions for additional legislative proposals.[2]

These displays of executive attention to social legislation, however, did little to heal the breach opened in January between the FORA IX and the Yrigoyen administration. According to the central Federación, unofficial anti-labor organizations like the Liga Patriótica Argentina and the Asociación del Trabajo, apparently with covert official blessing, continued to harass worker organization and activity. Officialdom, through the police, resurrected the Residence and Social Defense laws and applied these to "troublemakers." Hundreds of workers, the FORA IX said, were jailed because of participation in strikes in the early months of 1919.[3] Finally, the major labor organizations reacted to Yrigoyen's May legislative proposals much the way labor had responded to the 1904 González code. The executive measures, the Federación argued, implied restrictions on organization and activity that "would mean an attempt against the liberties and rights won by the syndically organized working class and would make impossible its syndical action in all the legitimate activities that are its own."[4] The FORA IX organized a large public rally in August to protest the proposals and threatened to call a general strike if they were approved.[5]

During 1919 the Socialist Party sought to draw closer to the Federación as the gulf between organized labor and the Radical government widened. Party representatives joined in the FORA IX's August meeting to add their objections to the Yrigoyen labor projects. In the Chamber of Deputies the Socialist delegation forced critical discussion of the excesses of the Liga Patriótica. In a debate that contained echoes of issues raised during Alfredo L. Palacios's first term in Congress, the Socialists were again embroiled in the question of nationalism. Nicolás Repetto, speaking on June 10, 1919, attacked the Liga for its hindrance of labor activity and its anti-foreign philosophy. Calling the league's actions during and since the "semana trágica" a serious overreaction to the momentary crisis and a main contributing factor to continued social disorder, Repetto expressed particular concern that members of the nation's armed forces had adhered to the Liga and participated in the group's public meetings.

Rogelio Araya, Radical deputy from the capital, saw the Liga Patriótica as a defender of order with as much right to exist in the republic as any labor organization. "The Liga Patriótica," he noted, "was formed as a reaction of Argentine feeling against the dissolution of our institutions that foreigners without roots in the republic tried to realize. The Liga Patriótica had its origins in the tragic week of January, in those days in which uncontrolled mobs assaulted the streets of this city, obliging its inhabitants to lock themselves into their houses, and commerce and industry to live frightened and fearful of new attacks more terrible than those already carried out."[6]

Socialist representatives clashed with Radicals on several other issues during the 1919 sessions. In May and June, Nicolás Repetto sought to interpellate the Minister of the Interior on government repression of recent agrarian disturbances, tying the Radical reaction to urban worker demands in January with a similar reaction to the strike movements of small farmers in April, May, and June.[7] In September, Juan B. Justo initiated the Socialists' annual critique of the national budget with the observation that so far as government fiscal policy was concerned there was little difference between the "new" UCR administration and the "old" conservative regime.[8]

On February 7, 1920, the Socialists of Buenos Aires met to select deputy candidates for the March 7 elections. The March contests would be the first under a new system of proportionate population representation based on the 1914 national census. The new alignment gave the capital thirty-two seats as opposed to its previous twenty. In March, twenty-three positions would be contested, sixteen to the majority and seven to the minority. Each party selected sixteen candidates. Those for the Socialist Party, as they appeared on the ballot, were Juan B. Justo, Agustín S. Muzio, Augusto Bunge, Enrique Dickmann, Federico Pinedo, Manuel González Maseda, Fernando de Andreis, Francisco Cúneo, Alfredo L. Spinetto, Esteban Jiménez, Alejandro Castiñeiras, Héctor González Iramain, Segundo Iñigo Carrera, Antonio Zaccagnini, and Felipe Di Tella. Illness forced Cúneo to abandon the list and Enrique Mouchet and Alberto Iribarne were added subsequently to round out the sixteen.

The final slate was composed of five doctors, four lawyers, two journalists, one tanner, one bookbinder, one employee, one traveling salesman, and one tailor. Middle-class professionals continued to dominate. The electoral program for 1920 included the basic features of that of 1918.[9]

During the campaign the Socialists aimed to shake loose Yrigoyen's popular support. The electoral proclamation of the executive committee began with the claim that the Socialists were entering the political contest once again in the never-ending struggle for the emancipation of working people. Attacking the Radical social policy as a fraud designed for political purposes, the proclamation specifically criticized tariff increases and charged the government with treating the privileges of the landowning classes as sacred.[10]

From the beginning of January the Radicals also campaigned intensively, focusing much of their attention on the Socialists. When the latter chose their list of candidates, *La Epoca*, the Radicals' principal journal, observed that the same names that had graced party slates from the early years of the century had reappeared again, implying an elite control of the party, a control of the professional middle class. "Doctors and doctors," *La Epoca* said of the Socialist candidates. "Between doctor and doctor a worker, to throw the voter off the track. A 'camouflaged' proletarian list. Above all, the inevitable re-elected [candidates]."[11]

The UCR of the capital did not finally choose its candidates until February 23, two weeks before the election. Of the sixteen men chosen, all but two carried the professional title "Doctor" before their names.[12] Despite the later time in selecting candidates as compared with the Socialists, the Radicals enjoyed improved organization and techniques. *La Epoca* carried announcements of party lectures, rallies, and committee meetings throughout January and February. Elections for the Radicals, like the Socialists, were becoming the culmination of many months of politicking.

Radical candidates ran on the bases of what they claimed were Yrigoyen's accomplishments. They stressed their roots as an original, national, Argentine political organization. They argued that an obstructionist Socialist-conservative alliance had stymied Radical initiatives in Congress, and called for party and national unity to defeat the obstructionists and to provide the Yrigoyen administration with an overwhelming majority in the Chamber of Deputies.

In the 1920 campaign, as in past contests, the UCR presented no concrete, articulated program. Candidate Leónidas Anastasi, however, at a pre-election rally, indicated that in the coming year his party would push for specific social legislation. "In matters of social policy," Anastasi began, "Radicalism has its own formula, which is neither blind adoration of capitalism, which the conservative parties profess, nor insensible admiration of the Soviet regime." The Radicals, he concluded, desired not conflict but "the collaboration of classes," achieved through enactment of measures that in most particulars echoed the program of the Socialist Party.[13]

The characteristics of the 1920 campaign were stamped from the same mold as deputy contests in the capital beginning in 1912. Socialists, Radicals, and Democratic Progressives gave speeches, provided detailed voting information, distributed leaflets, plastered the walls of the city with colorful posters, and held large street rallies to present candidates. The Radicals, with the support of the national administration, used the election period as a time to distribute foodstuffs free or at reduced prices to the populace of the capital. They emulated Socialist picnics with traditional *asados*, or barbecues of large sides of beef washed down with wine, for the faithful and prospective voters. The Socialists, for their part, introduced a new technique, the use of documentary and propaganda motion pictures to display the realities of social conditions in the republic. These were shown in theaters or meeting halls to supplement lectures and later from a special truck with a portable screen that could be set up in the open air.

The elections of March 7 took place in orderly fashion. The Radicals, with their leading candidate gaining 60,364 votes, took the sixteen-seat majority. The top Socialist vote-getter received 55,000 votes and the party captured the seven-seat minority positions. The PDP gained a little over 41,000 votes, while the PSI tallied almost 3,000 and the PSA about 2,700.[14]

Analysis of the results gave the three major parties grounds for cautious optimism. The Socialists regained advantages in *circunscripciones* two through four, six through eight, and fifteen, while the Radicals took *circunscripción* one and middle-class districts nine through thirteen as well as sixteen through eighteen. The Democratic Progressives made a very respectable showing, capturing fourteen, nineteen, and twenty, *circunscripciones* with heavy concentrations of owners and professionals. (See table 10.)

Radical triumphs in the provinces gave the UCR a total of 84 of the now 152 seats in the Chamber of Deputies. Groups bearing the Radical rubric, but in disagreement with party direction—the Blue Radicals of Córdoba, the Official Radicals of Jujuy, the Situational Radicals of Mendoza, the White and Black Radicals of Santiago del Estero, the Dissident Radicals of Santa Fe—controlled a combined total of 13 seats. The Democratic Progressives, who won the 9 majority seats from Córdoba in 1920, held 19 positions in the Chamber, the conservatives 14, the Socialists 10, and a scattering of conservative factions the remaining 12 seats.

Within the Radical-controlled Chamber of Deputies, the Socialists continued to register their opposition to the policies of the Yrigoyen administration.[15] In the sessions of 1920 and 1921 they tried to underscore further the few differences they saw between the UCR government and conservative administrations. They attacked monetary and

TABLE 10

DEPUTY ELECTIONS, FEDERAL CAPITAL, ABSOLUTE AND PROPORTIONATE VOTES BY CIRCUNSCRIPCIÓN, MARCH 7, 1920

Circun-scripción	UCR	%	PS	%	PDP	%	Voted	Registered	Turnout %
1	3,236	(38.4)	3,103	(36.8)	1,532	(18.2)	8,422	11,314	74.4
2	2,288	(33.4)	3,039	(44.6)	1,137	(16.7)	6,814	9,308	73.2
3	4,502	(38.9)	4,640	(40.1)	2,010	(17.4)	11,579	15,694	73.8
4	3,752	(35.5)	4,717	(44.6)	1,535	(14.5)	10,578	15,276	69.2
5	3,711	(43.4)	2,272	(26.6)	2,432	(28.4)	8,552	11,505	74.3
6	3,096	(37.2)	3,178	(38.2)	1,700	(20.4)	8,319	10,904	76.3
7	2,547	(35.7)	2,613	(36.7)	1,570	(22.0)	7,129	9,630	74.0
8	3,097	(34.4)	3,541	(39.4)	2,240	(24.9)	8,998	11,993	75.0
9	2,998	(36.7)	2,826	(34.6)	2,192	(26.9)	8,136	10,969	74.4
10	1,672	(38.8)	1,467	(34.1)	1,176	(27.3)	4,304	5,789	74.3
11	1,638	(36.2)	1,340	(29.7)	1,666	(36.9)	4,519	6,575	68.7
12	3,765	(44.8)	2,424	(28.6)	2,005	(24.9)	8,400	11,429	73.5
13	3,185	(40.7)	2,052	(26.2)	2,442	(31.2)	7,834	11,268	69.5
14	2,632	(37.1)	1,665	(23.5)	2,853	(40.2)	7,093	10,443	67.9
15	2,750	(36.4)	2,894	(38.3)	1,391	(18.4)	7,565	10,405	72.7
16	3,102	(37.4)	2,495	(30.0)	2,379	(28.6)	8,304	11,359	73.1
17	2,859	(37.2)	2,450	(31.9)	2,035	(26.5)	7,690	10,777	71.4
18	4,162	(35.0)	3,947	(33.2)	3,271	(27.5)	11,901	16,115	73.9
19	3,632	(34.9)	3,100	(29.8)	3,748	(36.0)	10,419	14,233	73.2
20	1,776	(32.2)	1,299	(23.5)	2,310	(41.8)	5,520	7,444	74.2
Totals	60,400	(37.3)	55,062	(34.0)	41,561	(25.6)	162,103	222,430	72.9

Source: Darío Cantón, Materiales, II, 49.

budgetary policies, argued for legislation that would regulate the activities of privileged and protected monopolies, and brought to light abuses in public administration. In one of the most spectacular and highly-publicized events of this period, the Socialists played a key role in bringing charges of conflict of interest against Yrigoyen's Minister of Finance, Domingo E. Salaberry. In April 1921 a vote of censure against Salaberry failed by only four votes.[16]

Important economic issues occupied the attention of both Radicals and Socialists. A crucial question, more and more debated, was the role of foreign investment. World War I had emphasized the republic's dependence on world markets for exports and foreign manufacturing for imports. The interruption of trade and the neglect of foreign owned and operated businesses and services during the wartime crisis highlighted Argentina's vulnerability to economic forces beyond its control. Increasing attention was paid to the exploitation of vital natural resources essential for developing a more self-sufficient national economy. At the forefront of concern was petroleum, especially the large reserves discovered in 1907 at Comodoro Rivadavia in the national territory of Chubút. In 1910 the Comodoro Rivadavia field was divided into zones of state and private exploitation. However, subsequent administrations failed to formulate a coherent petroleum policy to determine rights of ownership as between national and provincial governments and rights of exploration and exploitation as between public and private concerns. These ambiguities caused increased public concern in the war years and immediately thereafter when the Comodoro Rivadavia field, as well as potential sources in Salta and Mendoza provinces, became targets of investment by large foreign companies like Standard Oil of New Jersey and Royal Dutch Shell.

President Yrigoyen, in his inaugural message to Congress, continuously emphasized the need to increase petroleum production and the vital importance of this resource for the future of the country. The shutting off of petroleum imports during the war highlighted the need for increased local exploitation. By mid-1918 the president traveled south to Comodoro Rivadavia to view the state and private enterprises first-hand.

More than a year after his trip to the fields, Yrigoyen, through his Minister of Agriculture, Alfredo Demarchi, a past president of the Unión Industrial Argentina, introduced legislation to strengthen national control of petroleum. The first project, presented on September 23, 1919, provided for a continuation of the mixed public-private system but affirmed the state as original owner of all petroleum deposits in the republic. The chief executive was given authority to exploit this state property either directly, through provincial governments, or by concession, under tight regulation, to private companies, domestic or foreign. Other articles stated that exploitation should be primarily for internal use rather than export and that concerns engaged in petroleum mining and refining should give preference to Argentine citizens, all other conditions being equal, in appointing manual labor and administrative personnel. A second measure, presented three days later, began with the provision that the national executive "will realize in all the territory of the republic exploration and exploitation of petroleum deposits." To this end the legislation provided for the establishment of a government oil company, Yacimientos Petrolíferos Fiscales, to be part of the Ministry of Agriculture and thereby under the ultimate control of the president of the republic. When the Radical-controlled chamber refused to consider this legislation, Yrigoyen issued an executive decree on June 3, 1922, that put into effect the second of his proposals, creating officially the Dirección General de Yacimientos Petrolíferos Fiscales.[17]

Political considerations very probably played a major role in Yrigoyen's presentation of these proposals. Sensing the growing popularity of a nationalist stance with regard to petroleum, he attempted to garner the electoral benefits of a seemingly aggressive position on this issue. However, his initiatives at this time were neither innovative nor particularly nationalistic, and they still left overall petroleum policy vague and unsatisfactory. Yrigoyen's failure to push as strongly as he might have for his proposals after the 1920 congressional elections added substance to the opposition's argument that the measures were based more on politics than on concern for the nation's economic well-being. Finally, Yrigoyen's administration failed to provide the state owned and operated facility at Comodoro Rivadavia with necessary support or direction and the public enterprise was forced to operate under a series of handicaps that did little to improve performance.[18]

Nicolás Repetto was the leading exponent of the Socialist position on the oil question, a position that favored greater state control but also maintenance of the mixed public-private arrangement. During the final years of the Yrigoyen administration Repetto analyzed the workings of the state owned field and sought to undercut Yrigoyen's seeming political advantages on this issue. In several congressional speeches he attacked the government for its alleged failures in management at Comodoro Rivadavia. According to Repetto, the public enterprise was not doing well in comparison with private companies. Public production was stagnant or decreasing while private production steadily increased. He blamed the national administration for poor handling of a labor dispute in the fields that lasted for three months in 1919. When in July 1922 Repetto called for an investigation of the state concern, he argued that the government was concealing its many deficiencies in oil management. It was one thing, he said, to talk about national resources and the importance of public management, and quite another to administer these. Inadequate financing and a lack of technical skill hampered government operations. But most serious, he argued, was the Radical executive's failure to develop a coherent and consistent plan for the nation's petroleum reserves. Finally, Repetto warned, the failures of the state enterprise would further the case of the private companies, increase international competition for Argentine reserves by large foreign monopolies, and endanger national control of a crucial commodity.[19]

Dubious of the efficiency of state control, at least under Radical management, the party was nevertheless still critical of the abuses of foreign capital, and in the early 1920s it attacked these in Congress. In September 1921 a congressional committee reported favorably on the granting of a new line concession to the British-owned Central Córdoba Railroad. Socialist deputy Héctor González Iramain, on the Communication and Transportation Committee, offered several amendments. These included requirements that negotiations and financial arrangements for the concession be made public, that reports on construction, management, costs, and profits be made regularly available in Spanish, that the company provide in-country representatives with the authority to settle labor disputes, and that the company be obligated to accept the arbitrational powers of Argentina's chief executive.

During the debate on these amendments Juan B. Justo spoke out strongly against foreign investors in the republic. "We appear to have," he began, "political independence and liberty in form, but basically we depend today, as more than a century ago, on the authority and power of foreigners; and there is no power more absolute, more absorbent, more tyrannical than the power of monopoly, than the power of capitalist enterprises. . . . We are subjects of the great foreign railroad companies of the country. The only national lines transport almost nothing. The great enterprises are well known. All have their seat in London and all hide their transactions." If the concessions were to be granted, Justo concluded, the chamber at least had the right to impose its own conditions.

The Socialist language was strong, but their proposed remedies were moderate. They did not suggest a cancellation of the concession or nationalization of the line. They simply argued for regulation of certain practices. Even these moderate regulations, however, were apparently too much for the majority of deputies. Radical Roberto M. Ortiz, deputy from the capital and a lawyer for the railroads, led the counterattack. The González Iramain amendments were defeated after long and impassioned debate, and the concession was approved.[20]

In the early 1920s the realm of social problems again provided another area of congressional combat between Socialists and Radicals. Yrigoyen and the Radicals continued to present social legislation to the Congress. In the 1920–1922 interval the president and his party urged the passage of legislative projects that would provide pensions for railroad workers, workers employed by private enterprises engaged in public services, and bank employees, all of which were eventually approved. On June 8, 1921, the Radical executive introduced a comprehensive labor code covering such items as working conditions, labor-management relations, minimum wages and maximum hours, and accident compensation.[21] Inspired by the Washington Labor Conference, it echoed many of the planks of the Socialist program and was reminiscent of the González proposal of 1904. Like the earlier government-inspired comprehensive "Código de Trabajo," the Yrigoyen initiative languished in committee, although certain items from the code later were transformed into law.[22]

The Socialists, for their part, continued to press for the social reforms that were their trademark. Year after year they introduced and reintroduced measures to establish an eight-hour day, minimum wages, and a comprehensive social security system. They waged vigorous campaigns against alcoholism and prostitution, sought to enact equal legal rights for women, and championed divorce (which Yrigoyen strongly opposed). Party delegates urged the strengthening and broadening of existing social legislation and called public officials, and particularly the Labor Department, to account for not strictly enforcing the regulatory provisions of labor statutes. In Congress they picked holes in Yrigoyen's proposals, usually focusing on the ambiguous wording or the partial coverage implied in the projects. The various pension plans, Augusto Bunge argued, were "demagogic, false, and dangerous." Poorly written and conceived, he charged, they created privileged professional sectors within the working class. In place of particular proposals for particular groups he urged the establishment of a sweeping government-sponsored pension and social security system to cover all workers.[23]

The Socialists also continued to focus on social problems in other areas. In February 1922 party deputies brought to the chamber's attention a matter involving official repression in the national territory of

Santa Cruz. In November 1920 workers on the extensive sheep ranches of that region, at the southern tip of the country, presented to their owners, mostly British, a list of demands for improved conditions. These demands were: 1) an increase in salary; 2) an improvement in living quarters, with a limit on the number of men assigned to a room and a mattress for each worker; 3) the right to arm in self-defense when working in isolated and dangerous regions; and 4) the payment of monthly salaries in hard currency. To enforce their demands, the workers occupied some ranches and sheep-shearing operations. The owners, through the Sociedad Rural de Santa Cruz (Rural Society of Santa Cruz), agreed to these conditions and the first phase of the strike ended with little disturbance.

In late 1921, however, when the price of wool on the world market dropped dramatically and previously-agreed conditions were ignored, managers and workers squared off again. The laborers, organized in the Sociedad Obrera de Río Gallegos (Workers' Society of Río Gallegos), again occupied ranches. The owners formed a private corps of armed men, *guardias blancas* (white guards), and prepared to meet this new challenge with force. Local government officials, who were Radicals, supported the owners. Telegrams to Buenos Aires painted a picture of roaming bands of mounted men pillaging and looting the countryside and asked for national assistance. In November 1921 Yrigoyen directed Lieutenant Colonel Héctor Varela to lead a combined military-police column against the strikers. From late November 1921 to early January 1922 Varela methodically rounded up the leaders and the rank and file of the Sociedad Obrera. Some were exiled, some imprisoned, and some executed on the spot. Grisly tales of mass executions by machine-gun fire and decapitations by machete began to spread to the federal capital. Hundreds, perhaps thousands of workers lost either their lives or their freedom as the strike was broken. During Yrigoyen's administration an urban disturbance earned the appellation "semana trágica." The same adjective was later applied to the rural strike in Santa Cruz in 1921–1922: "la Patagonia trágica."[24]

These events took place in an area far removed from Buenos Aires. Few Argentines had traveled to the distant regions of the south. Most *porteños* probably knew more about Paris than Patagonia. Communications were rudimentary, the only rapid way to reach Santa Cruz being by ship, as no railroads penetrated much past Bahía Blanca. President Yrigoyen himself seemed poorly informed as to the exact nature of the dispute. Newspaper reports were one-sided and inaccurate. Most articles in *La Prensa* repeated the assertions and positions of the local officials and the owners. Two organs that tried to present the other side were the FORA IX's *La Organización Obrera* and the Socialist *La Vanguardia*.

In the Chamber of Deputies Antonio de Tomaso introduced a resolution on February 1, 1922, that Congress appoint a five-man committee to investigate the situation in the south. In his supporting speech de Tomaso tried to present the workers' side of the conflict in contrast to the prevailing pro-owner propaganda. He declared that the methods used in breaking the strike were responsible for "a horrible tragedy." Further, he castigated the excesses of police and military and denounced Colonel Varela "for having abused his functions, for having covered the armed forces of the nation with opprobrium, . . . for having ordered, personally or through his subordinates, mass shootings, in the field itself, of men chosen by lot and charged with being the leaders of the movement."[25]

De Tomaso's motion came at the end of the extraordinary sessions of 1922 and was not acted upon. The Socialists later used the Santa Cruz massacre as campaign ammunition against Yrigoyen and the Radicals, citing the sending of Varela as one more example of the basic anti-labor position of the UCR regime. In Patagonia the movement to improve conditions for the ranch workers was crushed. Events in the south remained only a distant concern for most politicians in the federal capital throughout the rest of the decade.

While Socialist deputies rose to the defense of working-class interests in Congress, actual relations between the party and the major labor organization, the FORA IX, steadily deteriorated. Socialists still sat on the federal council of the Federación, but the years 1920 to 1922 represented a period of increasing tension and fragmentation for the FORA IX. The syndicalists, who continued to dominate, found their organization increasingly pulled in three separate directions: toward anarchism, communism, and socialism as these forces attempted to make their respective positions prevail within the Federación.

Relations between the FORA IX and the party had never been close. The syndicalists cast a suspicious eye on Socialist attempts to organize the proletariat and guarded jealously their own apolitical nature. The Socialists, for their part, had accommodated the Federación in the dispute over attempts by party members to create Socialist unions, had backed the workers' cause in Congress, and had joined the central union in joint protest of repression and restrictive legislation. In September and October of 1920 the Socialists had requested the federal council of the FORA IX to participate in a national campaign to reopen the Caja de Conversión and to press for lower rents and a lower price for sugar. The leadership of the Federación steadfastly refused to become part of the Socialist campaigns, arguing that such participation would jeopardize the FORA IX's principles.[26] The Socialists responded that action to improve the lot of the working classes transcended partisan lines, and they accused the labor leadership of complicity with the Radical government in refusing to protest official economic policies.

Another ingredient in the brewing stew of discontent was added at the eleventh congress of the FORA IX (January 29–February 5, 1921, in La Plata). There the credentials of Socialist Agustín Muzio, in representation of the Unión Obreros Curtidores, were rejected. The majority based their objections on the somewhat contradictory grounds that Muzio had temporarily ceased being a worker when he became a national deputy and as a deputy had not sufficiently defended working-class interests.[27]

The stew simmered during a brief general strike in June 1921. The FORA IX accused the party of opposing the protest and hindering its progress. The Socialists, in turn, credited their parliamentary pressure with producing the release of prisoners following the strike action. The ensuing debate, fought largely in the pages of *La Vanguardia* and *La Organización Obrera*, let loose a torrent of charges and countercharges. Attacks became personal and petty. The Federación saw Muzio as the villain of the piece, embittered against the FORA IX from the eleventh congress. The Socialists charged the secretary-general of the Federación, former Socialist Pedro C. Alegría, with being an alcoholic and an incompetent. In July the printers of *La Vanguardia* refused to allow the printers of *La Organización Obrera* to use their press facilities.

The escalating antagonisms came to a head in September. The party printed a list of eight specific charges against "the small group of charlatans and traitors who have the FORA in their hands. . . ." Included were accusations that Alegría was personally unfit for leadership, as was the director of *La Organización Obrera*, Luis Lotito. But the major thrust of the eight points sought to taint the Federación's leadership with selling out to the Radical government. The Socialists questioned the vacillating actions of the federal council in the recent general strike and asked why Radical lawyer and deputy Leónidas Anastasi had been employed to provide legal services for the Federación and why Radical deputy José Tamborini had been invited to appear at a FORA IX rally. They also accused the labor leadership of failing "to place itself in resolute opposition to reactionary forces and to free itself from the taming influences of the government, today as visible as deplorable."

In its own defense, the FORA IX denied the major charges of complicity with the government. Anastasi, they countered, had proved a lawyer less partisan and more effective than those connected with *La Vanguardia*. Tamborini had been invited to a FORA IX rally (but did not appear) as one concerned with social problems and not for partisan reasons. The leadership further claimed an active and aggressive action against repression, resulting in days and weeks in jail while Socialist deputies lolled in the plush chairs of Congress. Finally, the Socialist attack on the Federación seemed to align the alleged working-class party with reactionary groups like the Liga Patriótica Argentina and the Asociación del Trabajo.[28]

The bitter exchanges between Socialists and syndicalists subsided in the final months of 1921. Both groups turned to other concerns. For the FORA IX the conflict with the Socialist Party was merely one dispute among many. In February 1921, the five Partido Socialista Internacional members of the federal council resigned in protest of the Federación's refusal to join the new Federación Sindical Internacional Roja (Red International Syndical Federation) with its seat in Moscow.[29] In March 1922 a labor congress from the capital tried to put some of the fragmented pieces of the Federación back together. Anarchists, communists, Socialists, and syndicalists met in a convention reminiscent of the first decade of the century. After debates in which each faction tried to gain the upper hand, the apolitical syndicalists again prevailed. From the meeting a new central organization emerged, the Unión Sindical Argentina (USA) (Argentine Syndical Union). The anarchists refused to join the new entity and continued to go their separate way. The Socialists no longer enjoyed representation on the federal council. The direction of the USA was syndicalist and communist, but it was direction over a seriously weakened central organization. The bitter in-fighting had taken its toll. As one labor historian put it, by 1922 "the workers were weary [of internecine strife] and turned their backs on organization in general, initiating a new period of inaction and of weakness in labor combativeness."[30]

The first half of the Yrigoyen administration had witnessed the growth of the FORA IX into Argentina's largest and most successful labor confederation. The second half of the Radical term, symbolically divided by the "semana trágica," saw the steady disintegration of the Federación. Favorable government actions and attitudes had contributed to the ascendancy of the FORA IX; a less favorable posture after

January 1919 accompanied its decline. Also contributing were the unchecked activities of anti-labor organizations, a halt to the ever-increasing inflation of the war years, and the renewal of internal, partisan differences. The Socialist Party was a major factor in this latter development. By 1922 the Socialists had divorced themselves almost completely from the central labor leadership. But in political terms the divorce had occurred at a propitious moment, a moment when the labor movement itself had returned to a state of weakness, division, and confusion.

The overall growth and expansion of Argentina's Socialist Party continued unabated during the years of Radical rule. At the thirteenth national congress, held at Pergamino in Buenos Aires province, July 6 through 9, 1916, delegates from 129 groups were in attendance. *La Vanguardia* mentioned an additional 28 centers affiliated but not attending because of failure to keep current in payment of dues. The 129 groups at the congress claimed to represent a total of 6,604 members. Twenty-nine groups with 2,832 affiliates were from the federal capital, one hundred with 3,752 affiliates from the interior.[31] By 1918 the number of groups had grown to 176 (28 in the capital) and the number of members to 8,575 (2,961 in the capital). In 1917 and 1921 the party suffered schisms, the second of which will be discussed in more detail below. As a result, the number of affiliates in 1921 dropped to 8,339 (2,264 in the capital), although the number of groups climbed to 184 (29 in the capital).[32] Membership still represented only about 10 percent of the total Socialist vote in national elections, an indication that the party depended heavily on the support of independents and disaffected partisans of other parties for success at the polls.

Despite the large number of Socialist groups in the interior, basic party strength was still rooted in the city of Buenos Aires. Socialist votes in deputy contests in the provinces remained at less than 5 percent of totals.[33]

The most significant gains for the Socialists in the interior were still at the local level. In 1920 the party elected its first representative to the provincial legislature of Tucumán. A Socialist also sat in the provincial chamber of Mendoza during this period. Four Socialists served in the provincial assembly of Buenos Aires. In elections to the city council of Avellaneda, held in November 1919, four Socialist representatives were elected along with eleven Radicals and eleven conservatives. In January 1920 Socialist Jacinto Oddone was chosen mayor of that city as a compromise candidate.[34] In the seaside resort city of Mar del Plata four Socialists captured council positions and the selection of mayor went to thirty-one-year-old Socialist Teodoro Bronzini. By 1920 the party had affiliates as city council members in thirteen municipalities of Buenos Aires province.[35]

Other Socialist successes were achieved in municipal elections in the city of Buenos Aires. In 1917 a Socialist-sponsored reform had extended the basic aspects of the Sáenz Peña law to elections held for the thirty positions on the Concejo Deliberante (City Council) of the capital. In the first contest held under the new law, in October 1918, the Socialists defeated the Radicals 47,977 to 47,139 to capture ten seats on the council.[36] The party continued to perform well in biennial municipal elections and to enjoy a strong voice in capital government throughout the 1920s. Within the Concejo future Socialist deputies gained valuable political and legislative experience and managed to enact measures and force consideration of issues reflective of party concerns at the national level.[37]

In the 1920s *La Vanguardia* began to publish lists of party members proposed by centers in the capital to run for public office. From these lists the party chose its final slate for national deputies and municipal councilmen. Between 1920 and 1926 a total of 123 affiliates were noted by name, occupation, and age upon entering the party. With regard to age, 21 were between seventeen and nineteen when they affiliated, 69 between twenty and twenty-nine, 27 between thirty and thirty-nine, 5 over forty, and one for whom no information on age was printed. As table 11 shows, the men listed were overwhelmingly engaged in white-collar occupations, with some representation of skilled workers. Among those sufficiently advanced in party ranks to compete for public office, then, patterns of party adherence seemed consistent from the turn of the century. Socialists, at least from this sample, were commonly men who entered the party in their twenties and who belonged to the middle sectors of society. Missing from their number were representatives from the extreme upper and lower societal strata.

In April 1920 the party collected figures on the occupations of all members in the federal capital. (See table 12.) This sample showed a somewhat more heterogeneous occupational pattern than that discussed above with regard to candidates for office. Except for somewhat larger percentages in the artisan and small merchant category, and somewhat smaller proportions in the owner and professional categories, the occupational make-up of the party generally paralleled that of the capital's overall voting population. Employees represented the largest single occupational group in the party. Other blocs with significant representation were merchants (231), students (156), mechanics (144), masons

TABLE 11

OCCUPATIONS OF NOMINEES FOR CANDIDACY
TO PUBLIC OFFICE BY CENTERS OF THE SOCIALIST PARTY,
FEDERAL CAPITAL, 1920–1926

1. Agent (1)	21. Lithographer (1)
2. Architect (1)	22. Machinist (1)
3. Artist (1)	23. Mason (4)
4. Barber (1)	24. Mechanic (3)
5. Bookbinder (2)	25. Merchant (10)
6. Bookkeeper (3)	26. Painter (1)
7. Bronze-worker (1)	27. Peon (1)
8. Carpenter (1)	28. Photographer (1)
9. Chauffeur (2)	29. Plumber (1)
10. Chemist (1)	30. Public accountant (4)
11. Decorator (1)	31. Seaman (3)
12. Doctor (6)	32. Solicitor (5)
13. Electrician (1)	33. Student (5)
14. Employee (26)	34. Tailor (1)
15. Engineer (2)	35. Tanner (1)
16. Harnessmaker (1)	36. Teacher (4)
17. Industrialist (1)	37. Traveling salesman (1)
18. Jeweler (2)	38. Typographer (2)
19. Journalist (8)	39. Veterinarian (1)
20. Lawyer (10)	40. Weaver (1)

Sources: Compiled from *La Vanguardia* editions of February 2, 1920, p. 3;
   October 17, 1920, p. 2; February 12, 1924, p. 2; and January 7, 1926, p. 3.

TABLE 12

MEMBERS OF THE SOCIALIST PARTY BY OCCUPATION,
FEDERAL CAPITAL, ABSOLUTE AND PROPORTIONATE, 1920

Occupational Category	Absolute	Percentage
Worker	732	20.0
Artisan and small merchant	1,382	37.8
Employee	1,155	31.6
Owner	24	0.7
Professional	293	8.0
Various	73	2.0
Total	3,659	

Source: "Cuadro estadístico de los afiliados a los centros de la Capital," *La Vanguardia* (April 10, 1920), p. 7.

(130), printers (125), tailors (117), painters (97), carpenters (89), iron-workers (81), and electricians (77).

The convening of regular party congresses continued to parallel overall growth. But while important matters of general interest were discussed at ordinary congresses, the most significant changes in party direction occurred at extraordinary congresses. The third extraordinary congress of 1917, already discussed, saw debate over the Socialist position vis-à-vis World War I. The momentous fourth extraordinary congress, held at Bahía Blanca from January 8 to 10, 1921, considered specifically the party's relationship with the Second and Third Socialist Internationals.

The Russian Revolution and the establishment of the Bolshevik regime produced a predictably adverse reaction from the Argentine right. On the left, reactions were more mixed and complex. For some the Bolshevik Revolution meant a glimmer of hope for progressive improvements in a war-torn world. Within Socialist circles initial reaction was generally favorable, especially to the overthrow of the Czar and the appearance of what seemed a social-democratic regime. The original enthusiasm of many party members cooled, however, after the Bolshevik takeover in late 1917. An important turning point in Socialist attitudes came in 1919. In the early months of that year Juan B. Justo and Antonio de Tomaso traveled to Europe to meet at Berne and Amsterdam with leaders of other parties and labor organizations. There, they discussed ways and means to re-establish and revitalize the international socialist movement. Meeting primarily with moderate socialists, they received disturbing reports about some of the dictatorial and coercive methods employed by the Bolshevik regime to revolutionize Russian society. These reports they relayed later to their colleagues in South America.[38]

By 1919–1920 the Russian Revolution had raised serious political dilemmas for Argentina's Socialist Party. On the one hand, the party could not dissociate itself from the Bolshevik regime without seeming to align with the Argentine right and to strain even further its relations with affiliates who believed that the party was moving away from the concerns of the proletariat. How to deny the first successful Marxist revolution? On the other hand, too close an identification with the revolutionary Bolsheviks meant going directly against twenty-five years of reformist, non-violent, parliamentary and political party history. These dilemmas were intensified, clarified, and to a certain degree resolved in the debate over adherence to the Third International at the fourth extraordinary congress in 1921.

From its early years the Argentine Socialist Party had affiliated with the Second International. Following its founding in 1889, the Second International had represented Marxist and non-Marxist, reformist and revolutionary socialist political parties and labor organizations. The Argentines, finding their own views compatible with those of the leaders of the Second International, frequently sent representatives to regular meetings held in Europe. When the Second International collapsed at the outbreak of World War I, the Argentine party shared the general socialist disillusionment and disappointment.

In the Soviet Union, Lenin determined to construct a more revolutionary body to replace the discredited Second International. In March 1919 he founded the Third International, or the Comintern, and issued his famous twenty-one conditions for membership. In Argentina, Socialist Party members began in late 1920 to take sides on affiliation with the Third International. Some who supported such an affiliation, mostly young, new adherents to the party, published a journal entitled *Germinal*, subtitled "A Single International: The Third," to express their views. They argued in the pages of *Germinal* that there could only be two alternatives: to join the Third International or to form a new Second International. The latter course meant a return to defunct reformism; the former, a commitment to a revolutionary alternative. The reformism that characterized the party throughout its history, they conceded, had been justifiable and previously efficacious. But war and the Russian Revolution had created new conditions and now the party must adapt to these.[39]

Those within the party who opposed adherence to the Third International founded their own publication, *Democracia Socialista*, in November 1920. The editors, men of long standing in the party, defended the past action and orientation of the party and viewed the present controversy as one more attempt to engage it in sterile, impractical, and visionary violent activity. They objected to Comintern control over local organizations and called the twenty-one conditions unreasonable and tyrannical demands inapplicable to the Argentine situation.[40]

Juan B. Justo, though not actively involved in *Democracia Socialista*, nevertheless shared its sentiments. As the fourth extraordinary congress approached he threw his support behind the formulation of a new International that would continue to embody the reformism of the Second. Drawing up a "Program of International Socialist Action" to be presented by the parliamentary group to the congress, he agreed with the general criticisms of the Second International. The major factor in the Second International's failure to survive the crisis of war, he argued, was neglect of international economic problems. Members of the Second International had been "subconscious imperialists," unaware of the economic root causes of international rivalry and unable to resist the pull of nationalism at the crucial moment. The Third International, he continued, also failed to deal with these issues. The twenty-one conditions sought control over the internal affairs of individual parties and labor movements but said nothing about basic changes in international economic structures. The Socialist Party of Argentina, Justo concluded, should contribute to the creation of a new International that would avoid the mistakes of the Second and the oversights of the Third. Specifically, the new international socialist program would recognize racial equality, support international application of labor legislation, abolish trade barriers, end the abuses of foreign capital, and establish an international and uniform monetary system and system of weights and measures.[41]

All of these points of view came together at the Bahía Blanca congress. The meeting opened on January 8, 1921. Justo was elected presiding officer. Debate began the following day on two resolutions. One, the majority report, called for sympathetic support of the Russian Revolution, separation from the Second International, and the adoption of an international socialist program along the lines suggested by Justo. The minority report called for complete separation from the Second International and adherence to the Third.

In sharp contrast with previous congresses, the discussions on these two resolutions took place in an atmosphere of relative calm, mutual respect, and serious consideration. The speakers for the majority proposal represented the party's office-holding establishment. They repeated in the congress the arguments against adherence to the Third International previously enunciated in the pages of *Democracia Socialista*. Antonio de Tomaso, who had accompanied Justo to Europe in 1919, was the strongest proponent of those who rejected affiliation with the Comintern. Unlike others in his camp, he was openly critical not only of Soviet international policies but internal developments as well.[42]

Generally, those who spoke on behalf of the minority report were not prominent figures. These delegates claimed to represent the left wing of the party—the young, the working class, the revolutionaries, and those who did not hold office. But their principal spokesman was an exception.

Enrique del Valle Iberlucea had been the sole Socialist in the Argentine Senate for eight years. In that conservative-dominated body he had witnessed project after project of Socialist-inspired legislation defeated or ignored. From 1917 he had viewed developments in Russia with in-

terest and sympathy. By 1920 he had determined that the peaceful parliamentary approach of the Socialist Party was fruitless. The class struggle, he concluded, could only be resolved through revolution. And
revolutionary change could only be achieved through the dictatorship
of the proletariat.[43]

At the fourth extraordinary congress Senator del Valle Iberlucea
spoke in favor of adherence to the Third International. He began with
the argument that support for the Bolshevik Revolution and allegiance
to the Comintern could not be separated. He then criticized the reformism of the Argentine Socialist Party, predicting that even if Socialists won parliamentary majorities, the bourgeoisie would forcibly stymie working-class demands. "The emancipation of labor," the senator
proclaimed, "can only be effected by means of a revolution." "The dictatorship of the proletariat is essential for the emancipation of the
working class," he continued, "but cannot be a definitive form of government, [and] will exist only during the period necessary to effect the
conquest of public power." Countries throughout the world, he noted,
were on the verge of revolution and adherence to the Third International implied solidarity with these revolutionary aspirations. But adherence did not mean for del Valle Iberlucea that revolution would
occur immediately in Argentina or that past political action should
be abandoned. Socialists should not withdraw from parliament, he
concluded, but rather should seek to strike a more revolutionary stance
within Congress and within the political system.[44]

The final speech of the congress terminated soon after midnight of
the meeting's third day. Voting then began. According to *La Vanguardia*, the separation of the Argentine Socialist Party from the Second
International was approved by an overwhelming majority. The congress passed unanimously and with a standing ovation a sympathetic
salute to the Russian Revolution. The general international program
for the party, written by Justo and accepted by the parliamentary
group, was approved by 4,494 to 4,138. A proposal to help reconstruct
the Second International was defeated 4,520 to 4,242. Finally, the crucial issue—unconditional adherence to the Third International—was
defeated 5,013 to 3,656. Juan B. Justo concluded the congress with a
brief statement of hope that the final results would not produce any
separation within the party. When the assembled delegates finally de-
parted the hall it was five o'clock in the morning.[45]

Justo's hope soon proved in vain. Shortly after the Bahía Blanca
assembly, many of those who had supported the minority report left
the Socialist Party and joined the newly-formed Argentine Communist

Party, essentially a continuation of the Partido Socialista Internacional, which had accepted the twenty-one conditions, joined the Comintern, and changed its name to Partido Comunista in December 1920.

Enrique del Valle Iberlucea did not leave the Socialist Party, but his actions at the fourth extraordinary congress did cause him eventually to lose his Senate seat. A federal judge in Bahía Blanca initiated proceedings against del Valle Iberlucea and demanded that his senatorial privileges be revoked—meaning virtual impeachment—because of the senator's views as expressed in January. The Senate considered the matter in July 1921. Once again del Valle Iberlucea had to defend his right to sit in the upper house. In three sessions of debate he argued his case on the basis of constitutional guarantees of freedom of personal expression. He concluded with the observation that, "Come what may, the world will not collapse! The Socialist Party will continue advancing, overcoming all obstacles, destroying all barriers, conquering all public positions!" The majority, however, remained unconvinced and voted 17 to 5 to uphold the charges against the Socialist.[46] Del Valle Iberlucea, already in poor health, was in effect expelled from the Senate and died shortly thereafter in late 1921.

For the Socialists, the period 1916 through 1921 was difficult and trying. At home they had done battle with the Radical administration of Yrigoyen with at best inconclusive results. Legislative measures with Socialist signatures were less in evidence than in past years. In capital elections the party held its own but did not gain strength at previous rates. In the provinces the Socialists, with a few local exceptions, remained an inconsequential minority. Socialist relations with organized labor, experiencing severe ups and downs, had bottomed out by 1921. International issues of war and revolution had divided the party, exposing serious weaknesses and producing schisms that threatened to become endemic. As Argentine politics entered a new decade the Socialist Party strove to regain the impetus that had carried it through the difficult first years of the century and on to electoral successes after 1912.

9. Socialists and the Alvear Administration: 1922–1927

> Besides being a *simpático* man of the world, and a discreet and prudent politician, what has Doctor Alvear done to deserve the high honor with which he has been distinguished?
>
> *La Vanguardia* on the presidential candidacy of Marcelo T. de Alvear in 1922

In March 1922 the national convention of the Unión Cívica Radical met in Buenos Aires to choose its presidential ticket for the elections of April 2. Several luminaries of long standing in the Radical movement aspired to succeed Yrigoyen, who was constitutionally prohibited from running again. The incumbent, however, let it be known that he preferred a relatively lesser light in UCR ranks. On March 12 the convention acquiesced in their leader's choice and selected Marcelo T. de Alvear to head the presidential ballot. Soon thereafter, on March 19, the Radical convention of the capital named ten candidates to run for national deputies and one, Tomás Le Bretón, to compete for del Valle Iberlucea's vacant Senate seat.[1]

The Socialists had decided at their sixteenth ordinary congress (November 1921) to enter the presidential campaign and chose a ticket of Nicolás Repetto and Antonio de Tomaso. Socialist Party candidates for capital deputies were selected on February 12. Most of the names were familiar: Nicolás Repetto, Antonio de Tomaso, Angel M. Giménez, Adolfo Dickmann, Carlos Manacorda, Manuel T. López, Antonio Zaccagnini, Alfredo L. Spinetto, Jacinto Oddone, and Miguel Briuolo. Mario Bravo was chosen as the party's senatorial candidate. Doctors and lawyers dominated, but López (employee), Zaccagnini and Oddone

181

(journalists of working-class origins), and Briuolo (lithographer) provided some occupational diversity.[2]

The party entered the campaign with its usual gusto. Most efforts were directed against Hipólito Yrigoyen and the record of his administration. Little attention was paid to Alvear, an unknown quantity dismissed as the "official" candidate selected to perpetuate the policies of Yrigoyen.[3] And the party concentrated on discrediting those policies. Editorials in La Vanguardia accused Yrigoyen of misusing public funds, expanding the bureaucracy needlessly to repay or gain political favors, and contributing with tax, tariff, and monetary measures to an increased cost of living. Socialist cartoonists aided the attack, depicting the Radical president as either a brooding ogre or, more commonly, a hypocritical politiquero (political schemer) who claimed sympathy with working-class interests while in reality defending the positions of the privileged.[4]

Socialist criticisms, however, had little effect. As the polls closed on election day, April 2, the Radicals predicted a convincing victory. The prediction proved more than just bravado. In the presidential contest Alvear won 422,136 popular votes and 235 electoral votes, easily besting the conservative runner-up with 222,840 popular votes and 60 electoral votes. The Socialist ticket won 77,918 popular votes and 22 electoral votes for a distant third-place finish.[5] If seen as a plebiscite on the Radicals' first term, the results of the 1922 presidential race must be regarded as a solid popular vote of confidence in the policies of Hipólito Yrigoyen and a testament of faith in the man chosen to continue as his successor.

In the capital congressional elections, the Radicals maintained their margin of several thousand votes over the Socialists, their leading vote-getter polling 65,847 votes to the Socialist leader's 60,081. The candidates of the Concentración Nacional (National Concentration), a new conservative party, won some 22,000 votes; the PDP and the UCR Principista, a splinter of the UCR, averaged about 10,000 votes each; and the Communist Party received about 4,200 votes. Radical Tomás Le Bretón defeated Socialist Mario Bravo in the senatorial race by a vote of 67,105 to 62,366.[6] (See table 13.)

In addition to the capital, the Radicals also won the majority of deputy seats in nine provinces. When the chamber opened its ordinary sessions in May 1922, the UCR had a total of 91 deputies. The rest of the seats were divided among Conservatives (14), conservative factions and coalitions (11), Democratic Progressives (14), Radical factions (10), and Socialists (10).[7]

Congress met from May to October during Yrigoyen's "lame duck"

TABLE 13

DEPUTY ELECTIONS, FEDERAL CAPITAL, ABSOLUTE AND PROPORTIONATE VOTES BY CIRCUNSCRIPCIÓN, APRIL 2, 1922

Circunscripción	UCR	%	PS	%	PDP	%	CN	%	UCRP	%	Voted	Registered	Turnout %
1	3,613	(36.4)	3,248	(32.7)	345	(03.4)	1,158	(11.6)	495	(04.9)	9,912	13,083	75.8
2	2,529	(33.4)	2,880	(38.1)	272	(03.5)	961	(12.7)	409	(05.4)	7,557	10,447	72.3
3	4,533	(36.7)	4,614	(37.4)	523	(04.2)	1,155	(09.3)	790	(06.4)	12,322	16,775	73.5
4	4,158	(35.9)	5,057	(43.7)	442	(03.8)	737	(06.3)	521	(04.5)	11,563	16,420	70.4
5	4,144	(41.7)	2,587	(26.0)	437	(04.4)	1,390	(14.0)	897	(09.0)	9,918	13,103	75.7
6	3,656	(37.3)	3,428	(34.9)	405	(04.1)	1,280	(13.0)	586	(05.9)	9,800	12,587	77.9
7	2,732	(34.6)	2,872	(36.4)	471	(05.9)	803	(10.1)	554	(07.0)	7,889	10,523	75.0
8	3,161	(31.7)	3,708	(37.2)	436	(04.3)	1,473	(14.7)	766	(07.6)	9,963	13,185	75.6
9	2,890	(34.0)	2,943	(34.6)	524	(06.1)	956	(11.2)	738	(08.6)	8,483	11,566	73.3
10	1,941	(39.0)	1,706	(34.2)	279	(05.6)	501	(10.0)	428	(08.6)	4,976	6,618	75.2
11	1,738	(33.6)	1,673	(32.3)	373	(07.2)	780	(15.0)	480	(09.2)	5,168	7,154	72.2
12	4,204	(44.6)	2,753	(29.2)	437	(04.6)	1,021	(10.8)	629	(06.6)	9,421	12,667	74.4
13	3,430	(39.8)	2,462	(28.5)	524	(06.0)	1,233	(14.3)	731	(08.4)	8,610	12,250	68.8
14	2,684	(34.4)	2,281	(29.2)	598	(07.6)	1,343	(17.2)	665	(08.5)	7,794	11,538	67.5
15	3,362	(36.2)	3,030	(32.6)	613	(06.6)	870	(09.4)	523	(05.6)	9,267	12,420	74.6
16	3,527	(37.6)	2,734	(29.2)	633	(06.7)	1,258	(13.4)	475	(05.0)	9,357	12,622	74.1
17	3,167	(36.6)	2,575	(29.8)	645	(07.4)	979	(11.3)	553	(06.4)	8,637	11,923	72.4
18	4,492	(35.0)	4,102	(31.9)	1,075	(08.3)	1,367	(10.6)	802	(06.2)	12,829	17,305	74.1
19	3,913	(33.9)	3,720	(32.2)	1,014	(08.7)	1,599	(13.8)	869	(07.5)	11,533	15,595	74.0
20	2,157	(35.0)	1,708	(27.7)	519	(08.4)	1,193	(19.3)	443	(07.1)	6,159	8,517	72.3
Totals	66,031	(36.4)	60,081	(33.2)	10,565	(05.8)	22,057	(12.2)	12,354	(06.8)	181,158	250,864	72.2

a. Sources: Individual party results are from *La Prensa* (April 21, 1922), p. 10. Voters and registered were not available for the deputy contests. The figures above are for the presidential race, registration being the same for both elections and number of voters sufficiently close to establish proportions. Taken from Darío Cantón, *Materiales*, II, 65.

b. The main parties in competition were the Unión Cívica Radical (UCR), Partido Socialista (PS), Concentración Nacional (CN), Partido Demócrata Progresista (PDP), and the Unión Cívica Radical Principista (UCRP).

period in office. The election of Alvear and his impending inauguration did not deter the Socialists from their unrelenting attack on the incumbent chief executive. The tone was set during the second meeting of the new sessions, May 10, when party deputy Héctor González Iramain made a stinging criticism of the political practices of the Yrigoyen administration. González Iramain noted that, for the most part, elections and the counting of ballots were carried out honestly within the spirit of the 1912 reform. He questioned, however, Radical fairness and impartiality in the pre-election period. In preceding contests, and particularly in the one just completed, he charged undue executive pressure and the renewal of discredited practices common under the political regime of the nineteenth century. The Socialist listed police intimidation of the opposition, the use of government employees to get out the Radical vote, and an alleged connection between the administration and gambling interests to raise funds and to sway voters as abuses of the new spirit of political democracy for which the UCR assumed so much credit.[8] On July 19 the Socialist delegation followed up this speech with a legislative proposal that would add to the electoral reform law a provision for eight months in prison for those who distributed material favors such as clothes, food and drink, or money to influence voters.[9]

In mid-1922 Socialist deputies hit Yrigoyen on a number of other fronts. They called into question administration enforcement of Radical-approved legislation to regulate work in the home, criticized UCR pension projects as piecemeal and politically motivated, and introduced a series of old and new proposals based on their own electoral program.[10] The Socialists saved their major blow for the period terminating Yrigoyen's presidency and the transition to Alvear. Budgetary discussions provided the occasion, and the principal critic, in a retrospective summary of the past six years, was Juan B. Justo.

Beginning with the assertion that "it is necessary and urgent from all points of view to mark how vicious and corrupt the administration of Yrigoyen has been," Justo brought together a decade of Socialist criticism. The Radicals came to power, Justo stated, virtually unknown after a quarter of a century as a party. "The purposes of señor Yrigoyen before coming to government were perhaps stated confidentially to officials of the army with whom he conspired to realize his revolutions . . . but never were they made known to the general public." Once in office, Justo continued, Yrigoyen simply intensified the worst aspects of the old regime. There were no basic changes in budgetary and fiscal policy. Under Yrigoyen provincial autonomy almost disappeared, while those groups most closely associated with the oligarchy—

estancieros, the military, and the church—continued to receive official support and special favors. "Empleomanía," the excessive expansion of useless bureaucratic positions, "the old recourse of the oligarchy," was used to solidify and expand Radical political advantages. Political corruption and the gaining of personal fortunes through administrative power continued unabated and even intensified as the former "outs" enjoyed the spoils of being "in." Finally, the Radicals failed miserably in the social realm, Justo asserted, advocating and maintaining economic policies that increased costs of consumer goods and defending the interests of the bourgeoisie. While presenting some new social legislation, the administration failed to enforce existing regulations to protect the rights of the working man. In sum, the promised "national regeneration" had not occurred.[11]

Partisan sentiment obviously colored the Socialist view of Yrigoyen's first term. Socialists and Radicals had squared off in political competition for almost three decades. At times, Socialist opposition to the Radicals under Yrigoyen seemed almost a kind of impulsive negativism, based on personal dislike and narrow political concerns. Seen in perspective, however, without denying the partisan content, it is difficult to imagine how the result could have been any different. Socialists and Radicals viewed Argentine society in opposing terms. These distinctions had been drawn, reiterated, and re-emphasized from the 1890s. For the Socialists, the vague Radical position on major issues failed to inspire confidence. Even in areas of agreement, collaboration was almost impossible with UCR deputies under the personalistic control of a president who had little use for Congress.

A definite judgment on the accuracy of the Socialist critique of Yrigoyen's term must await further investigation of this important and complex period. But from the available evidence, Justo does not seem to have been too wide of the mark. In few concrete ways did the first UCR government move in dramatically different paths from preceding conservative regimes. Possible exceptions were a shifting and more favorable attitude toward labor and the beginnings of economic nationalism. Moreover, historians generally have viewed favorably Yrigoyen's respect for individual liberties and constitutional guarantees, continued adherence to the provisions of the Sáenz Peña reforms, and an accelerated expansion of public education. The overall political atmosphere was free; political parties continued to grow and to express themselves; and no restrictions were placed on the rights of the opposition.

But these statements require qualification. Administration sympathy for labor diminished greatly after the "semana trágica." Economic nationalism was not clearly articulated nor did Radical politicians clearly dissociate themselves or their interests from foreign investors. The general respect for citizens' rights must be tempered with the observation that the special restrictive legislation of the first decade of the century was maintained and sometimes employed. Also, no attempts were made to expand political participation to include foreigners and women, two large and disenfranchised groups. Little was done, moreover, to shake established institutions and ways of doing things. Yrigoyen and the Radicals did support the church and the military. The interests of the *estanciero* class were well represented and well protected under the new regime. Administrative deficiencies—personalized and centralized control, corruption, the use of public positions for personal and political favors—were glaring. In the final analysis, the basic foundations of Argentine society remained unchanged, and the severe social problems that had come to light at the turn of the century remained unattended and unresolved.

Marcelo T. de Alvear became President of the Argentine Republic on October 12, 1922. It seemed that the man and the moment had met. Reassuring to conservatives and acceptable to Radicals, Alvear roused few strong reactions. Known as a sportsman (he had co-founded the fencing room of the Jockey Club) and a smiling *bon vivant* who enjoyed attending cultural and social events, he promised a sharp contrast in personality from the dour and secretive Yrigoyen.[12] Moreover, although his first months in office coincided with a post-war recession, the bulk of his presidency was a time of general prosperity and growth. As Argentina's European markets recovered and reopened, the country saw an expansion of its export trade reminiscent of the pre-war years. A renewed flow of foreign capital, an ever-increasing percentage of which came from the United States, helped stimulate expansion in the industrial, commercial, transportation, and public service sectors. Immigration resumed, some 843,000 foreigners entering Argentina between 1922 and 1926. Internal growth was sufficient to maintain full employment during this period. Overall, the cost of living declined while real wages rose.[13]

Socialists and Radicals alike assumed that Alvear would follow in the path of his predecessor. Both were in for some surprises. On October 6, 1922, the soon-to-be-inaugurated president appointed a cabinet composed of men generally not closely affiliated with the UCR or with Yrigoyen.[14] His uninspiring and diffuse inaugural address implied disagreement with Yrigoyen's personalistic methods of government and a reassurance that the constitutional powers of the president would, in apparent contrast with the immediate past, be strictly observed by the new regime. There were no words of praise for and scarce mention of the preceding administration.[15]

Once in office, Alvear began to replace Yrigoyenists in public administration and the military with his own men. These moves signaled a declaration of independence from the control of the former president, a process that eventually evolved into an open split between the two men and the most important division in Radical ranks since the early 1890s.[16]

For the Socialists, the beginnings of the Radical division at first had little appreciable impact. In Congress, the party delegation pressed just as hard on the Alvear administration as it had on that of Yrigoyen. On December 20, 1922, for example, Juan B. Justo initiated a critical interpellation of Finance Minister Rafael Herrera Vegas, asking the minister what the government planned with regard to the export of gold and the reopening of the still-closed Caja de Conversión. Unsatisfied with the vague responses he received, Justo observed bitterly that "unfortunately we have been and we shall continue to be governed by members of the financial oligarchy, by men who take more into account the opinions of bankers than the opinions of the deputies of the people."[17] When budgetary discussions began in early 1923, Justo greeted the Alvear proposals with the same arguments he had been repeating in the chamber since 1912. In the final extraordinary sessions of the 1922–1923 period, the Socialists joined conservatives and Democratic Progressives to oppose, unsuccessfully, a Radical-inspired intervention in the province of Córdoba.[18]

Although the Socialists continued their traditional opposition to the party in power, there were increasing signs that they might profit from the split within the UCR. The most hopeful of these was the election on February 4, 1923, of Mario Bravo to a Senate seat from the federal capital. In the contest, Bravo defeated Alvearist candidate Arturo Goyeneche by a vote of 77,505 to 70,706. Bravo had run for the same office eleven months earlier and had lost to Radical Tomás Le Bretón, who soon thereafter resigned his seat to become Alvear's Minister of Agriculture, by a vote of 67,155 to 62,395.[19]

Throughout 1923 the split in the Unión Cívica Radical dominated Argentine politics. In the Chamber of Deputies, the large Radical majority indicated potential for the initiation and passage of significant legislation. Generally, however, this potential was wasted in intra-party feuding and the reluctance of Alvear to formulate, present, and push for new projects.

In the 1923 Congress the Socialist delegation played its usual role.

Under the leadership of Justo, the nine party deputies (with Bravo gone to the Senate) assailed the budget, called for official investigations of working conditions in the northeastern forests, opposed expenditures intended to modernize the navy, and introduced measures to amplify Sunday rest and work accident legislation. Proposals to increase tariffs on imported goods occupied many of these sessions. Despite violent Socialist objections, a bill to raise customs assessments by 60 percent and specific duties 25 percent became law in November.[20] Socialists could take some comfort, however, in final Senate passage of an anti-trust law that the party, in the person of Juan B. Justo, had helped create.[21]

In 1923 the Radical schism produced few discernible legislative benefits for the Socialists. In three roll call votes on three separate issues, the Radicals voted *en bloc* to stymie Socialist initiatives. On June 11, 1923, Adolfo Dickmann proposed to interpellate the ministers of Finance and Public Works about the recent contracting of a foreign loan. Sixty Radicals and two Democratic Progressives joined to override thirty-three Socialists, conservatives, and Democratic Progressives to block Dickmann's project.[22] Two months later, on August 23, forty-three Radicals, with the support of sixteen conservatives, defeated twenty-two opposition votes on a Socialist-inspired resolution to bring charges of misconduct against the same federal judge in Bahía Blanca who had initiated the impeachment proceedings against Enrique del Valle Iberlucea.[23] An October proposal from Juan B. Justo to have the executive explain the government's failure to collect license fees and taxes from certain commercial and industrial establishments in the federal capital was opposed by a solid front of fifty-nine Radical votes over thirty-two for the Socialist, Democratic Progressive, conservative coalition.[24] The Radical front might have been cracking in 1923, but the fissures were not yet deep enough, judging by these votes, to cause the kind of defection that could give the Socialists a balance of power in the Chamber of Deputies.

The March 23, 1924, congressional elections in the federal capital gave the Socialists an occasion to follow up their recent senatorial victory. In early February the Federación Socialista de la Capital (Socialist Federation of the Capital) called its affiliates to a general meeting. Juan B. Justo was chosen to run for a vacant Senate post. The thirteen deputy nominees were Enrique Dickmann, Augusto Bunge, Héctor González Iramain, Agustín S. Muzio, José D. Castellanos, Francisco Pérez Leirós, Raúl Carballo, Fernando de Andreis, José Luis Pena, Jacinto Oddone, Pedro Revol, Joaquín Coca, and Eugenio Albani. The list included two doctors, two lawyers, four journalists, two employees, one tanner, one customs dispatcher, and one engineer. All the candidates, with the exception of Carballo, who joined in 1916, had been members of the party for at least ten years.[25]

After the February meeting, the smoothly-operating Socialist campaign machine moved into high gear. Written propaganda concentrated on the perceived weaknesses of the Radical opposition. One article charged the UCR with ignoring the spirit as well as the letter of the Sáenz Peña electoral reform. "The Radical government," it stated, "practices electoral fraud where it can; venality is exercised against many citizens individually and against great electoral sectors collectively; and violence is the normal recourse that the Radical governors of the interior use to win elections."[26] Another article accused Alvear of continuing the bad habits of his predecessor, supporting oligarchical interests, and tying himself and his government to the purse-strings of foreign investors.[27]

The Radicals, meanwhile, were having their troubles. The division between Alvearists and Yrigoyenists slowed the selection of candidates. Finally, on March 11 the UCR of the capital voted a pro-Yrigoyen slate. Pablo Torello, Minister of Public Works in the first Radical administration, was chosen to run against Justo for the Senate.

Campaigning in the *circunscripciones*, the Radicals stressed familiar themes. They reminded the electorate of the party's national and patriotic character, its commitment to democracy, and its "social conquests" based on "sound principles." Radical speakers sought to remind voters in the capital's southern districts of "the benefits that workers had received from the fully just and humane government of the UCR under Yrigoyen."[28] Other speakers promised to continue the struggle against "exotic socialism" and the "regime."

Election day, like the campaign, passed peacefully. As the votes were counted it became clear that the Socialists were on their way to a major triumph. In the first nine districts, Socialist deputy candidates defeated the UCR in eight. The margin there gained, added to victories in sections eleven and fifteen through nineteen, was sufficient to give the Socialists thirteen new deputy seats. The party's leading vote-getter, Héctor González Iramain, polled 77,373 tallies. The UCR won six seats, led by Guillermo Sullivan's 71,074 votes. (See table 14.) In the senatorial race, Juan B. Justo defeated Pablo Torello by a vote of 80,543 to 70,610.[29]

La Vanguardia attributed the victory to strength in working-class areas and the support of many independent voters.[30] Mario Rivarola, writing in the *Revista Argentina de Ciencias Políticas*, agreed in part

TABLE 14

DEPUTY ELECTIONS, FEDERAL CAPITAL, ABSOLUTE AND PROPORTIONATE VOTES BY CIRCUNSCRIPCIÓN, MARCH 23, 1924

Circun-scripción	UCR	%	PS	%	PDP	%	Voted	Registered	Turnout %
1	4,282	(43.4)	4,621	(46.8)	234	(02.3)	9,862	16,363	60.3
2	2,974	(39.0)	3,858	(50.6)	174	(02.2)	7,617	12,145	62.7
3	4,751	(42.0)	5,438	(48.1)	341	(03.0)	11,287	18,741	60.2
4	4,149	(37.9)	5,905	(53.9)	250	(02.0)	10,942	18,280	59.9
5	4,232	(46.6)	3,706	(40.8)	404	(04.4)	9,071	15,163	59.8
6	4,093	(43.8)	4,292	(46.0)	346	(03.7)	9,327	14,286	65.3
7	2,811	(39.2)	3,438	(48.0)	447	(06.2)	7,156	11,726	61.0
8	3,239	(35.9)	4,792	(53.2)	330	(03.6)	9,006	14,500	62.1
9	3,209	(41.0)	3,582	(45.7)	498	(06.3)	7,823	12,626	62.0
10	2,020	(43.7)	2,015	(43.6)	252	(05.4)	4,617	7,320	63.1
11	2,011	(42.4)	2,015	(42.5)	385	(08.1)	4,741	8,027	59.1
12	4,599	(50.0)	3,658	(39.7)	390	(04.2)	9,195	14,545	63.3
13	3,750	(46.4)	3,317	(41.0)	457	(05.6)	8,074	14,254	56.6
14	3,278	(44.9)	2,926	(40.1)	602	(08.2)	7,285	13,366	54.5
15	3,933	(42.2)	4,152	(44.6)	659	(07.0)	9,304	15,510	60.0
16	3,689	(42.0)	3,815	(43.4)	611	(06.9)	8,783	14,634	60.0
17	3,161	(39.9)	3,474	(43.9)	658	(08.3)	7,909	13,537	58.4
18	4,607	(38.6)	5,212	(43.7)	1,515	(12.7)	11,926	19,512	61.1
19	4,057	(38.7)	4,741	(45.2)	1,076	(10.2)	10,482	17,351	60.4
20	2,545	(43.7)	2,411	(41.4)	498	(08.5)	5,811	10,300	56.4
Totals	71,390	(41.9)	77,368	(45.5)	10,127	(05.9)	170,218	282,176	60.3

a. Sources: Individual party results are from *La Prensa* (April 5, 1924), p. 12. "Voted" and "Registered" are from República Argentina, *Memoria, 1923–1924*, p. 287.
b. Parties listed are Unión Cívica Radical (UCR), Partido Socialista (PS), and Partido Demócrata Progresista (PDP).

with the Socialist analysis. He noted that many voters had become disillusioned with the vague and non-programmatic Radicals. But he placed greater stress on the divisions within Radicalism as the main key to the Socialists' win. The Alvear government had withheld administrative support for the Yrigoyenist slate, removing an important ingredient of previous UCR election victories. Moreover, some Radicals, he observed, had voted for the Socialist ticket in protest against the management of their own party.[31]

When congressional sessions began in May 1924, the Socialist Party made an overt move to take further advantage of the Radical schism. The first order of business was to elect presiding officers for the term. It had been Socialist practice to vote for the candidate of the majority bloc for president, for the second-ranking bloc for first vice-president, and the third-ranking bloc for second vice-president. In 1924, however, they abandoned these criteria and supported the Alvearist candidate, Mario M. Guido. Guido's faction probably ranked no better than third in the Chamber, while the Yrigoyenists were the majority. The Socialist votes, plus those of conservatives, Democratic Progressives, and Alvearists, placed Guido in the president's chair. Forty-four Radical deputies temporarily left the Chamber in protest. They called the election the work of an anti-Yrigoyen coalition that they labeled the "contubernio" (collusion) and that included the Socialists.[32]

The next order of business again found the Socialists involved in the Radical dispute. During the first sessions, capital and most provincial deputy elections and diplomas for 1924 were approved *pro forma*. The elections in Córdoba, however, proved a special case. In that province conservative Governor Julio A. Roca held sway in the early 1920s. In 1923 the Radical deputies had voted *en bloc* to intervene in Córdoba for the purpose of overturning Roca's control. Alvearist senators and conservatives, however, refused to approve the intervention, and the president hesitated to take unilateral action. The Radicals, who had carried the deputy contests in Córdoba in 1922 by a vote of 47,953 to 31,393 over the Democratic Progressives, abstained in 1924 to protest federal inaction on the intervention. As a result, in 1924 the PDP captured six majority seats in Córdoba, with their leading candidate garnering 27,634 votes. The three minority seats went to Socialists Ricardo Belisle (1,809), Edmundo S. Tolosa (1,809), and Juan F. Remedi (1,775). Combined votes represented only 36,507 of 190,617 voters registered in the province.[33]

Debate on the seating of the three Córdoba Socialists lasted from early June to mid-August. Radicals argued against ratifying the diplomas in light of the small number of votes cast. The Socialists, pleased with a major gain in the interior, defended the right of their men to take seats in the Chamber. Radical abstention and intransigence, they pointed out, was hardly their fault. The party had entered an honest, regular, constitutionally-correct election and the results had to be honored.

The final vote came on August 14. After two ties at sixty-two votes apiece, President Guido broke the deadlock in favor of the three Socialists. The opposition had been uniformly Radical. Those in favor of approval had been a mixed group of conservatives, Democratic Progressives, Socialists, and eighteen Radicals.[34] Eight of the Radicals who had voted with the "contubernio" had previously voted in 1923 in favor of intervention in Córdoba.

Guido's decisive vote and the Radical defection was the final tear in the fabric of UCR unity. In August, in the federal capital, the Unión Cívica Radical split formally into two opposing groups. The supporters of Alvear, or perhaps more accurately the opponents of Yrigoyen, formed the Unión Cívica Radical Antipersonalista (The Antipersonalist Radical Civic Union). The "Antipersonalist" rubric referred to disagreement with Yrigoyen's personalistic control of government and the Radical Party. Those who continued to support the former president were called "Personalist" Radicals and retained the UCR title. In ensuing months Radical Party members throughout the republic aligned with these competing factions. What had been a behind-the-scenes disagreement was finally out in full public view. As Félix Luna put it, "For the first time since its foundation, Radicalism suffered a great, profound, and irreducible schism."[35]

The seating of the Córdoba deputies, their first from the interior, gave the Socialists their largest representation in the chamber to date. With eighteen deputies, the party ranked second overall.[36] The Radicals, with seventy-two seats, plus thirteen representatives from splinter groups, were still the first-ranking party. The conservatives and Democratic Progressives, with fourteen deputies each, and twenty-two representatives of conservative local parties rounded out the chamber.

The Radicals, then, had lost their clear-cut majority. Against a united opposition they had to have the backing of splinter groups to carry their initiatives. Moreover, they needed opposition help to achieve the two-thirds majority necessary to override decisions of the still-conservative Senate. In the fluid and volatile political situation of 1924 and 1925 these alliances were difficult to realize.

In the Chamber of Deputies the Socialists, voting as a unified bloc, were in an advantageous position to affect the course of legislation. In

1924 and 1925 they held the long-desired balance of power. Their effective use of this power, however, was hampered by growing fundamental differences among their own forces. These differences, as with the Radicals, were of long standing and began to come to the surface more frequently as the party became more successful at the polls and more influential at the national level.

The main issue producing strains within the party at this time involved individual behavior versus the demands of party discipline. The specific case concerned Antonio de Tomaso and was brought to the view of Socialist affiliates at the seventeenth party congress, held in Mar del Plata, October 12–14, 1923. There, de Tomaso was charged with having represented legally the manager of the Colón Opera during a labor dispute with the theater's employees. De Tomaso admitted the charge and defended his right and duty as a lawyer to accept any client who requested his services. The executive committee decided not to impose sanctions in this instance, and the congress agreed by a vote of 3,211 to 1,920, with 55 abstentions.[37]

Juan B. Justo had attempted unsuccessfully in 1921 to define clearly the relationship between professional practice and the responsibilities of party membership. In 1923, as an apparent aftermath of the de Tomaso case, he again proposed such a definition, which this time was approved by a general vote. The ensuing resolutions forbade Socialist office-holders "to have professional or pecuniary relations with concerns or managers who have or manage contracts, concessions, or franchises of the state or municipalities." Also, Socialist affiliates who "might be solicited to undertake the defense or professional representation of indicted public officials, accused or denounced, only can do so when they have obtained authorization from the national executive committee."[38]

While these measures were being prepared and voted upon, Nicolás Repetto resigned from the Chamber of Deputies. One of Justo's closest allies, Repetto shared the party founder's concern with the decline in standards of Socialist behavior as symbolized in the de Tomaso affair. Accordingly, he sacrificed his congressional position to concentrate on internal party matters. To this end he began, with like-minded Socialists, a journal entitled *Acción Socialista* (Socialist Action), intended, in his words, "to provoke a movement of clarification and straightening within our own ranks."[39]

On the other side, those affiliates against whom *Acción Socialista* and the disciplinarians leveled their criticisms counterattacked with arguments of their own. Their main complaint was that new disciplinary regulations were excessively restrictive of individual freedom. Federico

Pinedo, for example, stated that the disciplinarians hoped to make of the party a "capilla," or monastery, of obedient and loyal adherents. Politically, he observed, this orientation would doom the party to a minor role in national politics since "not all men have been born to be monks."[40]

Following the resolutions of the 1923 party congress, Pinedo joined fellow lawyers Mario Bravo, Antonio de Tomaso, and Héctor González Iramain to protest the restrictions placed on professional activity. Mario Bravo even offered to resign from the party and his recently-won Senate seat. In putting forth his resignation, Bravo noted his objection to submitting to "arbitrary impositions" and his "firm purpose of safeguarding [his] personal independence."[41] The executive committee refused to accept the resignation, claiming that Bravo's reaction was "disproportionate to the facts that motivated it." Bravo, a party leader from the early years of the century, acquiesced in the decision and resumed his party and senatorial duties.[42]

Bravo's return to the fold did not signal a general healing process. De Tomaso's defense of the manager of the Colón, Repetto's resignation and founding of *Acción Socialista*, and Bravo's threatened abandonment of the party were all manifestations of a deep and growing division. As the gulf widened, two men emerged as spokesmen and leaders of the opposing factions: Nicolás Repetto and Antonio de Tomaso. Their actions and reactions, and those of the men aligned with them, Repettists and Tomasists, ultimately produced a serious and significant schism.

The congressional sessions of 1924 and 1925 were confusing, chaotic, and, from the standpoint of legislative accomplishment, unproductive. Politics dominated. A complex competition for power and jockeying for position took place within and between all parties. Among Radicals, Antipersonalists struggled for the advantage over Personalists. Although the Socialist split did not yet reveal itself openly, subtle shifts in attitudes and positions forecast future realignments. All political eyes focused on the congressional elections of 1926 and the all-important presidential contest two years later.

With its expanded representation, the Socialist delegation in 1924 dealt with a broad array of issues. Generally, party actions followed the pattern of previous years. Each deputy made a contribution, usually handling a matter of specific individual interest. Ordinarily, those with more experience were at the forefront of initiatives and interpellations, while the newer congressmen gradually became accustomed to their surroundings. With Justo gone to the Senate and Repetto retired, the parliamentary group seemed to lack the unified leadership of the past. The Dickmann brothers, Adolfo and Enrique, led many debates, while de Tomaso and Augusto Bunge assumed leadership of the opposing faction. On most matters at this time, however, the Socialists worked more or less in harmony.

Socialist initiatives were predictable and familiar. On June 25, 1924, de Tomaso spoke for a divorce law and Bunge for a basic social security measure. Party deputies pushed for the entrance of certain Brazilian agricultural products duty free and on September 3 Muzio introduced proposals intended to improve the living and working conditions of persons employed in coastal shipping. Socialist interpellations of ministers centered on monetary policy, particularly the continued closure of the Caja de Conversión, and the treatment of workers in the far-flung territories of Tierra del Fuego in the south and El Chaco in the north. As in the past, Socialist initiatives remained in committee and interpellations produced no more than a public airing of some issues.

One of the major matters discussed in these sessions was of special interest for the Socialists. In November 1923 Congress had approved social security legislation, introduced earlier by the Yrigoyen administration. The first article of law 11,289 had provided for the establishment of social security funds for workers and employees in the merchant marine, industry, commerce, journalism, and the graphic arts. In September 1924 certain Radical-formulated modifications, at this time with both Alvearist and Yrigoyenist backing, were introduced for consideration. The Socialists opposed both these changes and the law itself. Augusto Bunge, who led the attack, argued, as he had in the past, that social security legislation should cover all workers. Piecemeal plans for specific groups, he contended, divided the labor movement and set groups of workers one against the other.[43] Joaquín Coca went so far as to call the law an employers' plot to split labor and judged its actual results as a total failure.[44]

In the voting, fifty-seven Radicals voted in favor of the modifications. All eighteen Socialists voted against, in alliance with conservatives, Democratic Progressives, and a handful of Radicals. Their total, however, reached only fifty-two and the modifications were approved.[45]

The chamber sessions of 1925 produced further frustrations for the Socialists. Caught in the fluctuating political situation of the period, they could neither ally with their traditional foes, the Yrigoyenists, nor support the conservative Alvear government. Socialist attempts to interpellate government ministers on the fulfillment of social legislation were rejected, criticisms of budgetary policy ignored, and legislative initiatives sent to stagnate in committee.

Symbolic of these sessions for the party was Alvear's veto of a Socialist measure to close all commercial establishments in the federal capital at eight o'clock in the evening. Another example was an attempt by Adolfo Dickmann to reform the process of voter registration. In the opening session of the year, Dickmann described the many faults of the existing system: the incompleteness of registration, low voter turnout, even with obligatory voting, and inadequate federal regulation of the entire process. To correct these faults he formulated a series of reforms, which were discussed at length but not acted upon.[46]

On one issue, however, the Socialists did achieve a measure of success. During the first session of the year, Jacinto Oddone suggested that a special congressional commission investigate charges that Radical deputies Luis Olmedo and José A. Núñez, both of Mendoza, had illegally obtained money from the Bank of Mendoza Province. The five-man committee reported to the chamber in September. Their conclusions were that the charges of malfeasance were true, that the two deputies should be expelled from Congress, and that the details of the investigation should be sent to the proper legal authorities in Mendoza. On September 23, in a rare show of unanimity, seventy-eight deputies, including all eighteen Socialists, voted to approve the majority report. Only two UCR deputies voted in the negative.[47]

Congressional actions occurred against the background of the growing split between Repettists and Tomasists. By 1925 the Tomasists controlled or were in the process of controlling most of the major directive organs of the party, including the executive committee and the editorial board of *La Vanguardia*. At the eighteenth party congress, held in Buenos Aires between October 11 and 13, 1925, the Repettists sought to regain control. They bombarded the assembly with critical charges of "improper" Socialist behavior on the part of the Tomasists. These ranged from criticisms of the actions of the executive committee to exposure and expulsion of a Tomasist who had used the party for personal gain to a motion of censure against de Tomaso himself for attending a luncheon aboard a battleship of the Argentine navy. Despite these attacks and charges, the Tomasists emerged from the congress relatively unscathed.[48] A few months later, however, a statutory reform approved by a general vote of the party undercut the centralized mechanisms by which the Tomasists had taken power and promised a return to dominance for the Repettists.[49]

The transfer of power back to the Repettists came slowly. In the meantime differences remained and festered. And nowhere were these differences more apparent than in preparations for the capital deputy elections of March 7, 1926. On the surface, the Socialists appeared to gird to face the Radicals. Editorials in *La Vanguardia* castigated the Alvear administration as a perpetuation of the worst features of *yrigoyenismo*.[50] But under the surface of anti-Radical unity, the Socialists battled bitterly against one another. The first major encounter was the selection of deputy candidates. Tomasists and Repettists tried to control the list. The final decision, which took place at the end of January, was a standoff. The ten candidates were evenly divided between the two factions, the Repetto group nominating its principal spokesman, Nicolás Repetto, along with Adolfo Dickmann, Rómulo Bogliolo, Alberto Iribarne, and Esteban Jiménez. Antonio de Tomaso was also chosen, along with four of his followers—Alfredo L. Spinetto, José Rouca Oliva, Germinal Rodríguez, and Felipe Di Tella. The program for these candidates was basically similar to those of 1922 and 1924, with the only major difference being article one, which demanded the abrogation of law 11,289 and the establishment of a national social security plan to cover illness, invalidism, old age, and maternity benefits.[51]

Soon after this meeting, Repetto charged that the de Tomaso faction had falsified votes from sympathetic centers to assure places on the list. This accusation prompted a violent polemic between the two men, played out in public view in letters to *La Vanguardia*. In the emotional heat of the debate, Repetto brought to light de Tomaso's legal defense in 1917 of a notorious murderer who had killed his wife and then destroyed the cadaver by fire. De Tomaso replied with the assertion that Repetto had supplied medical evidence for the defense. Repetto denied the charge and called for an impartial investigation to support his innocence.[52]

Like many such controversies in Socialist Party history, no firm resolution occurred. But the barrage of charge and countercharge further divided the party and seriously weakened its electoral effort. These exchanges, consuming numerous pages of Socialist print and an inordinate amount of time and energy, diverted attention from the campaign at hand and gave ready ammunition to the Radical opposition. Nor did the dispute abate as election day approached. Two days before the balloting, the Repetto deputies protested the naming of certain *fiscales* (election observers), arguing that they were Tomasist sympathizers who would try to influence the count in favor of their five choices.[53]

While the Socialists squabbled, the Personalist Radicals faced the election with certain advantages. In contrast with 1924, the internal division in the UCR was no longer a bothersome sore but a clean break. The Personalists, unencumbered with obstructions in their own group, began to campaign in early January with enthusiasm, dedication, and unity. Although candidates were not selected until February 18, they were chosen quickly and smoothly in what those in charge described as a harmonious, open, and widely representative meeting.[54] After the convention, UCR spokesmen stressed the twin and interrelated goals of party unity and discipline. They contrasted the alleged achievements of the Yrigoyen administration with the "do-nothing" Alvear regime. They lumped Socialists with the Antipersonalists as members of the "contubernio," obstructing the initiatives of the Yrigoyenists, particularly in areas of social and economic reform.

The personal appearance of Hipólito Yrigoyen at several rallies underscored the Radical commitment to victory in 1926. Although there is no evidence that the former president actually spoke to the assembled faithful, his appearance on a balcony or public podium seemed to stimulate party spirits as well as announce his return to the public arena.

The election took place as scheduled on March 7. Because of challenges, some irregularities, and a slow count, the final results were not published until the end of the month. However, from the scrutiny of the first five *circunscripciones*, it was apparent that the Personalist Radicals had notched a major victory. In addition to the usual win in section five, the Radicals also carried one, two, and three, the Socialists retaining only the faithful fourth. Thereafter the UCR went on to sweep the remaining districts of the capital, improving its overall showing from 1924 by some 8,000 votes. The Socialists, on the other hand, lost strength across the board, declining by some 14,000 tallies from their previous performance. Many of their losses seemed to go to the Antipersonalists, whose 37,487 votes probably came from conservative and independent voters who had supported the Socialists in 1924. The Communists continued to average a little over 4,000 votes.[55] (See table 15.)

In terms of strength in Congress, the elections of 1926 were not as disastrous for the Socialists nor as encouraging for the Radicals as the capital results implied. As a single bloc, the Socialists still retained second place, actually increasing their representation from eighteen to nineteen. The Personalists, in addition to their impressive showing in the capital, captured majorities in the provinces of Buenos Aires, Catamarca, and La Rioja, for a total of sixty seats. Although still the

TABLE 15

DEPUTY ELECTIONS, FEDERAL CAPITAL, ABSOLUTE AND PROPORTIONATE VOTES BY CIRCUNSCRIPCIÓN, MARCH 7, 1926

Circunscripción	UCRP	%	UCRA	%	PS	%	Voted	Registered	Turnout %
1	5,653	(43.4)	1,858	(14.2)	4,428	(34.0)	13,007	19,459	67.8
2	3,627	(40.0)	1,306	(14.4)	3,394	(37.4)	9,057	13,615	66.5
3	5,222	(41.7)	1,585	(12.6)	4,562	(36.4)	12,512	19,475	63.7
4	4,017	(32.5)	2,957	(23.9)	4,549	(36.8)	12,359	19,499	63.2
5	4,870	(43.1)	2,733	(24.1)	2,927	(25.9)	11,296	16,859	65.4
6	4,549	(42.1)	1,854	(17.1)	3,664	(33.9)	10,798	15,649	68.1
7	3,099	(38.6)	1,275	(15.8)	2,927	(36.4)	8,020	12,398	64.5
8	3,858	(39.0)	1,594	(16.1)	3,677	(37.1)	9,889	15,117	65.1
9	3,420	(39.0)	1,761	(20.1)	2,943	(33.6)	8,757	13,657	60.1
10	1,978	(38.6)	1,310	(25.5)	1,498	(29.2)	5,119	7,925	64.2
11	2,113	(39.3)	1,410	(26.2)	1,514	(28.1)	5,372	8,825	60.1
12	4,461	(45.2)	1,915	(19.4)	2,821	(28.5)	9,869	15,088	65.4
13	3,667	(43.0)	1,793	(21.0)	2,491	(29.2)	8,529	14,837	56.7
14	3,250	(41.1)	1,995	(25.2)	2,178	(27.5)	7,904	14,258	55.4
15	5,179	(42.9)	1,424	(11.8)	4,278	(35.5)	12,047	18,624	64.6
16	4,139	(39.1)	2,414	(22.8)	3,177	(30.0)	10,585	16,533	64.0
17	3,952	(42.5)	1,501	(16.1)	2,954	(31.8)	9,287	14,720	63.1
18	5,615	(41.4)	2,398	(17.6)	4,489	(33.1)	13,557	20,833	65.1
19	4,381	(38.5)	2,709	(23.8)	3,415	(30.0)	11,371	18,089	63.0
20	2,421	(38.5)	1,695	(26.9)	1,715	(27.2)	6,284	10,825	58.0
Totals	79,471	(40.6)	37,487	(19.2)	63,601	(32.5)	195,619	306,285	63.8

a. Source: República Argentina, *Memoria, 1925–1926*, p. 181.
b. The main parties in competition were the Unión Cívica Radical Personalista (UCRP), the Unión Cívica Radical Antipersonalista (UCRA), and the Partido Socialista (PS).

largest party, the Personalists declined by twelve seats from 1924. The major gains in 1926 went to the Antipersonalists, who, under a variety of titles, swept contests in six provinces, producing a total of thirty-three deputies. The conservatives retained fifteen seats, local conservative parties twenty-one, and the Democratic Progressives nine.[56]

These elections also returned Nicolás Repetto and Antonio de Tomaso to the chamber. In the first months of the new sessions, their differences remained hidden. The one major exception, according to Repettist Joaquín Coca, was an attempt by de Tomaso to block the acceptance of diplomas for UCR deputies from Buenos Aires province. Coca analyzed this maneuver as an effort by de Tomaso to ally with the "contubernio."[57]

Discussions over the seating of the Buenos Aires deputies took up the first two months of these sessions. Ultimately, the Socialist parliamentary group voted in favor of admitting the Yrigoyenist congressmen. Enrique Dickmann, speaking for the party bloc, deplored the delay in consideration of more serious business while this debate proceeded, and averred that although such arguments provided ripe opportunities for political maneuvering, "the nineteen Socialist deputies are not going to enter into any illicit combination; we are not going to lend ourselves to any parliamentary maneuver; we are going to proceed scientifically and conscientiously, consulting always the collective good."[58]

The rest of the 1926 sessions went rather well for the Socialists. The party division remained quiescent and the nineteen deputies continued to vote in a unified manner. Party representatives attended almost all sessions with customary punctuality and regularity, in sharp contrast with Radical and conservative deputies, who had high rates of absenteeism. Although only one-sixth of the chamber, the Socialists expanded their numerical influence with many initiatives and interpellations. For example, Enrique Dickmann proposed a minimum wage law for employees of state owned and managed public utilities and transportation services (July 2), Nicolás Repetto suggested the creation of special national credit facilities for small farmers (July 14), and Enrique Dickmann and Antonio de Tomaso jointly sponsored legislation to protect working women before and after childbirth (July 21).

Socialist interpellations of Alvear's ministers in 1926 belied the "contubernio" thesis. On July 21 Jacinto Oddone began several days of grilling the Minister of Education on the inadequacies of primary and secondary schools in the republic, a questioning that other party deputies, representing both factions, joined. De Tomaso, also in July, interpellated the Minister of the Navy on the acquisition of new ships.

Repetto, not to be outdone, in August called the Minister of War to account for alleged abuses in implementing military justice, finally calling for the impeachment of the minister. At the same time, other Socialists interrogated Minister of the Interior José P. Tamborini as to repeated violations of and non-compliance with established social legislation.

These interpellations, plus the usual criticism of the budget at the end of the year, seemed to indicate no change in the Socialists' criticism of the ruling party. On the face of it, there was little evidence that the Socialists were engaged in any tacit agreement with the Antipersonalists to strengthen their hand vis-à-vis the Yrigoyenists. It should also be mentioned, however, that the major thrust for most criticism of the Alvear administration seemed to come more from the Repetto faction than from those who followed de Tomaso.

Unlike previous congressional years during Alvear's presidency, the 1926 sessions produced some important legislation. Several of these measures were Socialist-inspired. They included prohibition of night work in bakeries, the long-sought granting of civil (not political) rights to women, provisions for loans to cooperatives, and suspension of law 11,289. Also, Congress passed two measures, first suggested by Adolfo Dickmann, to stiffen the provisions of the Sáenz Peña law. One, law 11,386, set up a new and more comprehensive system for registering voters. The other, law 11,387, provided for stricter regulation of the electoral rolls and the election process.

Along with these accomplishments came some frustrations. The chamber overcame Socialist objections and voted funds for a new Argentine Embassy in Italy. The lower house also refused to override the president's veto of a Socialist proposal to close commercial establishments in the capital at 8:00 p.m. The proponents of the law, including all nineteen Socialists, failed by two votes to reach the necessary two-thirds to overcome the veto.[59]

The internal disputes of the 1920s did not prevent the Socialist Party from increasing its membership. After a slight decline following the 1921 schism, the party grew from 184 groups in that year to 262 in 1925, and from 8,339 adherents to 10,914 for the same period. Patterns of party growth were the same as in previous years. The capital showed a steady rise in adhered groups and affiliates. Buenos Aires, province and city, the two major centers of Socialist strength, counted about half of the total party groups and almost two-thirds of all party members. In the interior, Mendoza showed significant increases, more than doubling its numbers between 1923 and 1925. The party also enjoyed continued if somewhat erratic strength in Córdoba, Santa Fe, and Tucumán.[60]

Socialist groups outside the capital continued to run candidates for national office. They registered some gains in the provinces of Buenos Aires and Mendoza, but still lagged far behind Radicals and conservatives.[61] The Socialists did manage to elect three deputies from Córdoba in 1924. Although Socialist spokesmen tried to depict the election as a sign of growing vitality in the provinces, a more realistic assessment led inevitably to the conclusion that the victory was a fluke, related more to Radical abstention than to Socialist expansion.[62]

Most Socialist power in the provinces still centered in urban areas, particularly the coastal and suburban cities of Buenos Aires province. The most notable Socialist gains were in Mar del Plata. From 1922 to 1926 the party won every municipal election in that city to retain control of the government there.

Socialist expansion in the 1920s was probably best represented with the inauguration of new national headquarters in January 1926. The three-story Casa del Pueblo (House of the People), located in central Buenos Aires only a few blocks from the national Congress, served as the focal point for all party activity in Argentina until its destruction in 1953 by a Peronist mob. Housing an extensive library, party offices and files, and, after 1927, the presses of *La Vanguardia*, the new building was the most spacious, well-equipped, and permanent seat the party had known since its founding.

With regard to labor, there were few of the violent confrontations during the Alvear administration that had scarred previous presidents. Except for two brief general strikes in 1923 and 1924, labor militancy clearly declined in the 1920s. Prosperity undoubtedly contributed to labor's lethargy. Prices stayed stable while wages registered slight increases. Furthermore, partisan divisions added to the decreased effectiveness of central labor confederations. The anarchist Federación Obrera Regional Argentina passed through a period that its principal historian called "the least interesting and also in part the most negative" of its history.[63] Because of doctrinal disputes between anarchists, communists, and "fusionists," the number of unions adhering to the FORA dropped from around 400 in 1920 to 111 in 1927.[64] The Unión Sindical Argentina, direct descendant of the successful syndicalist FORA IX, suffered many of the same difficulties and experienced the same decline as its anarchist competitor. From an estimated membership of 397 unions in 1920, the USA fell to 161 unions by 1925.[65]

Relations between the Socialist Party and the central labor organizations were not good in the early 1920s. Contact was maintained with the USA through the active participation in positions of leadership by Socialists Agustín S. Muzio of the Tanners' Union and Francisco Pérez Leirós of the Municipal Workers' Union. In 1924, however, the USA expelled both these men after their election to the Chamber of Deputies.

Following their expulsion, Muzio and Pérez Leirós helped form a new central organization, composed of unions with a generally Socialist orientation. The new entity, the Confederación Obrera Argentina (COA) (Argentine Workers' Confederation), emerged from a February 1926 meeting at the Buenos Aires headquarters of the railroad workers' union, La Fraternidad. Pérez Leirós was named pro-secretary (second-in-command) and Muzio served as one of the members of the directive committee. The municipal workers, the tanners, cutters, tailors, and costumers of Buenos Aires, as well as La Fraternidad, were well-represented among the leadership. But the core of the new group was the Unión Ferroviaria (Railroaders' Union), formed in 1922 to represent those rail workers not in La Fraternidad. In the 1920s the Unión Ferroviaria was Argentina's single most important union. José Negri of the UF was chosen secretary general of the new Confederación and the railroad union supplied about two-thirds of the COA's total membership.[66]

From its founding, the Confederación professed its apolitical nature. The first editorial of its newspaper, *La Confederación*, stated that the new organization "has no determined political, patriotic, or philosophic character. . . . The COA is free from all bonds with political or ideological groupings, even when these groupings might pursue identical ends by different means."[67] In addition, the *carta orgánica* urged the working class "to organize in the union area to achieve better conditions of work and remuneration."[68] But other statutes allowed flexibility of tactics. Unlike the FORA and USA, the COA admitted the usefulness of working for social and economic legislation through the parliamentary process. Strikes, both general and partial, were not forbidden or discouraged, but strict statutory regulation sought to assure unanimity and careful organization before a walkout was called.[69]

The Socialist Party enthusiastically supported the founding of the Confederación Obrera Argentina. Although the COA formally stated its apoliticism, its sympathies clearly lay with the party. Any direct connections or open electoral support would have been politically unwise. But the presence of Muzio and Pérez Leirós in the leadership, as well as the new confederation's general reformist orientation, attested to a commonality of interest.

From 1926 to 1930 the COA was Argentina's largest and most influential labor organization. For the first time since the turn of the century, the Socialist star outshone that of the anarchists and syndicalists. But this achievement was soon diminished by the continued internal division within the party. Indeed, the two Socialists serving as leaders of the COA were on opposite sides of the party fence, Pérez Leirós a Repettist and Muzio a Tomasist. In 1927 this division openly split the party at a time when it appeared to have won the firm foothold among the organized working class that Socialists had pursued for more than thirty years.

10. Schism: 1927–1930

> We are a civil army and we face the enemy in perma-
> nent political warfare. An army shoots a soldier who
> deserts in the face of the enemy; we expel him. We
> are in constant civil war over ideas, sentiments, pur-
> poses, led by the democratic procedures of liberty
> and equality. Some tire of the struggle: let them sur-
> render their posts to others; some are ambitious for
> other things: let them go elsewhere.
>
> > Enrique Dickmann, discussing the
> > recent Socialist schism in the
> > Chamber of Deputies, July 27, 1927

The division that had festered within the Argentine Socialist Party
since 1923 ultimately produced a final and irrevocable schism in 1927.
The process of this Socialist split, the fourth serious party fragmentation in thirteen years, was complicated and confusing, occurring within
the context of jockeying for political position and power both within
the party itself and on the national level.

Personalists versus Antipersonalists and their struggle to capture the
presidency in 1928 provided the larger framework. Meeting in the city
of Buenos Aires in late April, 1927, eleven months before the presidential contest, the Antipersonalists selected their ticket of Leopoldo
Melo for president and Vicente C. Gallo for vice-president, choices that
enjoyed the sanction of Marcelo T. de Alvear and that attracted tacit
conservative support. The Personalists had not yet chosen their candidate, but it was widely assumed that Hipólito Yrigoyen would be the
UCR standard-bearer. The Socialists would later enter their own ticket
of Mario Bravo and Nicolás Repetto.

Buenos Aires province was the key to the 1928 election. From 1918 through 1927 the province had been in Yrigoyenist hands, sending UCR majorities to the Chamber of Deputies and electing UCR provincial governors and legislatures. In 1925 Antipersonalist senators had proposed a federal intervention in the province, intended to swing Buenos Aires into the Alvearist camp through the appointment of an Antipersonalist interventor. The measure passed the Senate but was blocked by Personalists in the Chamber of Deputies. The Socialists had also voted against the measure. Senator Juan B. Justo, speaking for the party delegation, labeled the proposed intervention openly partisan and politically motivated. The Socialists historically had opposed interventions of this type. Justo also indicated, however, that an intervention to redress serious social or economic inequities would receive Socialist support.[1]

By 1927, as Buenos Aires province was the key to the presidency, the nineteen Socialists in the chamber were the key to a successful anti-Yrigoyenist intervention in that province. On March 3 Juan B. Justo called a caucus of the Socialist parliamentary group and urged that they initiate a proposal for a federal intervention in Buenos Aires. The intervention, he argued, was aimed at a February decision of the provincial government to allow the establishment of gambling casinos. On May 19, 1927, Adolfo Dickmann, acting for Justo and his other Socialist colleagues, introduced the intervention proposal. He based his initiative, the first such ever brought to congressional consideration by the Socialists, on long-standing party opposition to gambling, "a terrible plague that threatens to dissolve the morality and the good and healthy custom of the people of the republic."[2] In Buenos Aires province, furthermore, the proceeds from gambling went to finance Radical political activities. There existed a strong connection, he alleged, between the men who controlled casinos, race tracks, and the lottery and those who served in the governmental and legal structure of the province.

Yrigoyen, master of the political maneuver, responded easily to the Socialist challenge. He directed his followers in Buenos Aires province to eliminate the *raison d'être* of the Socialist proposal. They obeyed and closed the casinos, halted the horse races, and suspended the lottery. The Socialist parliamentarians, in a public manifesto, expressed their pleasure in these moves and took credit for "abolishing in the province the game of chance as a public institution" and freeing the working class from the possibility and the temptation of impoverishing themselves even more. "It is," the statement concluded, "a splendid political triumph in the best sense of the word."[3]

And indeed it was, but the triumph belonged to Yrigoyen and not to the Socialists. By resolving the gambling issue the Radical *jefe* had undercut the intervention proposal, which the Socialists were forced to withdraw from consideration in early June, and had protected the bulwark of his electoral strength.

The most important final outcome of the entire intervention episode was its effect on the internal life of the Socialist Party. Soon after the parliamentary group made its decision to retract the May 19 initiative, Deputy Raúl Carballo, a Tomasist, began to publish in *La Prensa* criticisms of the party's leadership for its handling of the entire intervention matter. He labeled the original proposal as political, contrary to the best interests of the party, and forced on Socialist legislators by Justo and Dickmann. The appearance of these criticisms in the bourgeois press, which Carballo later claimed he had to use because the pages of *La Vanguardia* were closed to him, led the parliamentary group to meet on June 8 to decide proper disciplinary action. The Repettists called for immediate censure, the Tomasists suggested the case be brought before the next party congress. Neither side prevailed. But at another meeting a few days later the group voted unanimously to recommend that Carballo resign his congressional seat.

Following this resolution, the matter of Carballo's status was put to a general vote of the party. Affiliates voted 4,149 to 356 in favor of the offending deputy's resignation from Congress and 3,925 to 580 for his expulsion from the party.[4] Carballo, however, claimed that the vote was rigged and refused to leave his chamber position. His case then became a rallying point for the Tomasist faction, which may purposely have manipulated the entire affair to provide an issue with which they could leave the party and begin a new organization. In May Tomasists formed their own newspaper, *Crítica y Acción*, and began to criticize the party leadership, now predominantly Repettist.[5]

In late June and early July the controversy became more public and more bitter. On July 20 the Socialist division had its first clear-cut impact on the Chamber of Deputies. The Tomasist deputies, joining conservatives, Antipersonalists, and Democratic Progressives, voted for their colleague Héctor González Iramain to serve as second vice-president of the chamber. The eight other Socialists (Castellanos, Coca, Adolfo Dickmann, Enrique Dickmann, Oddone, Pena, Pérez Leirós, and Repetto) voted with the Yrigoyenist Radicals for a UCR candidate, coming out on the short end by a tally of 63 to 47.[6] Thereafter the two factions began to operate in the chamber independently of one another, introducing separate legislative proposals and supporting separate and different points of view on many issues. On July 27 the

Socialist deputies spent several hours in a turbulent congressional session expressing publicly their respective positions. The details of the Carballo affair were explained and debated, as well as the underlying causes of the party schism, now open and seemingly irrevocable.[7]

Following these debates, the de Tomaso faction prepared to form a new and distinct party. Meeting in Buenos Aires on August 7, at a constituent convention attended by representatives from 24 capital groups and several provincial delegates, presided over by Antonio de Tomaso, the dissidents organized the Partido Socialista Independiente (PSI) (Independent Socialist Party). De Tomaso and his colleagues retained the program of the old party and, with some minor changes, the same basic organizational structure. They resolved to found another newspaper, a daily entitled *Libertad!*, which began to appear regularly in mid-August. Headquarters were established in mid-town Buenos Aires.[8]

The Socialist split, once formalized, produced an outpouring of journalistic invective of the kind usually reserved for the bourgeoisie. Writers for *La Vanguardia* and *Acción Socialista* labeled the dissidents "libertines," in reference to their refusal to adhere to party rules and regulations, and also as "traitors" for having left the Socialist Party. *Crítica y Acción* and *Libertad!* called the party leaders "dictators" trying to impose their will on all Socialists.

The barrage of charges and countercharges in 1927 often obscured rather than clarified the causes of the Socialist schism. Seen in perspective, the underlying and basic factor was a struggle within the leadership for dominance over the direction of Argentina's largest and most influential Socialist organization. Personalities and ideologies played subordinate roles to the simple question of who would rule. In this instance the group of men who had followed de Tomaso's lead lost in the battle with those who rallied around Repetto, and as a result of their loss they left to form their own party.

Although the PSI claimed to have the same general orientation as the Socialist Party, it also professed to assume a more nationalistic position on some issues. This alleged nationalism was invoked in 1927 to set the two parties apart on the crucial question then being debated in Congress: Should the state own and exploit all of Argentina's petroleum reserves? This debate, like that over intervention in Buenos Aires province, occurred within the larger context of the impending presidential election. Yrigoyen, abandoned by many of the leading personalities of the Radical Party who had allied with Alvear, increasingly based his strength on the newer, younger, lesser known, and more militant members of the UCR. He and they believed that a strong nationalistic stand on the petroleum question would satisfy not only their own sentiments but also appeal to the majority of the electorate, already alerted to the activities of private oil companies in Latin America. Therefore, Yrigoyen instructed his deputies in 1927 to support legislation that would not only assure national ownership of all Argentine oil reserves but also provide for a state monopoly over exploration and exploitation and include expropriation of foreign-owned properties.[9] The Alvear administration and the Antipersonalists approved the concept of national ownership but opposed the state monopoly as unrealistic and expressed preference for the continuation of a mixed system.

The Socialists, now officially divided, took opposing stands. After lengthy discussions, the Independents let it be known that they would back the Yrigoyenist position favoring a state monopoly, although objecting to expropriation of private concerns. By so doing, de Tomaso and his followers, aligning with the Personalists on the most important issue of the day, momentarily stood the "contubernio" thesis on its head. The old-line Socialists branded the PSI position as cynical political opportunism, which it probably was. The popularity of both the nationalist monopoly principle and Yrigoyen among the Argentine electorate was increasingly manifest in 1927. The de Tomaso maneuver, Joaquín Coca later stated, was an attempt to associate with that popularity and gain electoral support in the capital in 1928.[10]

As the petroleum debate unfolded, the Socialist deputies approved national ownership and favored a stronger state role in exploration and exploitation. However, they rejected the state monopoly. Such a monopoly, they concluded, was unheard of in any other country and they doubted that the Argentine government alone was capable of directing such an enterprise in a productive and efficient fashion. Moreover, they argued, such a proposal was primarily politically motivated and in the long run unrealistic since the predominantly conservative Senate would never approve the monopoly concept. In contrast, they supported retention of the mixed public-private arrangement, with stringent state controls over private enterprise.

The petroleum question was the major subject of discussion for the 1927 sessions of the chamber. Debate was long and exhausting, taking place within an arena of intense parliamentary and political maneuvering. On September 1 national ownership and control of the country's petroleum reserves was approved by a vote of eighty-eight to seventeen, with both Socialist groups supporting the proposal.[11] After some tactical delays the most important vote came on September 8, when the following amendment to the discussed petroleum measure was proposed: "The exploration and exploitation of such resources [petroleum reserves] will be made exclusively by the national state in all the territory of the republic." The chamber passed this amendment by a vote of sixty-five to fifty-five. The Yrigoyenist Radicals voted *en bloc* in favor, but it was the eleven Independent Socialists who provided the margin of victory. The eight Socialist Party deputies voted with the Antipersonalists, conservatives, and Democratic Progressives in a losing cause.[12] Following this vote, refinements were made in the legislative proposal to strengthen the state role and to eliminate any provisions for a mixed system. The Personalists wanted to push for immediate expropriation of private companies, but the PSI refused to back that measure. The Socialist deputies managed to include articles that would guarantee workers in both private and public companies an eight-hour day, a forty-four–hour week, the right to organize, and a minimum wage. At the end of September the historic legislation was sent on to the Senate, where it was destined to languish without ever being considered.[13]

Juan B. Justo, by 1927 the "Grand Old Man" of Argentine socialism, did not become directly involved in the schism. Although he was clearly the key figure on the "disciplinarian" side, the dissidents were very circumspect in criticizing the revered party founder and usually attacked him only by implication. Following the withdrawal of the Buenos Aires intervention project, Justo let his lieutenants carry on the partisan struggle while he concentrated on his senatorial duties. In the upper house, in alliance with Mario Bravo, he introduced legislation to establish divorce and to separate church and state. Many of his speeches centered on issues arising from foreign control of Argentina's economy. In August 1927 Justo sought to deny a Senate seat to Rudecindo S. Campos, chosen to replace a deceased senator from the northern province of Jujuy. Campos, Justo pointed out, had served as a lawyer for Standard Oil in the north. At a time of increasing concern over the activities of international monopolies, the Socialist argued, persons so closely tied to foreign capital should not be allowed to assume positions in national legislative bodies. In the voting for Campos, the two Socialist senators were joined in opposition by three Yrigoyenist Radicals, but thirteen senators voted in the affirmative and Campos took his seat.[14]

At the end of the senatorial sessions Justo traveled to a small farm in Buenos Aires province to rest from the rigors of a strenuous year. There he read, planned future legislative activities, and worked in the fields and gardens. Early in the morning of January 8, 1928, he suffered a heart attack and died peacefully in bed. His body immediately was returned to Buenos Aires and interred on January 9.[15]

Justo's death was a profound blow to the party. Gone was the man who had provided the principal direction for Argentine socialism from 1893. Justo's public career paralleled the growth of the party. It was he who had traced the main lines of theory and practice through the difficult early years and into the post-1912 period when the party registered its first significant electoral victories. It was almost inevitable that a man of such ability, energy, and forceful convictions would leave an indelible stamp. But Justo, with the aid of others, had striven to make the Socialist Party something more than a personal vehicle, something that would survive the passing of one figure, something new on the Argentine political scene—a modern party. And Justo built well. Recovering from the shock of his death, the Socialist leadership pledged to resume the work begun in the 1890s. And the men who had been closest to Justo—Mario Bravo, the Dickmann brothers, Nicolás Repetto—provided the necessary continuity of leadership, having shared party responsibilities with their "maestro" from the turn of the century. Justo had founded the Argentine Socialist Party with a handful of men meeting around a single table in a café. When he died in 1928 the party, even with its recent schism, was firmly established in every part of the republic. Its main founder and leader for thirty-five years was gone, but the party, with its structure and its program, remained and endured, and this was the most eloquent of all the many tributes to Justo's memory.

The 1928 deputy elections in the capital supplied the first major test of the party's viability following the twin shocks of the most recent schism and Justo's death. With their habitual anticipation the Socialists chose deputy candidates for the April 1 contest in February. In addition, the party selected a presidential ticket of Mario Bravo and Nicolás Repetto. Repetto, who had assumed titular leadership of the party, was also its candidate for senator from the federal capital.

In the campaign the Socialists focused intensely, almost ferociously, against what they called "Yrigoyenismo." A March 31 executive committee "Manifesto to the People," for example, reviewed the previous Yrigoyen administration in critical terms and warned the electorate they could expect little improvement the second time around.[16]

Most party comments on the Independent Socialists tended to ally the dissidents with the Yrigoyenist forces. Generally, however, the former affiliates received secondary attention, usually as an afterthought to some attack on the Personalists. The PSI, for its part, convened in late January to select candidates and a program for the upcoming elections. Deciding not to enter a presidential ticket, it chose instead to focus on the capital congressional contest. The meeting selected Alfredo L. Spinetto to run for the Senate and picked twelve well-known former Socialists to compete for deputy seats. Seven of the twelve previously had served in the chamber, two others had been councilmen in the municipal government of the capital, and three more had been prominent Socialist militants for some time.[17]

The PSI platform echoed traditional Socialist dogma. It carried many of the same planks as the Socialist Party's program. The major difference was in article one of the sixteen-point plan, which advocated "nationalization of the petroleum reserves of all the republic, *and* exploitation by the state." Using the petroleum issue as a touchstone, the Independents attempted to portray themselves as more nationalistic, more concerned with defending Argentine national interests and natural resources than the Socialist Party.

As the 1928 campaign progressed, PSI spokesmen expressed confidence that their party would capture the minority seats in the capital. The tone of their pre-electoral activity was moderate and positive. They did not openly support Yrigoyen, but neither did they attack the Personalists in the bitter terms of the old party. With regard to their colleagues, they also spared invective in most cases. Instead, the Independents stressed their nationalism, their openness, and their newness.

On the face of it, the PSI seemed to combine in 1928 a well-articulated program of basic change with a strong nationalist orientation. It could march with the Yrigoyen bandwagon and enjoy the benefits thereof without actually climbing aboard. Moreover, although only formed in August of the previous year, it suffered few of the drawbacks of a new party and reaped most of the benefits. It could identify itself as something different on the Argentine political scene, while at the same time presenting recognizable candidates and a familiar program. In addition, organization posed few problems. Internal party structure paralleled that of the old Socialist Party in most particulars, and by early 1928 the PSI had centers in each of Buenos Aires's twenty *circunscripciones*. The Independents, then, could call on experienced hands to organize rallies and speeches, distribute leaflets, provide voter information, chauffeur sympathizers to the polls, and generally do the difficult legwork essential to any successful campaign. In sum, the 1927 schismatics were far better organized than the 1915 Partido Socialista Argentino, essentially a one-man show and now defunct, and much better known and much more within the Argentine mainstream than the 1917 Internationalists and the 1921 Communists. Therefore, they posed a correspondingly more serious threat to the established Socialist Party, which had won either majorities or minorities in every capital deputy election since 1912.

Yrigoyen's Radicals, confident of victory, readied for the April 1 elections at a more leisurely pace than either of their Socialist rivals. The strategy of the Radical campaign was simple: to stress the achievements of the first Yrigoyen administration and to promise a follow-through in 1928–1934 of the work begun in 1916–1922. In the capital, prior to the selection of Radical candidates, UCR leaders toured *circunscripciones* to remind voters of President Yrigoyen's personal concern for the welfare of the individual Argentine.[18]

In the federal capital in 1928 the seven parties that competed for the twelve deputy seats and one senatorial position were all either the result of or affected by internal schisms that occurred in the 1920s. On the Radical side were the Personalist UCR, the odds-on favorite to win, and the Antipersonalist UCR, which had drawn conservative support to its cause. The Socialists, who in the past had provided the Radicals with their principal competition, were divided between the Socialist Party and the PSI. The Communists, who had participated in capital elections throughout the 1920s without winning much over 2 percent of the vote, were in 1928 divided into three factions.

The electorate to which these parties hoped to appeal was quantitatively quite different in 1928 from when Radicals, Socialists, and conservatives had first done battle in 1912. The number of registered voters had grown from 126,303 to 303,712. Although exact figures as to population in 1928 are not available, the municipal census of 1936 listed a city population of 2,415,142, up from 1,575,814 in 1914.[19]

In terms of *circunscripción* growth, a pattern begun in the pre-war years persisted in the 1920s and early 1930s. Sections in the center of the capital remained relatively stable, while outlying districts, particularly *circunscripciones* 1, 15, and 16, registered phenomenal increases (see Appendix B). By 1936, moreover, even with the renewed immigration of the 1920s, the capital was reasserting a balance of native born over foreign born, 1,543,107 Argentines to 870,722 non-Argentines. The census also showed that of the 870,722 capital inhabitants born abroad, only 66,572 (63,634 men and 2,938 women) had become naturalized citizens.[20]

Election day, April 1, passed peacefully throughout the country. The outpouring of voters was the largest in Argentine history. In the nation as a whole, 1,461,581 voters of 1,807,566 registered, a little over 80 percent, went to the polls. In the capital, where voter turnouts were traditionally higher than in the interior, 278,252 of 303,712 registered voters cast their ballots, a percentage of 91.61 percent. As these votes were counted it became clear that a massive turnout had produced a massive victory for Hipólito Yrigoyen and the Personalist Radicals. The final tally gave the Radical ticket of Hipólito Yrigoyen and Francisco Beiró almost 840,000 votes, 57.41 percent of all those cast. The Antipersonalist-conservative slate gathered about 440,000 votes, the Socialist team of Bravo-Repetto picking up about 65,000. The dimensions of the Yrigoyen victory were staggering. The Personalists carried every province but San Juan, rolling up overwhelming majorities in the capital and the provinces of Buenos Aires, Córdoba, Santa Fe, and Tucumán.[21] When the Electoral College met, Yrigoyen received 245 votes to 74 for his opponents.[22]

In the capital the Yrigoyenist candidate for senator, Diego Luis Molinari (139,073), swamped both Repetto (43,342) and the PSI's Spinetto (29,409). In the deputy contests the results were much the same. The Radicals, who had lost the majority to the Socialists in 1924, and had recaptured it in 1926 by a 16,000 vote margin, crushed the opposition by more than 75,000 votes in 1928. The Socialists were even beaten by their Independent rivals for the minority, failing thereby, for the first time since 1912, to elect a single capital congressman.

In the voting for the twelve majority seats, Radical Daniel Talens led his ticket with 127,411 votes. Héctor González Iramain topped the PSI slate, which took the six minority seats, with 51,273 votes. Enrique Dickmann was the leading Socialist vote-getter with 45,225 votes. Juan José Bonifacio led the Antipersonalists with 28,153, and the three Communist groups averaged between 1,500 and 2,000 votes.[23] In the contest the Yrigoyenists swept every *circunscripción* and the Independent Socialists defeated the Socialists in thirteen of twenty. (See Table 16.)

Socialist Party analysts tried to brush off the Personalist victories as the result of "peculiar psychological" factors of the moment. Party journals argued that the inherent contradictions in both the UCR and the PSI would eventually lead to their dissolution and the ultimate triumph of socialism.[24] But the Socialists could not completely shrug off their serious losses in 1928. One of the bases of their political strength, both for action and for education on the issues, the parliamentary group, had shrunk to three men—Mario Bravo in the Senate, Nicolás Repetto and Adolfo Dickmann in the Chamber of Deputies. After sixteen years of participation, they were back to the level of their congressional numerical representation in 1913. The dissidents had shaken the party and beaten them at the polls, while the Yrigoyenists, Socialist *bêtes noires* from the 1890s, controlled the national administration. The task for the near future was clear: to heal internal wounds, define

TABLE 16

DEPUTY ELECTIONS, FEDERAL CAPITAL, ABSOLUTE AND PROPORTIONATE VOTES BY CIRCUNSCRIPCIÓN, APRIL 1, 1928

Circunscripción	UCR	%	UCRA	%	PS	%	PSI	%	Voted	Registered	% Turnout
1	13,110	(51.1)	1,924	(07.5)	4,120	(16.0)	3,799	(14.8)	25,612	27,516	93.1
2	5,229	(44.1)	1,391	(11.7)	2,455	(20.7)	1,747	(14.7)	11,857	12,849	92.3
3	7,479	(46.3)	1,292	(08.0)	3,578	(22.1)	2,356	(14.6)	16,120	17,375	92.8
4	6,371	(43.5)	2,345	(16.0)	3,085	(21.0)	1,875	(12.8)	14,643	16,411	89.2
5	7,234	(45.3)	2,370	(14.8)	2,121	(13.3)	3,025	(18.9)	15,946	17,196	92.7
6	6,442	(43.9)	1,440	(09.8)	2,643	(18.0)	3,033	(20.6)	14,669	15,666	93.6
7	4,211	(41.4)	1,078	(10.6)	2,069	(20.3)	2,021	(19.8)	10,167	10,992	92.5
8	5,191	(43.6)	1,127	(09.4)	2,365	(19.8)	2,329	(19.5)	11,893	12,753	93.3
9	4,321	(42.0)	1,446	(14.0)	1,667	(16.2)	2,275	(22.1)	10,279	11,129	92.4
10	2,720	(43.8)	990	(15.9)	934	(15.0)	1,257	(20.2)	6,200	6,778	91.5
11	2,568	(39.5)	872	(13.4)	881	(13.5)	1,563	(24.0)	6,490	7,288	89.1
12	5,449	(50.8)	1,123	(10.4)	1,619	(15.1)	1,881	(17.5)	10,706	11,643	92.0
13	5,489	(45.6)	1,426	(11.8)	1,475	(12.2)	2,681	(22.3)	12,021	13,582	88.5
14	5,050	(41.3)	1,544	(12.6)	1,302	(10.6)	3,327	(27.2)	12,204	13,975	87.3
15	12,900	(49.7)	1,864	(07.1)	4,416	(17.0)	3,803	(14.6)	25,955	27,900	93.0
16	10,206	(50.0)	2,480	(12.1)	2,661	(13.0)	3,027	(14.8)	20,391	21,903	93.1
17	6,893	(47.3)	1,447	(09.9)	2,083	(14.3)	2,569	(17.6)	14,551	15,836	91.9
18	8,168	(47.2)	1,904	(11.0)	2,686	(15.5)	3,088	(17.8)	17,269	18,736	92.7
19	5,477	(40.6)	1,604	(11.9)	2,106	(15.6)	3,112	(21.1)	13,468	14,895	90.4
20	3,053	(39.0)	1,363	(17.4)	895	(11.4)	1,834	(23.4)	7,811	9,289	84.1
Totals	127,756	(45.9)	31,140	(11.2)	45,420	(16.3)	51,314	(18.4)	278,252	303,712	91.6

a. Source: República Argentina, *Memoria, 1927–1928*, p. 27.
b. The four major parties in competition were the Unión Cívica Radical (UCR), the Unión Cívica Radical Antipersonalista (UCRA), the Partido Socialista (PS), and the Partido Socialista Independiente (PSI).

differences with the opposition, and regroup to regain lost electoral and congressional strength.

In 1928 the election victories of the Personalist UCR gave the Yrigoyenists political predominance in almost all branches of government. Eight provincial governments were under Radical control. Personalist majorities had swept deputy contests in the provinces of Buenos Aires, Córdoba, Entre Ríos, Mendoza, San Luis, Santa Fe, Santiago del Estero, and Tucumán, as well as in the federal capital. When the lower house sessions began in June 1928 the Radicals enjoyed a clear majority position with ninety-two deputies. Antipersonalists and other Radical factions numbered nineteen deputies, conservatives controlled thirty-five seats, the Independent Socialists had eight representatives, and the Socialist Party two seats. The Yrigoyenists failed, however, to capture the Senate, where nine conservatives, nine Antipersonalists, and one Socialist easily outnumbered the eight Radical Personalists.

Despite, or perhaps because of, the large UCR majority in the chamber in 1928 and 1929, the tone and legislative production of Congress changed little from the immediately preceding years. The Yrigoyenist bloc, while presenting a considerable number of important proposals, often took an intransigent stand with regard to the opposition. The Radicals' favorite tactics were to delay the opening of sessions and fail to appear to provide a quorum when a vote contrary to their wishes was to be taken. The opposition conservatives, Antipersonalists, Independent Socialists, and Socialists in turn reciprocated with unending calls for ministerial interpellations and with anti-Yrigoyen political speeches in the chamber having little to do with debated legislation. The partisan maneuvering of the pre-1928 presidential election period continued unabated after Yrigoyen gained office for a second term.

The second presidential inauguration of Hipólito Yrigoyen occurred on October 12, 1928. His advantages seemed many, especially in comparison with 1916. The Radical victory had been a clear triumph, indicating a popular mandate for *yrigoyenismo*. The conservative elements, which had weakened Radicalism internally, were separated from the movement. Yrigoyen could now draw upon six years of administrative experience and a seasoned knowledge of the workings of government. Radicals controlled a majority of provincial governments and were in a position to increase their margins even more. Although the national Senate remained anti-Radical, the Chamber of Deputies had a sizeable UCR majority. Finally, Yrigoyen's widespread personal popularity could not be doubted. His overwhelming victory had come on the heels of an administration, that of Alvear, that had overseen a six-year period of peace and prosperity. Clearly, the electorate believed Yrigoyen would continue economic growth, maintain social harmony, and also introduce new changes to strengthen these overall conditions.

Most of these seeming advantages, however, were more illusory than real, and most of the high expectations of 1928 were doomed to frustration. Many of the Radicals who had gained administrative experience in 1916–1922 were now on the side of the Antipersonalists. Yrigoyen, therefore, was forced to appoint new and untried men to important administrative positions, where they not only lacked experience but also frequently succumbed to the tendency to fatten themselves in office. The president himself, though retaining many of his political skills, was seventy-six years old in 1928. Advanced age exacted its toll and Yrigoyen's weaknesses were accentuated in his second term. He dealt personally with petty administrative details and to reward the faithful allowed the bureaucracy to swell out of all reasonable proportion. He increased centralization of authority through provincial intervention and treated the legislative branch with disdain. A cult of personality began to develop around him that he did little to discourage, arousing unreasonable expectations that the Radical "caudillo" had almost supernatural powers to deal with any situation, any crisis. Finally, the opposition, which had been caught somewhat off guard in 1916, was now seasoned, strong, and ready to resist any and all initiatives that bore the Yrigoyenist mark.

The Socialist Party, while remaining aloof from alliance with the "contubernio," nevertheless contributed greatly to the anti-Yrigoyen opposition. *Acción Socialista* greeted the Yrigoyen inauguration with expressions of concern over "the atmosphere of calculated occultism that surrounds his action" and "the remembrance of the previous presidency, so full of administrative deals and scandals, tolerated and consented to by the *jefe único*." At seventy-six years of age, the editorial noted, few changes could be expected: "All points, on the contrary, [to the certainty] that we shall have a re-edition, corrected and revised, of the first presidency of sad and lamented memory." In consequence, the Socialist Party "will maintain firmly and serenely its clear position in the field of political forces, and will exercise the delicate and difficult task of watching over, in defense of the interests of the working people, the administrative action of the new government."[25]

True to this pledge, Dickmann and Repetto spent a good part of the 1929 Chamber of Deputy sessions seeking interpellations of Yrigoyen's ministers. The administration, in turn, tried to stymie interpellation, at first by abstaining from initial sessions. Finally, on June 12 Repetto managed to introduce a resolution that the Minister of Public Works appear to explain what the government had done to lower rail rates for transfer of agricultural goods, an important item at a time when the effects of the world depression were beginning to hurt Argentina's farmers. In response, Radical Romeo David Saccone of the capital presented the majority bloc's position on interpellations. When used to gain information to formulate legitimate legislative proposals, he contended, questioning of ministers before Congress was right and proper. Repeated interpellations for political purposes, however, were an unjustifiable intrusion of the legislative branch into the prerogatives and authority of the executive. Therefore, as the anti-Yrigoyenists resorted automatically and systematically to interpellations for partisan ends, so, too, would the UCR automatically and systematically vote against such requests. The Independent Socialists supported the Socialists' right to interpellate under any conditions, but in the final voting the Radicals predictably prevailed.[26]

For most of July and the first part of August the Radicals either abstained from attending or walked out *en masse* when votes were called to question ministers. Finally, on August 22 a quorum was present to hear Nicolás Repetto resolve to call the Minister of the Interior to explain to Congress the fulfillment of the provisions for the national Labor Department to mediate labor-management disputes. The resolution was in reference to Yrigoyen's deployment of federal troops to break an agrarian workers' strike in Santa Fe province.[27] After the introduction of the resolution, Radicals and Socialists squared off in a lengthy and impassioned exchange over the rights and wrongs of Yrigoyen's actions.[28] At a later session, on September 5, Repetto's resolution was defeated by a vote of 55 to 41 along the usual party lines.[29]

This congressional tug of war continued into special sessions of October 1929 through January 1930. The anti-Yrigoyenists, claiming to uphold their constitutional rights and duties, consistently sought to interpellate the cabinet. The Yrigoyenists, averring that they sought to protect administrators from undue harassment in the performance of their functions, just as consistently hindered these attempts. No minister appeared before the Chamber of Deputies in 1929. Meanwhile, in the midst of this struggle, some significant legislation emerged, measures that enjoyed generally broad support. Law 11,563 provided for a national census of livestock, law 11,570 toughened provisions for enforcement of social legislation in the capital and national territories, and law 11,575 provided retirement benefits and pensions for bank employees. The real milestone of these sessions, however, was law 11,544, which read in its first article that "the duration of labor cannot exceed eight hours daily or forty-eight hours weekly for all persons occupied by another's account in public or private exploitations, even if non-profit." Specifically excluded from the law's provisions were agricultural workers, farmers, and domestic servants. Despite these limitations, the number-one plank of socialist organizations for forty years in Argentina finally had become law.

These legislative measures, however, offered little solace to Yrigoyen and his supporters. By the end of 1929 the political position of the administration was beginning to deteriorate badly. It was at this time that the impact of the world depression began to make its real mark on Argentina. The republic's vulnerable export-oriented economy suffered from lower prices on agricultural goods and the contraction of overseas markets. Exports of beef and grain began to fall, affecting the balance of payments and the stability of the peso. On December 16, 1929, Yrigoyen closed the Caja de Conversión, which Alvear had reopened in 1927, to prevent the drain of gold. The labor sector, relatively quiet in the mid-1920s, began to suffer adverse effects. After steady increases in employment from the mid-1920s, the first signs of unemployment appeared in 1929 and worsened in 1930. Real wages, which also had risen in the 1920s, began to decline at the end of the decade.[30]

Yrigoyen, who had experienced what had seemed a similar crisis during his first term, attempted a number of measures to deal with this new jolt to the economy, none of which proved very successful. At the same time, the political situation continued to worsen. The lines between Yrigoyenists and anti-Yrigoyenists became more sharply drawn and exchanges between the two groups more hostile. What many defined as a climate of violence descended on the political scene. Radical interventions in San Juan and Mendoza produced shooting incidents and required the dispatch of federal troops to maintain order. In early November the anti-Yrigoyenist political boss of Mendoza, Carlos Washington Lencinas, was shot to death by a Radical. Nicolás Repetto connected the assassination with the re-emergence of Yrigoyenist Radicalism to executive power, recalling the 1916 attempt against the life of Juan B. Justo. Repetto did not accuse the president directly of instigating violent acts, but implied that "around President Yrigoyen there is an ambiance of crime and it is very probable that from the ambiance of crime might have surged the crime of Mendoza." Violence and Radicalism, he concluded, were inseparable.[31]

As the Yrigoyenists entered their "time of troubles," the Socialist Party held its twentieth ordinary party congress at the Casa del Pueblo, October 10–13, 1929. Some 205 delegates, representing 171 centers and groups, met in an atmosphere of harmony and unity, free for the moment from the internal bickerings of the past. The congress concentrated primarily on social problems dealing with agricultural workers, vowing to devote more attention and resources to rural areas. The reports of the executive committee, parliamentary group, and press committee were all approved with little dissent. Finally, the congress sanctioned the party platform for the approaching deputy elections in the capital. The planks of the platform were basically the same as those for 1928. However, thanks to passage of law 11,544, for the first time in party history the Socialists did not need to demand legislation to establish the eight-hour workday. They did, nevertheless, include a provision to extend this reform to the "trabajadores del campo," workers in the countryside.[32]

Three and one-half months after the congress, the party chose its list of candidates for the March 2 congressional contest. "Solos contra todos," "Alone against all," was the theme for this election. The Socialists placed the principal blame for the "disastrous and chaotic" situation of the country squarely on the Yrigoyen government, but refused to associate with the growing anti-Yrigoyen coalition of Independent Socialists, Antipersonalists, and conservatives. Viewing that coalition as one inspired only by political opportunism, the Socialists claimed to have nothing in common with "the so-called opposition groups that have made of their hate against Yrigoyen a negative banner and program; and if, to the misfortune of the country, they should triumph, they would submerge the republic in disaster or perhaps civil war, by their known aversion to free institutions, of which universal and secret suffrage is the base and foundation."[33]

The PSI, which had floated with the Yrigoyenist tide in 1928, made unremitting opposition to the Radical regime the centerpiece of their campaign in 1930. Running on the same platform as that of two years ago, the Independents argued that it was essentially useless to speak of specific changes within a Congress controlled by a dictatorial administration that systematically ignored constitutional provisions defining the relationship between executive and legislative branches. Accordingly, the PSI promised supporters that its first order of business after the March elections would be to initiate impeachment proceedings against Yrigoyen and his entire cabinet "for reiterated violation of the National Constitution and the organic laws of the country and for badly performing their functions."[34]

The Radicals, for their part, fully realized the importance of the capital contest. It was in Buenos Aires where most anti-Yrigoyen sentiment and activity were located. A defeat for the UCR there could be a serious psychological blow for the government and the party throughout the republic. Yrigoyen's supporters, therefore, responded with one of the Radicals' best-planned campaigns in history. Lectures and rallies began in early February, organized by UCR committees established in each of the capital's twenty *circunscripciones*. On February 14, 118 delegates to the UCR capital convention selected ten candidates for deputy positions, all of whom had been elected to Congress in 1926 and were seeking re-election in 1930.

Although the UCR still eschewed a formulated program, its candidates clearly did run on one issue: support for the nationalization of petroleum. They also sought to use Yrigoyen's past performance in a variety of social and economic areas as a framework from which to appeal to the electorate. Defending Yrigoyen in the face of a rapidly eroding situation, the UCR representatives attacked the Socialist Party in familiar terms. Most Radical criticism, however, was focused on the "contubernio"—Independent Socialists, conservatives, and Antipersonalists.

On election day in the capital all three parties forecast victories. The turnout of 297,479 voters, or 86.13 percent of the 345,383 registered, only five percentage points below the showing in the presidential battle of 1928, attested to public interest in the contest. The first results, those for *circunscripción* one, became available on March 7. They showed a significant shift from 1928. In the presidential year the Radicals had carried this section, normally a Socialist district, with an overwhelming total of 13,110 votes as compared with 4,120 for the Socialist Party and 3,799 for the PSI. In 1930 the UCR totals dropped about 4,500 votes to 8,649, the Socialists more than doubled their tally to a winning 9,126, and the PSI made a respectable increase to 8,433. Reading these returns, the Independents attributed the Socialist margin to strength in the "politically and culturally most backward" sectors of the district. The Socialist Party, *Libertad!* predicted, would win in *circunscripciones* one through four and do well in district fifteen. But in the other districts, and in the city as a whole, the struggle would boil down to a fight between the Yrigoyenists and the PSI.[35]

When the final tally was completed two weeks later the PSI analysis proved correct. The Socialist Party carried *circunscripciones* one through four and fifteen. All but one of the remaining sections fell to the Independents. The Radicals carried only *circunscripción* twelve, Yrigoyen's home district, and that by a scant twenty-nine-vote margin. Even *circunscripción* five, which was to the Radicals what four was to the Socialists, fell by almost 2,000 votes to the new party. (See Table 17.) Overall, Antonio de Tomaso received 109,292 votes to lead the

TABLE 17

DEPUTY ELECTIONS, FEDERAL CAPITAL, ABSOLUTE AND PROPORTIONATE VOTES BY CIRCUNSCRIPCIÓN, MARCH 2, 1930

Circun-scripción	UCR	%	PS	%	PSI	%	Voted	Registered	Turnout %
1	8,649	(29.9)	9,126	(31.5)	8,433	(29.1)	28,906	33,000	87.6
2	3,124	(25.0)	4,409	(35.4)	3,130	(25.1)	12,453	14,225	87.5
3	5,043	(31.1)	5,655	(34.9)	4,407	(27.2)	16,169	18,857	85.7
4	4,549	(29.7)	6,228	(40.6)	3,403	(22.2)	15,313	18,342	83.5
5	5,080	(29.5)	3,961	(23.0)	7,062	(41.1)	17,177	19,499	88.1
6	4,192	(27.0)	4,322	(27.8)	5,935	(38.2)	15,506	17,403	89.1
7	2,464	(23.8)	3,132	(30.3)	4,177	(39.9)	10,312	11,755	87.7
8	3,332	(26.5)	3,860	(30.7)	4,416	(35.1)	12,552	14,236	88.2
9	2,735	(26.2)	2,765	(26.5)	4,348	(41.7)	10,417	12,021	86.7
10	2,603	(30.6)	2,078	(24.4)	3,253	(38.3)	8,482	9,926	85.5
11	1,698	(25.8)	1,493	(22.7)	3,036	(46.2)	6,564	7,953	82.5
12	4,035	(36.0)	2,463	(21.9)	4,006	(35.7)	11,208	12,847	87.2
13	3,444	(29.1)	2,275	(19.2)	5,472	(46.3)	11,816	14,415	82.0
14	3,231	(26.3)	1,966	(16.0)	6,449	(52.6)	12,244	15,287	80.1
15	7,925	(26.4)	10,224	(34.1)	9,217	(30.7)	29,926	33,890	88.3
16	6,234	(28.2)	5,562	(25.2)	8,389	(38.0)	22,031	25,203	87.4
17	4,561	(28.1)	3,813	(23.5)	6,616	(40.8)	16,198	18,724	86.5
18	4,632	(26.0)	4,700	(26.4)	7,330	(41.1)	17,800	20,367	87.6
19	3,742	(25.7)	3,666	(25.2)	6,328	(43.5)	14,537	17,128	84.9
20	1,955	(24.8)	1,372	(17.4)	3,973	(50.4)	7,868	10,305	76.4
Totals	83,251	(28.0)	83,076	(27.9)	109,323	(36.7)	297,479	345,383	86.2

Source: República Argentina, *Memoria, 1929–1930.*

PSI to a ten-seat majority victory. Nicolás Repetto got 83,076 votes for one Socialist seat, and Eduardo F. Giuffra 82,713 votes to lead the Radicals for three additional minority seats.[36]

The reversal was dramatic. In 1928 the UCR had carried every district in the capital. Although the Radicals had not outpolled the combined opposition, they had amassed 127,756 votes to the Socialist, PSI, and Antipersonalist total of 133,874. In the 1930 elections the anti-Yrigoyenist combined vote was 192,368 to 82,713.

After the March elections Argentina entered a period of virtual political paralysis. Economic difficulties continued to worsen while an old, sick, and isolated Yrigoyen did little to respond. The opposition coalition, in which the Independent Socialists played a prominent role, hammered away at the aging "caudillo." Most leading newspapers, student groups, conservatives, and a growing number of his own party stated or suggested that Yrigoyen should resign from office in view of his inability to cope with the crisis. The legislative branch of government came to a standstill. The Senate never convened. In the Chamber of Deputies the Radicals enjoyed a large majority of ninety-eight seats. However, in response to the militant criticisms of the opposition, the UCR delayed the opening of sessions from May until July. Once the lower house began to meet it became immediately bogged down in partisan issues, particularly the approval of diplomas from the recent election. These arguments dragged on through the winter, still occupying congressional attention at the end of August.

While the position of the civilian Radical government deteriorated, factions within the Argentine army planned to oust Yrigoyen from office and assume national leadership. For the Socialist Party the two impending alternatives for Argentina's future were equally unpalatable. The Socialists viewed the second Yrigoyen administration as an unmitigated disaster—inept, encouraging violence, and practically inviting revolution. A military coup, however, flew in the face of everything the party had stood for over its thirty-five–year history. An intervention by the armed forces would break a long tradition of civilian dominance and halt the democratic experiment begun in 1912. The Socialists could expect little influence in such a regime and very likely could anticipate the kind of official repression experienced at the turn of the century. Programmatically, the Socialists had consistently taken anti-military positions and in Congress had just as consistently voted against what they considered excessive military appropriations. As recently as 1928, Repetto and Dickmann had stated their objections to and cast their votes against pay raises for the officer corps.[37] Moreover, in the 1920s the Socialists had been leaders in sounding the alarm against the rise of European fascism in Italy and Spain. They noted the influence and impact of Mussolini's and Primo de Rivera's examples on certain sectors of Argentine society, particularly certain groups within the Argentine army.[38] A military coup, therefore, might mean more than just the overthrow of the civilian and democratically-chosen Yrigoyen government. It might also mean the first step toward the establishment of a fascist state.

Despite their objections and their opposition in 1930, however, the Socialists were powerless to prevent any military move. On August 28, 1930, Nicolás Repetto, the sole party deputy in the chamber, forecast that Argentina would soon follow the course of other South American republics and witness "the transfer of a dictatorship from civilian hands to military hands." Repetto blamed the Yrigoyenist government directly for this prospect. Representing the bourgeoisie, he argued, the Radicals had defended the economic status quo instead of introducing the kinds of basic changes that might have forestalled the present crisis. As the political and economic situation worsened in the late 1920s, Repetto claimed, the Radicals increasingly resorted to illegal and violent means, especially in carrying out provincial interventions, to maintain power. The example of government flouting the Constitution and the law inevitably spread to other institutions, in this case the army, to justify the use of force to settle political issues.[39]

A little more than a week after this speech, on September 6, the predicted coup occurred. Army units from the nearby Campo de Mayo marched into the capital and forced Hipólito Yrigoyen from the Casa Rosada. The coup was virtually bloodless; few defended the president who had been so overwhelmingly elected in 1928. General José F. Uriburu became provisional president and ruled by decree. The new executive initiated both a state of siege and martial law, closed the Congress, and ordered provincial interventions to replace Yrigoyenists with conservatives.[40] For the first time since the mid-nineteenth century a constitutionally elected president had been forced from office by a military coup. In 1930 the Argentine army, in the past non-interventionist and non-political in comparison with most other Latin American armies, assumed the political leadership of the republic. From that date to the 1970s the military would be the single most influential arbiter of the nation's destiny. Argentina's experiment with democracy had ended. In the 1930s, and thereafter, the party would face again the challenges of the pre-Sáenz Peña period: to withstand the pressures to meet violence with violence, revolution with revolution, in favor of peaceful political participation in a less than peaceful or honest political process.

The events of 1927 to 1930 had great impact on the Socialist Party's position in the capital and the Congress. The Socialists lost votes in 1928, regained them in 1930, and witnessed a drastic decline overall in the size and influence of their parliamentary representation. But the schism of 1927, the Radical victory of 1928, and the military revolt of 1930 had little apparent effect on the basic size and structure of the party itself. Indeed, it experienced continued growth in this period. Statistics for 1930 show only a slight drop in party membership following the PSI's formation in August 1927. The *Anuario Socialista* for 1932 placed total membership of the party as of November 1931 at 16,214 adherents in 345 groups. These included 436 women in three feminine centers and about 4,500 youth affiliates in 98 groups, additions not clearly delineated in previous tallies. Subtracting the combined figures for youth and women leaves a total of 11,278 voting male adherents in the party.[41]

In the interior the party ran true to past form, making only token showings in most provinces. In Buenos Aires province the leading Socialist vote-getter for deputy in 1930 polled 26,408 votes to the top Radical's 171,584.[42] Mar del Plata did remain under Socialist control, the party winning the 1928 municipal election there with 2,138 votes to the Radicals' 1,367 and the conservatives' 1,177.[43]

During this period the Socialist Party enjoyed a close collaboration with the Confederación Obrera Argentina. Although the COA constantly professed its apoliticism, there was little doubt as to where its sympathies lay. Prior to the 1928 elections, for example, *La Confederación* reminded its readers that while labor organizations could not support parties or candidates, there was nothing to prevent .individuals from so doing. In fact, not to do so would be a direct detriment to the working class when one of the competing parties, the Yrigoyenist Radicals, were "those who in the tragic week of January 1919 imprisoned and martyred defenseless proletarians, . . . sprinkled the soil of Santa Cruz generously with blood, . . . [and] sanctioned the railroad pension law, including article 11."[44] Later in 1928 the Confederación ousted Independent Socialist Agustín S. Muzio from its ranks, labeling him a "traitor to the country's working class" for not supporting a COA-sponsored boycott.[45] If the Confederación did not openly back the Socialist Party, it did it no little service in so attacking the principal opposition.

By the end of the 1920s organized labor in Argentina was still fragmented and weak. Socialist Francisco Pérez Leirós observed that in 1895 only 0.38 percent of the republic's population belonged to some sort of labor organization.[46] By 1928, the approximately 130,000 members of the COA, USA, and FORA were only 1.30 percent of an estimated ten million Argentine population. Unity of these small and disparate forces was essential for any future effectiveness. Accordingly, in 1929 the syndicalist USA and the Socialist COA began to discuss fusion. On September 27, 1930, members of both organizations convened in Buenos Aires to form a combined central union, the Confederación General del Trabajo (CGT) (General Labor Confederation).[47] The beginning was hardly auspicious, for it came three weeks after the military coup of September 6 brought into office a government unsympathetic to the working man and the rights of labor. But the CGT survived this difficult period and went on to be the republic's most enduring and effective central labor organization.

11. Conclusion

Following the military coup of 1930 the Socialist Party helped rally resistance to the conservative-military alliance known as the Concordancia that assumed control of Argentina's government. Never forsaking its reformist orientation, even with the imposition of regimes that often ignored provisions of the Sáenz Peña reforms and returned to the repressive and fraudulent policies of the past, the Socialists entered elections, sent representatives to local and national governing bodies, and tried to defend their positions and articulate their issues in the public forum.

In the early 1930s, with the Radicals temporarily reverting to intransigence and abstention in protest of military government, the Socialists won majority deputy seats in the capital and minority positions in Buenos Aires province. These victories gave the party forty-three representatives in the chamber by 1932, their highest total ever. With the added presence of Mario Bravo and Alfredo L. Palacios in the Senate, elected from the capital in 1931, the Socialists became congressional leaders of the opposition during the early years of Argentina's "infamous decade" under Concordancia control. From their congressional seats the Socialists focused on issues of economic nationalism and social justice, usually accomplishing little other than informing public opinion on these matters.

The Unión Cívica Radical re-entered the arena of electoral politics in 1935. This re-entrance, coupled with another Socialist schism in 1938, produced a drastic decline in Socialist Party strength at the national level. In the 1938 deputy elections the Socialists failed for only the second time since 1912 to elect a single representative to the chamber, their total bloc being reduced to five members. In 1940 the party made a small comeback, capturing the five minority seats in the capital. In 1942 it took the twelve minority positions from the same district, for a total of seventeen in the lower house. These gains, however, provided the last significant national representation for the Socialists until 1964. On June 4, 1943, a new military coup ousted a reactionary civilian government from office and paved the way to power for Juan Domingo Perón.

The Perón years (1946–1955) were traumatic for many Argentines, but perhaps none were more deeply affected than the leaders and adherents of the Socialist Party. Under Perón the political opposition, which included Radicals, conservatives, Democratic Progressives, and Socialists, suffered some of the restrictions and repressions of an authoritarian regime. But most galling for the Socialists, who bitterly opposed Perón from beginning to end, was the new caudillo's ability to bring about, seemingly overnight, many of the results for which the Socialists had struggled since the 1890s. Perón mobilized the working-class masses as a political force for the first time in Argentine history and brought them into national life on an unprecedented scale. Moreover, he managed to implement and make effective much of the party's social program, ranging from major issues like improved wages, hours, and fringe benefits to minor but symbolically important matters such as opening the Teatro Colón to the working populace. Finally, in alliance with his wife Evita, Perón in 1949 gave Argentine women the right to vote; thus he realized a long-standing Socialist goal and reaped the rich political benefits therefrom.

In addition to capturing the Socialist program, Perón also successfully imitated and expanded Socialist techniques of political propaganda. He was a master in the use of the mass demonstration, the torchlight parade, and the frenzied rally. Cleverly mixing nationalism and socialism, he easily bridged the gap that had frustrated so many Socialist Party efforts in the past. Maintaining absolute control over legislative and executive branches, he was also able to overcome the gulf between legal enactment of social measures and their actual implementation in practice. Finally, labeling the Socialists themselves as exotic, bourgeois, and elitist, Perón managed to turn his own proletarian followers violently against the party that had claimed and striven to represent working-class interests for more than half a century.

Socialists were prominent in the opposition to Perón and rejoiced in his overthrow in 1955. However, from that date the party has not been able to re-establish contact with the working class, which has remained firmly Peronist in sympathy and orientation. Fragmented, no longer attracting the able younger affiliates who gave vitality to the Socialist movement in its early years, and stubbornly adhering to reformism and programmatic stands formulated sixty years ago, the Socialists by the early 1970s were a negligible influence on the Argentine political scene.

Socialist difficulties and disappointments in the post-Perón era often have obscured the very real achievements of the party in the early twentieth century. Much of the social legislation either introduced or implemented by Perón, for example, originated with the Socialist Party. Largely through Socialist initiative in Congress such measures as Sunday rest, regulation of working hours and conditions, and the eight-hour day were written into law. While the Socialists were not the only group to support social legislation and social justice, they were the most persistent advocates of such change and the only political party in the republic to present the need for social reform in clearly articulated programmatic form.

The Socialists were also the first party to seek to mobilize the proletariat politically. Despite limited success, they did enjoy substantial working-class support in the federal capital, particularly in *circunscripciones* like two through four, six through eight, and fifteen, which the Socialists carried more often than not against Radical and conservative opposition between 1912 and 1930. Moreover, though party leadership was predominantly composed of university-educated doctors and lawyers, the party did present and elect to local and national office more representatives of working-class background and occupation than any other competing party. Also, the party itself provided an institution for mobility, offering educational and cultural opportunities and allowing workers to move up the status and professional ladder through party positions and election to office.

Contemporary critics have taken the Socialists to task for some of their positions on economic matters. Spokesmen for the nationalist revolutionary left have argued that defense of free trade blocked the growth of native industry and have suggested that the Socialists favored foreign over domestic capital.[1] Though valid criticisms of the Socialists' lack of foresight in perceiving the political advantages of protectionism and economic nationalism, these attacks come from the distorted perspective of partisan hindsight. They fail to explain how a party that claimed to represent the interests of the working class could at the same time adopt the high-tariff policies of organizations like the Unión Industrial Argentina. Moreover, although the party's moderate position on foreign capital investment is open to criticism, the early and consistent Socialist exposure of the abuses of such investment should not be ignored. From articles in *La Vanguardia* warning of the dangers of foreign finance and its influence to revelations in Congress of conflicts of interest between public officials and foreign companies, the Socialists brought to view the consequences of overseas capital and control of the Argentine economy. In many ways they contributed to the economic nationalism that emerged with the Radical government of Yrigoyen and later with Perón.

The Socialist Party also made significant contributions to the political development of the republic. Appearing at a time of great social and economic change, it helped stimulate the passage of the Sáenz Peña reform in 1912, participated without recourse to violence in elections from 1896 to 1930, and determinedly demanded expansion of the suffrage and respect for honest, open, democratic electoral and political procedures. Moreover, it mobilized and politicized many citizens who previously had not participated in politics, organized and articulated public opinion, and transferred that opinion to the centers of government decision-making. Finally, as a party, the Socialists set an example for other political groups in the republic, which gradually began to imitate Socialist organization and campaign techniques and even to adopt some aspects of the Socialist program.[2]

These achievements were accomplished despite considerable obstacles. Socialist theorizing notwithstanding, objective conditions in Argentina at the turn of the century were not propitious for the development of the Socialist Party. Like many socialist parties, the Argentine group at first faced bitter repression. Also, emerging nationalism, increasingly potent in the first decades of the century, often proved an insurmountable barrier for the new party. Furthermore, practical financial considerations impeded party growth. Depending for its funding on the dues of members, the salaries of elected officials, and the proceeds of ancillary organizations, the party lacked the wealthy contributors and backing of its chief political rivals. A lack of funds, in turn, hindered expansion from the federal capital into the interior and the formation of a truly national base for political action.

It should be noted, however, that a lack of funds was not the only reason the party failed to expand much beyond the federal capital. The presence of non-naturalized foreign-born tenants and workers, the scattered population, the strength of conservative traditions, and the power of provincial political bosses all contributed to Socialist failures in the interior, despite organizational and programmatic efforts to establish a rural and provincial base. Socialist perpetuation of Domingo Sarmiento's division of Argentina into "civilized" city and "backward" provinces may also have added to poor party showings outside of Buenos Aires. A more thorough analysis of this point is, however, beyond the scope of this study. It is to be hoped that future investigations into the details of provincial politics in Argentina will help shed light on this important problem.

These difficulties were not peculiar to the Argentine Socialist Party. Socialist groups throughout the Americas encountered similar obstacles. There were, however, certain special features about Argentina that further complicated Socialist development; probably the most important of these was the role of massive immigration. Although foreigners introduced radical European ideologies into the republic and provided the core of early labor and radical organizations, the most important feature of their presence in Argentina, so far as the Socialists were concerned, was that they represented the great bulk of the proletariat. In post-1912 Argentina their political potential was immense, but it was a potential never realized. Naturalization had to precede politicization, and to become naturalized was a step only a tiny minority of foreigners were willing to take.

Competing with revolutionary anarchists, apolitical syndicalists, and later pragmatic Radicals for working-class support, the Socialists became more and more frustrated with their inability to mobilize the proletariat. Accordingly, they began to shift their focus from exclusive labor concerns to issues of a more general nature to attract a broader constituency. The party also attempted to rationalize its failures with the argument that "the most advanced, cultured, and civilized" sectors of the proletariat did rally to its banner. This elitist concept, reflecting in part a consistent theme of traditional liberal thought in Argentina, probably further alienated "the ignorant, backward, and barbaric" sectors that would help bring Juan Perón to power.

Other related difficulties hindered Socialist efficacy. Argentina shared with most Latin American countries problems of inequitable concentrations of land and wealth, dependence on an agricultural economy oriented toward export markets, and depressed social conditions in both rural and urban areas. Many of the basic factors that either produced or portended revolution in most Latin American countries were present, but so, too, were some important safety valves: unparalleled prosperity before 1930, moderate political reform, and a relatively open and flexible social structure. The impact of these conditions on the immigrant again was critical for the Socialists. Although the foreign-born laborer might live in a *conventillo*, work twelve hours a day, and often see his wife employed in the most menial tasks, he apparently believed that his prospects were better in the New World than in the Old and that his children would enjoy ample opportunities for advancement up the social-economic scale.[3] Therefore, while the immigrant who longed to return to Europe maintained his foreign citizenship and ignored Socialist blandishments to enter into the Argentine political process, the immigrant who determined to stay in the republic might often have preferred the status quo, finding conditions far from good but still not so intolerable as to dictate a commitment to socialism. Moreover, some naturalized immigrants and second-generation sons may have preferred to identify more closely with Argentine traditions by supporting nationalist Argentine parties like the Radicals rather than the European-tainted Socialists.

Added to these external difficulties were internal strains and tensions. Dissension within Socialist ranks, often over external questions, produced several debilitating schisms between 1896 and 1930. Although fragmentation may have been salutary in the long run, achieving the cleansing and continuity that the dominant directors required, its immediate effects were often disastrous. Splinter factions took away votes in both national and local elections. Perhaps most important, the time and energy these disputes consumed distracted Socialist attention from concentration on other issues and weakened electoral campaigns against the non-Socialist opposition.

Various factors converged to produce ruptures. Ideological differences played an important role, especially the struggles over revolution versus reformism and nationalism versus internationalism. Important, too, but more difficult to measure, were clashes of personality and ambition, often obscured rather than clarified by the flurry of rhetoric that inevitably accompanied party splits.

A continuous thread in most cases of fragmentation was the very nature of party organization. Paradoxically, many of those features that led to Socialist viability and success also caused splintering. For example, the party's tight organization and discipline undoubtedly accounted in large measure for the party's ability to survive the difficult early years of the century and to triumph at the polls after 1912. But the emphasis on discipline, on a particular definition of proper socialist behavior, drove away not only independent spirits but also many who conscientiously believed that the strict application of rules and regulations hindered rather than aided effective socialist action.

Continuity of leadership engendered other tensions. According to party statutes, all affiliates periodically selected candidates for public office and chose party leaders. In practice, however, while lip service was paid to injecting new blood into positions of responsibility, essentially the same set of names consistently appeared and reappeared on the executive committee, in editorial offices, and on candidate lists for local and national office. Once elected to Congress in the 1912 to 1914 period, for example, Socialists like Mario Bravo, Enrique Dickmann,

Juan B. Justo, and Nicolás Repetto served as deputies or senators without interruption through the 1920s. Their names regularly topped Socialist ballots.

Opening up leadership to new faces was a particularly difficult problem for the Socialist Party. It was a minority party, with few congressional seats and a limited number of political plums to distribute. Furthermore, political effectiveness, especially in Congress, depended greatly on the cohesiveness and experience of the small Socialist bloc. Cohesiveness and experience came, naturally, only from working together over long periods of time. The practical necessities of the political situation, then, reinforced repetition in office. Repetition, in turn, frustrated others with aspirations to serve party and nation.

In summary, the Socialist Party faced a serious set of liabilities in its early years. Internally, the party seemed to suffer from some of the same contradictions that the Socialists perceived in capitalist society. Externally, the party had to deal with less than optimal objective conditions: a foreign-born proletariat; an overall prosperity that strengthened the bourgeoisie and often alleviated, at least momentarily, social pressures; and, a strong nationalism, which aided the opposition while it frustrated and fractionated the Socialists.

Despite these difficulties the Socialists organized, grew, and enjoyed substantial if relatively limited electoral success. They introduced new issues for public debate, brought new men into politics and national life, and provided models for political organization and behavior. Finally, the Socialists helped introduce a new political spirit and orientation into the republic. Committed to political democracy, social justice, and economic equality, they offered a real alternative to prevailing conditions and an opportunity for Argentines to achieve peacefully the basic revolutionary change that has eluded them for so long.

Appendices

APPENDIX A

REGISTERED VOTERS IN THE FEDERAL CAPITAL BY OCCUPATION AND BY CIRCUNSCRIPCIÓN, 1918, AND PERCENT OF TOTAL LITERATE BY CIRCUNSCRIPCIÓN, 1916

A			B			C			D		
Manual Workers			Artisans and Small Merchants			Employees			Owners		
Circ.	Number	Percent	Circ.	Number	Percent	Circ.	Number	Percent	Circ.	Number	Percent
4	5,732	45.48	2	2,530	35.16	20	3,443	38.83	20	465	7.73
15	2,444	32.01	7	2,553	33.00	14	3,376	37.67	14	458	5.59
2	2,171	30.17	6	2,844	32.95	19	3,322	37.51	19	501	4.39
1	2,456	29.04	16	3,174	32.59	13	2,777	33.92	13	360	4.06
17	2,232	27.32	8	3,094	32.31	11	4,098	32.62	11	197	3.89
3	3,179	25.30	9	2,799	31.79	10	1,483	32.47	10	151	3.31
16	2,306	23.68	10	1,439	31.49	12	2,777	31.54	12	283	3.16
18	2,934	23.04	15	2,341	30.66	9	3,014	31.48	9	275	3.12
6	1,916	22.20	18	3,891	30.47	5	2,335	30.18	5	275	3.10
8	1,997	20.85	1	2,554	30.20	18	2,577	29.86	18	354	2.70
7	1,562	20.19	3	3,712	20.54	16	2,488	29.41	16	250	2.57
19	1,984	17.37	17	2,260	27.66	17	1,443	28.47	17	204	2.50
12	1,544	17.23	19	2,989	26.18	6	3,617	28.32	6	211	2.44
5	1,509	17.02	11	1,325	26.14	7	2,273	27.82	7	188	2.43
9	1,386	15.74	12	2,300	25.67	15	1,653	27.48	15	174	2.28
10	641	14.06	4	3,231	25.63	1	3,077	26.94	1	186	2.20
13	1,058	11.95	13	2,002	24.87	8	2,617	26.87	8	186	1.94
20	681	11.32	14	2,024	24.73	3	1,820	25.29	3	224	1.78
11	547	10.79	5	2,097	23.65	2	1,905	24.95	2	119	1.65
14	681	8.32	20	1,385	23.02	4	2,876	22.81	4	68	.54
Totals	38,969	22.16		50,544	28.75		52,971	30.13		5,120	2.91

E

Professionals

Circ.	Number	Percent
20	1,774	29.49
11	1,466	28.92
14	2,167	26.47
19	2,684	23.50
13	2,034	22.97
10	792	17.34
9	1,456	16.54
5	1,341	15.12
12	1,340	14.95
18	1,772	13.87
7	980	12.67
8	1,175	12.27
17	997	12.20
16	1,107	11.37
6	956	11.08
3	1,169	9.30
15	618	8.09
1	602	7.12
2	451	6.27
4	508	4.03
Totals	25,389	14.44

F

Various and Without Profession

Circ.	Number	Percent
14	79	9.70
16	285	2.92
17	204	2.50
5	203	2.29
1	172	2.03
15	153	2.00
11	91	1.80
19	184	1.61
18	201	1.57
7	119	1.54
4	189	1.50
6	127	1.47
2	105	1.46
3	182	1.45
10	61	1.34
12	118	1.32
9	109	1.23
8	110	1.15
20	58	.96
13	77	.86
Totals	2,827	1.60

G

Totals		Literate	
Circ.	Number	Circ.	Percent
1	8,458	14	99.4
2	7,196	11	99.1
3	12,564	20	98.9
4	12,604	19	98.6
5	8,868	10	98.2
6	8,631	13	98.1
7	7,737	12	97.7
8	9,576	9	97.6
9	8,802	5	97.4
10	4,567	8	97.1
11	5,069	18	96.6
12	8,961	17	96.4
13	8,853	6	96.3
14	8,186	7	96.3
15	7,635	3	95.8
16	9,739	16	95.5
17	8,170	15	93.2
18	12,769	1	92.1
19	11,419	2	90.4
20	6,016	4	89.1
Totals	175,820		

Note: One of the major difficulties I encountered in describing and analyzing elections in the federal capital between 1912 and 1930 was to discover an accurate profile of the social and economic status of the voting population as judged by occupation. Some information came from the national census of 1914, which, as column G indicates, described the high percentages of the electorate able to read and write and detailed this information by *circunscripción* for 1916. The census also listed Argentine males by occupation, but only for the capital as a whole, not for voting districts. Accordingly, the figures on occupation above come from the actual lists of registered voters in the capital for 1918. The source consulted was República Argentina, *Registro Cívico de la Nación: Padrón Definitivo de Electores: Distrito Electoral de la Capital: 1917–1918*, four volumes, located in the basement of the Palacio de Justicia, Buenos Aires.

The year 1918 was chosen as a compromise. A lack of resources and time prevented further investigation of other registry lists, which grew considerably in bulk and number of registered voters as the 1920s progressed. The 1918 volumes can be used to gauge the occupational composition of most districts from 1912 to 1924. In the late 1920s, however, the enormous growth of out-lying *circunscripciones* and a corresponding increase in the number of voters there make the 1918 figures somewhat less useful for certain areas, although probably still reasonably descriptive for more central districts.

Certain difficulties complicated the gathering of these statistics. First, they had to be compiled by hand, a laborious process involving the notation of over 175,000 persons by occupation. Therefore, some margin of error must be allowed for difficulties in transcription. Second, it should be observed that discrepancies exist for total figures in each *circunscripción* and those listed officially as registered for the capital deputy election of 1918. (See chapter 7.) These differences result in part from the problems involved in determining who was eliminated from the rolls before or after 1918. At any rate, the number of voters listed provides a fair and adequate sample.

Once the occupational lists were compiled, the next problem was to assign larger categories that would allow election analysis. No clear formula exists for such categorization and some arbitrariness was inevitable in grouping various occupations. The five categories selected grouped persons who have ex-hibited tendencies to vote in a similar manner and to share similar political interests. Assigning class designations, as described in the text, also demanded certain subjective and arbitrary judgments. Generally, category A was clearly working class, category B contained a mixture of working and middle class, category C middle class, and categories D and E upper class. Undoubtedly, however, many overlaps and variations exist within and between these groups. Moreover, the very titles themselves sometimes added to the ambiguity. For example, was an *escultor* an artist or a construction worker; an *empleado* simply a man who fetched coffee or a white-collar clerk in a business or bu-reaucratic office? Finally, designated occupation in the *Registro Cívico* was determined through self-identification. In status-conscious Buenos Aires many enrolling voters might have inflated the nature of their occupations, persons engaged in unskilled pursuits, for example, adopting more glorified titles in the face of officialdom.

With several hundred different occupations listed in the *Registro Cívico*, the following are examples of the most numerous for each category:

A. Manual Workers: aparador, armador, armero, aserrador, ayudante, cal-derero, camarero, capataz, carrero, cartero, cartonero, cepillero, cochero, cocinero, compositor, conductor, cortador, criador, chófer, empajador, escultor, estibador, frentista, fundidor, grabador, guarda, hornero, jar-dinero, jornalero, lechero, linotipista, litógrafo, lustrador, maquinista, marinero, marinero mercante, marino, marmolero, matarife, minervista, motorista, mozo, mucamo, obrero, ordenanza, peón, pescador, pintor, planchador, portero, sereno, sirviente, tipógrafo, tornero, yesero.

B. Artisans and Small Merchants: abastecedor, agente, albañil, almacenero, alpargatero, aprendiz, armero, barbero, broncero, cantinero, carnicero, carpintero, cigarrero, cobrador, comerciante, comercio, comisionista, con-fitero, constructor, curtidor, chocolatero, decorador, dorador, ebanista, electricista, encuadernador, farmacéutico, fotógrafo, gasista, gráfico, herrador, herrero, hojalatero, joyero, librero, martillero, mecánico, molinero, mosaísta, mueblero, músico, panadero, peinador, peluquero, platero, plomero, procurador, relojero, repartidor, sastre, sombrerero, talabartero, tallista, tapicero, tejedor, tintorero, tonelero, vendedor, vidriero, zapatero.

C. Employees: calígrafo, clasificador, comisario, dependiente, empleado, empleado de la aduana, empleado comercial, empleado del banco, empleado de los correos, empleado del Ministerio de la Agricultura, empleado del Ministerio del Interior, empleado municipal, empleado nacional, empleado de la policía, enfermero, escribano, letrista, taquigráfico, telefonista, telegrafista.

D. Owners: agricultor, cambista, contratista, consignatario, empresario, estanciero, fabricante, ganadero, hacendado, industrial, patrón, propietario, rentista.

E. Professionals: abogado, actor, agrimensor, agrónomo, arquitecto, artista, contador, corredor, dentista, dibujante, educacionista, eclesiástico, escritor, estudiante, ingeniero, juez, maestro, médico, militar, periodista, perito, profesor, químico, reporter, sacerdote, técnico, tenedor de libros, traductor, veterinario.

F. Various: aspirante, idóneo, inspector, jockey, jubilado, operador, sin profesión.

A point should be made with regard to category C. Within the *Registro Cívico* a number of registered voters clearly designated themselves as government employees, some referring to a particular ministry with which they were associated, others simply labeling themselves *empleado municipal* or *empleado nacional*. Unfortunately, however, the total number of this important group clearly designated reached only 2,898. The 1914 national census listed 33,775 Argentine males in the capital as *empleados de gobierno o administración*. Therefore, it must be assumed that the great majority of government employees identified themselves only as *empleados* in the *Registro*. The 1914 census also listed 14,313 Argentine males as *empleados* under the category of "General Designations," presumably representing private employees. Using the 1914 data, then, it can be estimated that roughly two out of every three voters listed in the 1918 *Registro* as *empleados* were in fact government or public employees, composing one of the largest and most important blocs of voters in the city.

Finally, it should be observed that the information here provides only an occupational profile of each voting district. In analyzing specific elections and results I have noted where particular parties have won or lost in areas that have certain characteristics. I have not argued that particular occupational groups have voted necessarily for particular parties, although the results often lead to that assumption. There is, of course, no way of knowing exactly which voters supported which parties. The data here presented, however, do represent the most accurate and clearest picture of the social-economic status of the voting population of the city of Buenos Aires by district collected to date, and the best that can be hoped for without survey material. Furthermore, they provide a more sophisticated and scientific profile than can be constructed from journalistic sources and impressionistic accounts.

APPENDIX B
POPULATION GROWTH OF THE CITY OF BUENOS AIRES, BY CIRCUNSCRIPCIÓN: 1904–1936

Circun-scripción	1904	1909	1914	1936
1	17,275	47,917	103,358	330,982
2	36,985	53,466	70,628	88,997
3	84,792	94,965	104,188	103,262
4	60,878	65,370	76,024	73,631
5	24,046	46,600	79,660	123,396
6	36,820	61,007	77,705	105,837
7	33,489	50,930	67,007	78,401
8	67,449	78,246	81,095	72,634
9	65,959	72,999	83,252	84,712
10	37,687	45,869	42,293	44,262
11	37,304	38,746	43,530	51,791
12	63,728	68,236	73,165	74,950
13	67,144	68,178	75,064	81,307
14	62,578	57,493	62,598	74,809
15	16,176	48,381	106,716	396,369
16	29,447	52,146	89,866	228,959
17	19,515	48,596	76,182	115,532
18	63,773	103,007	111,939	123,047
19	71,105	74,990	86,968	99,427
20	48,592	45,596	49,748	62,837
River	6,149	8,960	14,828	NA
Totals	950,891	1,231,698	1,575,814	2,415,142

Sources: *Censo general de población, 1904*, p. 78; *Censo general de población, 1909*, pp. xiv–xv; *Tercer censo nacional, 1914*, II, p. 3; and *Cuarto censo general, 1936*, II, pp. 12–129.

Notes

Abbreviations Used
BDNT   *Boletín del Departamento Nacional del Trabajo*
BUIA   *Boletín de la Unión Industrial Argentina*
Diputados   Congreso Nacional, *Diario de sesiones de la Cámara de Di-*
                putados
Fuerzas armadas Ministerio del Interior, Subsecretaría de Informaciones, *Las*
                fuerzas armadas restituyen el imperio de la soberanía po-
                pular: Las elecciones generales de 1946
HAHR   *Hispanic American Historical Review*
Memoria   *Memoria del Ministerio del Interior, presentada al Hono-*
                rable Congreso de la Nación
Senadores   Congreso Nacional, *Diario de sesiones de la Cámara de Se-*
                nadores
RACP   *Revista Argentina de Ciencias Políticas*

Preface

1. For an overview of the evolution of socialist organizations in Latin America, see Victor Alba, *Politics and the Labor Movement in Latin America*, pp. 60–117.

2. A review of this phenomenon, with an attempt at typology, is Robert J. Alexander, "The Emergence of Modern Political Parties in Latin America," in Peter G. Snow, ed., *Government and Politics in Latin America: A Reader*, pp. 385–403. A commentary on the paucity of political party studies and methodological problems in their study is John D. Martz, "Dilemmas in the Study of Latin American Political Parties," in ibid., pp. 403–418.

3. An attempt to place political party development in Latin America within a coherent theoretical framework is Robert E. Scott's "Political Parties and Policy-Making in Latin America," in Joseph La Palombara and Myron Weiner, eds., *Political Parties and Political Development*, pp. 331–366.

4. See Alba, *Politics and the Labor Movement in Latin America*, pp. 62–82; Robert J. Alexander, *Labor Parties of Latin America*, pp. 22–28, and the same author's *Latin American Political Parties*, pp. 107–122.

5. The standard study on the Argentine Socialist Party is Jacinto Oddone's two-volume *Historia del socialismo argentino*. Oddone, a Socialist activist for

more than half a century, concentrates primarily on the period 1890–1910. He provides considerable documentary information, but most of his analysis is from a partisan's perspective. A more recent effort, José Vazeilles's *Los Socialistas*, brings the study up to date but provides little original information, relying instead on lengthy excerpts from the writings of party leaders.

Chapter 1: Emergence: 1890–1895

1. The economic growth of nineteenth-century Argentina is described in more detail in James R. Scobie, *Argentina: A City and a Nation*, pp. 112–135. Statistical indicators of economic expansion can be found in Ernesto Tornquist and Company, *The Economic Development of the Argentine Republic in the Last Fifty Years*.

2. Figures compiled from República Argentina, *Segundo Censo de la República Argentina, Mayo 10 de 1895*, 1, 650.

3. Ibid., II, p. cl.

4. Ibid., p. 6.

5. For the role of Great Britain in Argentina's nineteenth-century economic life, see H. S. Ferns, *Britain and Argentina in the Nineteenth Century*.

6. See Scobie, *Argentina*, pp. 88–159.

7. Tornquist & Co., *Economic Development of the Argentine Republic*, pp. 139–140.

8. Jacinto Oddone, *La burguesía terrateniente argentina*.

9. For a review of the living conditions of the rural poor throughout Argentina, see Carl Solberg, "Farm Workers and the Myth of Export-Led Development in Argentina," *The Americas* 31, no. 2 (October 1974): 121–138.

10. For a review of these nineteenth-century political developments, see José Luis Romero, *A History of Argentine Political Thought*. For an excellent description and analysis of the "Generation of Eighty," see Thomas F. McGann, *Argentina, the United States, and the Inter-American System, 1880–1914*.

11. Ysabel Fisk Rennie, *The Argentine Republic*, pp. 176–181.

12. Peter G. Snow, *Argentine Radicalism: The History and Doctrine of the Radical Civic Union*, p. 9. David Rock's *Politics in Argentina, 1890–1930: The Rise and Fall of Radicalism*, which appeared after the present monograph was in press, provides the most satisfactory description and analysis of the evolution of Argentina's Radical Party yet published.

13. For a detailed description of these developments, see Luis V. Sommi, *La revolución del 90*.

14. Ismael Bucich Escobar, *Historia de los presidentes argentinos*, pp. 276–295.

15. Félix Luna, *Yrigoyen*, pp. 15–73.

16. Snow, *Argentine Radicalism*, p. 12.

17. Gabriel del Mazo, *El radicalismo: Ensayo sobre su historia y doctrina*, I, 312–316.

18. For a definition of political parties, with delineation of their characteristics, see La Palombara and Weiner, eds., *Political Parties*, p. 6, and Sigmund Neumann, *Modern Political Parties: Approaches to Comparative Politics*, pp. 395–396.

19. José Panettieri, *Los trabajadores en tiempos de la inmigración masiva*

en Argentina, 1870–1910, p. 35. One author noted that the average number of workers in capital industrial establishments in 1895 was 8, rose to 12 in 1908, and dropped again to 8 in 1913. Adolfo Dorfman, *Historia de la industria argentina,* p. 286.

20. A statement of the conservative position is Lucas Ayarragaray, *Socialismo argentino y legislación obrera.*

21. Adrián Patroni, *Los trabajadores en la Argentina,* p. 3. All translations from the Spanish are mine.

22. Hobart Spalding, *La clase trabajadora argentina: Documentos para su historia, 1890–1912,* pp. 34–38.

23. For an excellent review of living and working conditions in Buenos Aires at the turn of the century, see James R. Scobie, *Buenos Aires: Plaza to Suburb, 1870–1910,* especially chapter 4.

24. Spalding, *La clase trabajadora argentina,* p. 194.

25. Dardo Cúneo, *El primer periodismo obrero y socialista en la Argentina.*

26. Oddone, *Historia del socialismo argentino,* I, 196–197.

27. Emilio J. Corbiere, "Socialistas y anarquistas," *Polémica* 42 (Buenos Aires, 1971): 36.

28. Oddone, *Gremialismo proletario argentino,* pp. 26–39.

29. Ibid., pp. 48–51.

30. Ibid., pp. 53–57.

31. Ibid., pp. 67–69.

32. For an analysis of *El Obrero,* see José Ratzer, *Los marxistas argentinos del 90,* pp. 93–112.

33. Oddone, *Historia del socialismo,* I, 200–201.

34. Cúneo, *Primer periodismo,* pp. 45–49; and *La Vanguardia: Número del cincuentenario de su fundación* (1944), pp. 98–99.

35. Juan B. Justo, *Obras de Juan B. Justo: La realización del socialismo,* p. 318.

36. Ibid., p. 273.

37. Justo was one of the few Argentines at the turn of the century to have studied Marx. Most Argentine socialists, like Justo originally, became converts without having read Marx. Luis Pan, *Justo y Marx: El socialismo en la Argentina,* pp. 130–131.

38. Much of the biographical information on Justo has been taken from Dardo Cúneo, *Juan B. Justo,* pp. 21–122.

39. See Leopoldo Zea, *Dos etapas del pensamiento en Hispanoamérica: Del romanticismo al positivismo,* p. 293.

40. Justo, *Obras,* pp. 25–26.

41. Oddone, *Historia del socialismo,* I, 230.

42. Ibid., pp. 233–234.

Chapter 2: Organization and Recruitment: 1895–1900

1. *La Vanguardia* (Buenos Aires, May 9, 1896), p. 1. At this time Argentine citizenship was not a requirement for membership in the party, but it was required for holding party office.

2. Jacinto Oddone, *Historia del socialismo argentino,* I, 265–266.

3. The entire minimum program is noted in ibid., pp. 270–271.

4. Ibid., pp. 271–277. The original statutes, plus later modifications, can be found in Pedro A. Verde Tello, *El partido socialista: Su actual forma de organización*.

5. *La Vanguardia* (March 7, 1896), p. 1.

6. Oddone, *Historia del socialismo*, I, 258–260.

7. *La Vanguardia* (March 14, 1896), p. 1.

8. *La Vanguardia* (March 10, 1900), p. 1.

9. *La Vanguardia* (March 17, 1900), p. 1.

10. Juan B. Justo, *Internacionalismo y patria*, pp. 216–217.

11. For more information, see Gino Germani, "Mass Immigration and Modernization in Argentina," in Irving Louis Horowitz et al., eds., *Latin American Radicalism: A Documentary Report on Left and Nationalist Movements*, pp. 341–342 and passim.

12. República Argentina, *Segundo censo*, II, cvii.

13. República Argentina, *Censo general de población, edificación, comercio e industrias de la Ciudad de Buenos Aires, levantado en los días 16 al 24 de Octubre de 1909*, pp. xxxi–xxxii.

14. S. Fanny Simon, "Anarchism and Anarcho-Syndicalism in South America," *HAHR* 26, no. 1 (February 1946): 39.

15. Jorge Larroca, "Un anarquista en Buenos Aires," *Todo es Historia* 4, no. 47 (Buenos Aires, March 1971): 45–57.

16. Diego Abad de Santillán, *La F.O.R.A.: Ideología y trayectoria del movimiento obrero revolucionario en la Argentina*, pp. 59–75.

17. Information from José Elías Niklison, "Acción social católica obrera," *BDNT* 46 (March 1920): 15–286.

18. Grote summarized his objections to socialism in *El socialismo: Breve exposición y crítica de sus doctrinas economicas y morales*.

19. For biographical information on these three men, see Sergio Bagú, *Vida ejemplar de José Ingenieros: Juventud y plenitud*; Mario Bravo, "Leopoldo Lugones en el movimiento socialista (1896–1897)," *Nosotros* 2, no. 26–28 (May-July 1938): 27–47; and Raúl Larra, *Roberto J. Payró: El novelista de la democracia*.

20. *La Montaña* (July 1, 1897), p. 5.

21. Enrique Dickmann, *Recuerdos de un militante socialista*, p. 66.

22. For example, E. Dickmann, *Ideas e ideales*.

23. Nicolás Repetto, *Mi paso por la medicina*, p. 11.

24. Repetto, *Mis noventa años: Escritos e intervenciones parlamentarias*, p. 248.

25. Repetto, *Mi paso por la medicina*, p. 278.

26. Repetto, *Mi paso por la política: De Roca a Yrigoyen*, p. 31.

27. E. Dickmann, *Recuerdos*, p. 101.

28. *La Vanguardia* (September 5, 1896), p. 1.

29. Juan B. Justo, *Obras de Juan B. Justo: La realización del socialismo*, p. 33.

30. Adolfo Dickmann, *Los congresos socialistas: 40 años de la acción democrática*, p. 12.

31. John H. Williams, *Argentine International Trade Under Inconvertible Paper Money, 1800–1900*, pp. 148–162.

32. A collection of Justo's writings on monetary problems is his *La moneda*.

33. *El Diario del Pueblo* (October 1, 1899) p. 1.
34. *El Diario del Pueblo* (November 8, 1899), p. 1.

Chapter 3: Repression and Growth: 1900–1910
1. Carl Solberg, *Immigration and Nationalism: Argentina and Chile, 1890–1914*, pp. 109–110.
2. The full text of the Social Defense law is in Jacinto Oddone, *Historia del socialismo*, II, 82–87. The major provisions of the laws of Residence and Social Defense remained in effect until the presidency of Arturo Frondizi (1958–1962).
3. Ismael Bucich Escobar, *Buenos Aires Ciudad*, p. 247.
4. República Argentina, *Memoria, 1912–1913* (1913), pp. 222–227.
5. Oddone, *Historia del socialismo*, I, 169.
6. Ibid., II, 15.
7. *La Vanguardia* (May 7, 1904), p. 2.
8. *La Vanguardia* (November 19, 1904), p. 1.
9. *La Vanguardia* (December 1, 1904), p. 1.
10. Ricardo Caballero, *Yrigoyen: La conspiración civil y militar del 4 de febrero de 1905*, pp. 7–137.
11. *La Vanguardia* (February 11, 1905), p. 1.
12. *BDNT* 9 (June 30, 1909): 295–300.
13. For more information on this strike, see Oddone, *Historia del socialismo*, II, 47–71.
14. *La Vanguardia* (January 14, 1910), p. 1.
15. *La Vanguardia* (January 24 and 25, 1910), p. 1.
16. *La Vanguardia* (September 30, 1910), p. 1.
17. Sebastián Marotta, *El movimiento sindical argentino, 1857–1907*, I, 103–117.
18. Oddone, *Gremialismo proletario argentino*, p. 95.
19. Diego Abad de Santillán, *La F.O.R.A.*, pp. 153–154.
20. Oddone, *Gremialismo*, p. 127.
21. Marotta, *El movimiento sindical*, I, 211.
22. Ibid., pp. 278–281.
23. Oddone, *Gremialismo*, p. 188.
24. Marotta, *El movimiento sindical*, II, 53.
25. Abad de Santillán, *La F.O.R.A.*, p. 118.
26. Oddone, *Historia del socialismo*, II, 151–152.
27. *BDNT* 5 (June 30, 1908) : 254.
28. *BDNT* 3 (December 31, 1907) : 374–375.
29. Hobart Spalding, *La clase trabajadora argentina*, pp. 88–89.
30. Enrique Dickmann, *Recuerdos de un militante socialista*, p. 204.
31. Adolfo Dickmann, *Los congresos socialistas: 40 años de la acción democrática*, pp. 13–20.
32. Mario Bravo, "Organización, programa y desarrollo del Partido Socialista en la Argentina," *RACP* 10 (1915): 119–150.
33. José P. Baliño, "El socialismo en la provincia de Buenos Aires," in Partido Socialista, *Almanaque del Trabajo* (1918), p. 148.
34. Benito Marianetti, *Las luchas sociales en Mendoza*, pp. 11–53; Ramón

Morey, "El Partido Socialista en Mendoza," in Partido Socialista, *Almanaque del trabajo* (1919), pp. 153–159.

35. Oddone, *Historia del socialismo*, II, 321–352.

36. Dardo Cúneo, *Juan B. Justo*, pp. 185–191.

37. A. Dickmann, *Los congresos socialistas*, pp. 13–14.

38. Bravo, "Mi primer contacto con el movimiento socialista," *La Vanguardia: Número del cincuentenario de su fundación* (1944), p. 127.

39. Juan Antonio Solari, *Mario Bravo: El político, el poeta, el hombre*.

40. William Belmont Parker, *Argentines of To-Day*, I, 315–316.

41. Carmelo M. Bonet, "El Diputado Antonio de Tomaso," *Nosotros* 8, no. 60 (April 1914): 97–100.

42. Biographical information from various editions of *La Vanguardia*.

43. Spalding, *La clase trabajadora argentina*, p. 74.

44. *La Vanguardia* (June 24, 1905), p. 3.

45. Oddone, *Historia del socialismo*, II, 206–208.

46. *La Vanguardia* (March 19, 1904), p. 1.

47. *La Vanguardia* (July 22, 1905), p. 2.

48. The specific planks of the 1910 platform were: 1) proportional representation of minority parties; 2) elected municipal government based on universal suffrage; 3) employer responsibility for on-the-job accidents; 4) reduction of taxes that increase the price of consumables, and progressive taxation on income derived from land ownership; 5) abrogation of the Residence Law; 6) abrogation of obligatory military service and creation of a citizens' militia; 7) separation of church and state; 8) work inspection; and 9) abolition of the death penalty. *La Vanguardia* (February 3, 1910), p. 1.

49. Ferri's remarks and Justo's response can be found in Justo, *Obras*, pp. 236–249.

50. For a summary of the Argentine nationalist reaction to foreign immigration, see Solberg, *Immigration and Nationalism*, pp. 132–157.

51. Justo, *Internacionalismo y patria*, pp. 233–237.

52. This position was forcefully stated in a party manifesto in response to a government charge that the May 1909 general strike in Buenos Aires was largely foreign-inspired. The manifesto was printed in the *Revista Socialista Internacional* 1, no. 6 (May 1909): 437–438.

53. These responses appeared in *Revista Socialista Internacional*, June 15, 1909, pp. 29–39; July 14–15, 1909, pp. 77–81; August 15, 1909, pp. 152–154; and October 15, 1909, pp. 278–280.

Chapter 4: Palacios: 1904–1908

1. República Argentina, Ministerio del Interior, *Boletín Demográfico Argentino* 5, no. 11 (January–July 1904): 19–26.

2. *Memoria, 1901–1904* (1904), pp. 97–98.

3. *Boletín Demográfico Argentino* 5, no. 11: 25.

4. Carlos Ibarguren, *La historia que he vivido*, p. 137. Following the Radical revolt of 1905, highlighting the conservatives' failure to accommodate the opposition or to bring them into the political process, President Figueroa Alcorta introduced legislation to annul the *circunscripcional* reform and return to the *lista completa*. Congress approved this legislation and temporarily halted the thrust for political change within conservative ranks.

5. Alfredo L. Palacios, *La miseria en la República Argentina*.

6. Palacios, "Socialismo ético," *Cuadernos Americanos* 17, no. 4–5 (July-October 1958): 201.

7. Palacios, *El nuevo derecho*, p. 175.

8. Ramón Columba, *El congreso que yo he visto*, I, 124.

9. República Argentina, *Censo general de población, edificación, comercio e industrias de la ciudad de Buenos Aires, levantado en los días 11 y 18 de setiembre de 1904*, p. 105.

10. *La Luz* (February 24, 1904), p. 2.

11. *La Prensa* (March 14, 1904), p. 5.

12. *Memoria, 1927–1928* (1928), pp. 65–73.

13. *Diputados*, I (May 9, 1904), 57–59. In making this motion Palacios invoked Article 63 of the Argentine Constitution, which states that "each one of the legislative bodies can call to their chambers the ministers of the chief executive to receive explanations and reports which they deem necessary." The Socialists in Congress often resorted to the device of interpellation, not only to gain information but also to force public confrontation between themselves and the executive branch. The right to interpellation was considered a vital congressional prerogative, especially in a governmental system where the preponderate authority rested with the executive. Accordingly, most deputies were reluctant to deny the right of interpellation even when it might embarrass the administration with which they were connected.

14. *Diputados*, I (May 9, 1904), 60–61.

15. *Diputados*, I (May 11, 1904), 149–164.

16. *Diputados*, I (May 27, 1904), 195–198.

17. *Diputados*, I (July 29, 1904), 572.

18. *Diputados*, III (October 7, 1905), 383–401.

19. See Hobart Spalding, *Argentine Sociology from the End of the Nineteenth Century to World War One*.

20. See Alvaro Yunque, *La literatura social en la Argentina*.

21. These plays were consulted in the Biblioteca de la Sociedad de Autores Argentinos in Buenos Aires.

22. Juan Bialet Massé, *El estado de las clases obreras argentinas a comienzos del siglo*.

23. The full text of the 1904 proposal can be found as an appendix to the first volume of *Diputados* for 1904.

24. *Diputados*, I (May 9, 1904), 65.

25. *Memoria, 1901–1904*, pp. 104–105.

26. Jacinto Oddone, *Historia del socialismo argentino*, II, 229.

27. José Ingenieros, *Sociología argentina*, p. 248.

28. *La Vanguardia* (August 13, 1904), p. 1.

29. Américo R. Guerrero, *La industria argentina: Su origen, organización y desarrollo*, pp. 109–110.

30. *BUIA* 18, no. 432 (December 15, 1904): 1–3.

31. *BUIA* 18, no. 431 (November 15, 1904): 1–2.

32. *BUIA* 19, no. 436 (April 15, 1905): 1–4.

33. *Diputados*, II (September 30, 1904), 621–628.

34. *BUIA* 19 (May 15, 1905): 1–4.

35. Palacios, *La justicia social*, pp. 188–189.

36. Ibid., p. 190.

37. *Diputados*, I (September 7, 1906), 788–789.
38. Guerrero, *La industria argentina*, p. 147.
39. Palacios, *La justicia social*, pp. 214–215.
40. Palacios, *Por las mujeres y los niños que trabajan*, p. 57.
41. Palacios, *La justicia social*, pp. 217–219.
42. *La Prensa* (March 10, 1908), p. 9.
43. *Diputados*, I (July 31, 1907), 645–651; ibid. (August 2, 1907), 653–665.
44. *La Vanguardia* (May 14, 1904), p. 2.

Chapter 5: Reform: 1910–1913

1. For more biographical information, see Fermín V. Arenas Luque, *Roque Sáenz Peña: El presidente del sufragio libre*, and Paul Groussac, "Roque Sáenz Peña," in Unión Nacional, *Sáenz Peña: La campaña política de 1910*, pp. 95–132.
2. Roque Sáenz Peña, *La reforma electoral y temas de política internacional americana*, pp. 42–63.
3. *La Prensa* (March 14, 1910), p. 9.
4. The complete texts of these laws are reproduced in *Fuerzas armadas*, I, 10–16.
5. Ibid., pp. 1–324.
6. *Diputados*, V (1911), 266–282.
7. Miguel Angel Cárcano, *Sáenz Peña: La revolución por los comicios*, pp. 210–213.
8. *La Vanguardia* (March 4 and 5, 1912), p. 1.
9. *La Vanguardia* (April 2, 1912), p. 1.
10. Cárcano, *Sáenz Peña*, pp. 213–214.
11. *Memoria, 1911–1912* (1912), p. 63.
12. *Memoria, 1927–1928* (1928), pp. 65–73.
13. Enrique Dickmann, *Recuerdos de un militante socialista*, p. 249.
14. *La Prensa* (April 21, 1912), p. 11.
15. *La Prensa* (April 23, 1912), p. 12.
16. The class composition of the electorate of Buenos Aires's twenty *circunscripciones* is based on an analysis of the occupations of the city's voters according to the 1918 Civic Registry. It has been listed once in an appendix rather than repeated for each election. For the details of this analysis, see Appendix A. For a review of the capital's class structure and location before 1912, see James R. Scobie, *Buenos Aires: Plaza to Suburb, 1870–1910*.
17. Dardo Cúneo, *Juan B. Justo*, p. 236.
18. After elections, the Chamber of Deputies reviewed the electoral process in each district and then voted whether to approve the entrance (*diploma*) of elected representatives. This was usually the first order of business for each new session.
19. *Diputados*, I (May 31, 1912), 74–78.
20. *Diputados*, I (June 19, 1912), 265–273.
21. *Diputados*, I (June 21, 1912), 319–321.
22. *Diputados*, I (July 22, 1912), 648–657.
23. *Diputados*, III (March 7, 1913), 768–786.
24. Palacios, *Por las mujeres*, pp. 141–233.
25. *La Prensa* (April 8, 1913), p. 13.

26. *La Prensa* (April 9, 1913), p. 9.

27. Sáenz Peña, *La reforma electoral*, pp. 120–129.

28. Quoted in Carl Solberg, *Immigration and Nationalism: Argentina and Chile, 1890–1914*, p. 126.

29. José Camilo Crotto, whose own parents were second-generation Argentines of Italian descent, was a successful businessman and lawyer. Active in the Radical movement in the 1890s, in 1907 he became chairman of the party's national committee. A close friend of Yrigoyen, he was elected senator in 1912 and governor of Buenos Aires province in 1918. William Belmont Parker, ed., *Argentines of Today*, II, 560–562.

30. The Crotto-Del Valle Iberlucea exchange can be found in *Senadores*, I (April 29, 1913), 18–49.

31. *Diputados*, I (May 15, 1913), 185.

32. *Diputados*, I (May 17, 1913), 247–285.

33. *Diputados*, I (May 29, 1913), 598. Names and affiliations of congressmen to determine· roll call alignments were taken from *Fuerzas armadas*, I, 340–437.

34. *Diputados*, I (May 20, 1913), 326–327.

35. *Diputados*, I (June 2, 1913), 755–779.

36. *Diputados*, II (August 6, 1913), 793–805.

37. *Diputados*, II (July 2, 1913), 390–392.

38. *Diputados*, III (September 3, 1913), 28–30.

39. *Diputados*, III (September 15, 1913), 256–264.

40. *Diputados*, III (September 26, 1913), 543–559.

41. *Diputados*, II (July 2, 1913), 432–436.

42. *Diputados*, II (August 20, 1913), 959–965. For information on the Argentine meat industry and its political power, see Peter H. Smith, *Politics and Beef in Argentina: Patterns of Conflict and Change*, pp. 32–81. The sugar industry, located in the northern provinces, although not as powerful as the meat interests, nevertheless had sufficient political influence to gain special tariff protection in 1912 and to enjoy special attention for its high cost production. Solberg, "The Tariff and Politics in Argentina, 1916–1930," *HAHR* 53, no. 2 (May 1973): 267–268.

43. *Diputados*, III (September 17, 1913), 323.

44. Quoted in Arenas Luque, *Roque Sáenz Peña*, p. 282.

Chapter 6: Elections, Congress, and the 'Palacios Affair': 1914–1915

1. The candidates, with their occupational background, were Mario Bravo (lawyer), Francisco Cúneo (mechanic-inventor), Enrique Dickmann (doctor), Angel Giménez (doctor), Nicolás Repetto (doctor), Antonio de Tomaso (lawyer), and Antonio Zaccagnini (journalist).

2. *La Vanguardia* (March 22, 1914), p. 2.

3. *Fuerzas armadas*, I, 358.

4. *Diputados*, I (June 3, 1914), 569–576.

5. *Diputados*, I (June 5, 1914), 618.

6. After debate and compromise a compensation of 2,000 pesos for each family was approved. *Diputados*, VII (1914–1915), 664.

7. *Diputados*, III (August 19, 1914), 802–805.

8. *Diputados*, IV (September 4, 1914), 52–53.

9. *Diputados*, III (August 5, 1914), 500.

10. *Diputados*, IV (September 30, 1914), 1,140–1,194.

11. *Diputados*, IV (September 4, 1914), 58–72.

12. Juan B. Justo, *Internacionalismo y patria*, pp. 187–188.

13. Ibid., pp. 239–240.

14. Nicolás Repetto, *Mi paso por la política*, p. 166. In a 1971 interview in Buenos Aires, former Socialist Deputy Américo Ghioldi told me that in these caucuses individuals generally agreed on subjects to present. Deputies could take an independent stand if they so desired, but such instances were rare. Interview, Américo Ghioldi, Buenos Aires, March 17, 1971.

15. *Diputados*, I (June 9, 1915), 397.

16. *Diputados*, I (June 21, 1915), 591.

17. *Diputados*, II (August 6, 1915), 487–499.

18. *Diputados*, III (September 3, 1915), 172–175.

19. *Diputados*, III (September 10, 1915), 287.

20. *Diputados*, III (September 25, 1915), 555–561. It should be noted that this legislation, like many social measures of the period, was limited in scope and infrequently enforced in practice.

21. *La Vanguardia* (April 2, 1912), pp. 1–2.

22. *La Vanguardia* (January 2–3, 1914), p. 1.

23. *La Vanguardia* (March 12, 1914), p. 1. Radicals were well represented in the Sociedad Rural Argentina. In 1918, for example, of the fourteen deputies who belonged to the Sociedad, eleven were Radicals and three were conservatives. The list of Sociedad members from which this information was taken is "Nómina de socios," in *Anales de la Sociedad Rural Argentina* 52 (February 1918): 116–134. I am indebted to Professor Carl Solberg of the University of Washington for bringing this list to my attention and supplying me with a copy.

24. *RACP* 10 (1915): 119–190.

25. Ibid.: 329–385.

26. Information on the PDP is from Carlos Ibarguren, *La historia que he vivido*, pp. 282–286; Raúl Larra, *Lisandro de la Torre: El solitario de Pinas*; and *RACP* 1 (1910): 76–95.

27. For comparison with the 1895 data, see chapter 1, table 2.

28. These developments are treated in more detail in Diego Abad de Santillán, *La F.O.R.A.*, pp. 207–254; Martín S. Casaretto, *Historia del movimiento obrero argentino*, pp. 116–122; Sebastián Marotta, *El movimiento sindical argentino: Su génesis y desarrollo*, II, 87–198; and Jacinto Oddone, *Gremialismo proletario argentino*, pp. 247–258.

29. *BDNT* 35 (December 1917): 64.

30. *La Vanguardia* (January 20 and 30, 1912), p. 1.

31. *La Vanguardia* (January 22 and 23, 1912), p. 1.

32. *La Organización Obrera* 3 (November 1915): 1.

33. For a review of the tenants' position, the development of the 1912 strike, and subsequent strike action in the farm belt of Argentina, see Solberg, "Rural Unrest and Agrarian Policy in Argentina, 1912–1930," *Journal of Inter-American Studies and World Affairs* 13, no. 1 (January 1971): 18–52.

34. *La Vanguardia* (July 12, 1912), p. 1.

35. *Diputados*, I (July 29, 1912), 828–837.

36. Solberg, "Rural Unrest," p. 29.

37. Mario Bravo, "Organización, programa y desarrollo del Partido Socialista in la Argentina," *RACP* 10 (1915): 132.

38. José P. Baliño, "El socialismo en la Provincia de Buenos Aires," Partido Socialista, *Almanaque de Trabajo* (1915), p. 153.

39. Ramón Morey, "El Partido Socialista en Mendoza," in Partido Socialista, *Almanaque del Trabajo* (1919), pp. 153–159.

40. Darío Cantón, *Materiales para el estudio de la sociología política en la Argentina*, II, 28.

41. *RACP* 10 (1915): 203–204.

42. Cantón, *Materiales*, I, 83.

43. *Humanidad Nueva* 4, no. 2 (1911): 148.

44. *La Vanguardia* (November 14, 1912), p. 2.

45. These were reprinted with relish by the Unión Industrial Argentina. *BUIA* 27, no. 540 (December 15, 1913): 1–3. Ugarte continued a career as essayist and journalist, best known for his nationalist pleas to Latin American nations to unite on the common base of their Iberian background to resist the cultural, diplomatic, and economic imperialism of the United States.

46. *La Vanguardia* (May 23 and 26, 1914), p. 3.

47. Adolfo Dickmann, *Los congresos socialistas*, pp. 21–23.

48. *La Vanguardia* (July 10, 1915), pp. 1–2.

49. Reprinted in Palacios, *La justicia social*, pp. 302–303.

50. Jaime Kanner, "Perfiles y figuras: Justo y Palacios," *Crítica Socialista* 1, no. 5 (September 1, 1915): 4–5.

51. Enrique Dickmann, *Democracia y socialismo*, pp. 119–134.

52. *La Vanguardia* (June 15, 1915), p. 3.

53. *La Acción: Organo del Partido Socialista Argentino* (November 17, 1915), p. 2.

54. *La Acción* (January 19, 1916), pp. 3–4.

55. Following his separation from the Socialist Party, Palacios remained active as leader of the PSA until the demise of that party in the early 1920s. Thereafter, he continued as an important public figure, helping in 1925 to form the Unión Latinoamericana, an organization that sought continental solidarity against the threat of North American imperialism. In the latter part of the decade Palacios became Dean of the Faculty of Law at the University of Buenos Aires. Throughout this period he wrote extensively on social and economic problems and in 1931 he rejoined the Socialist Party.

Chapter 7: Yrigoyen, War, and Labor: 1916–1919

1. *La Vanguardia* (February 7, 1916), p. 1; and (March 2, 1916), p. 3.

2. *La Vanguardia* (March 24, 1916), p. 1.

3. Biographical information from Diego Abad de Santillán, *Gran enciclopedia argentina*; William Belmont Parker, ed., *Argentines of Today*; and "Nómina de socios," *Anales de la Sociedad Rural Argentina* 52 (February 1918): 116–134.

4. *La Prensa* (April 3, 1916), p. 9.

5. *La Prensa* (April 14, 1916), p. 11.

6. Ibid.

7. Ibid.

8. The attack is described in more detail in Dardo Cúneo, *Juan B. Justo*,

pp. 269–274. An official investigation of the incident produced no clues as to the identity or motive of Justo's assailant other than the supposition that he was "a subject with some mental imperfection, stirred by other disturbing factors, such as the ambiance or mistaken ideas of the social action of the victim." *Diputados,* IV (January 13, 1917), 3,595.

9. *Diputados,* IV (December 15, 1916), 2,812–2,832.

10. Tornquist and Company, *The Economic Development of the Argentine Republic in the Last Fifty Years,* p. 140.

11. Ibid., pp. 267–269.

12. Guido Di Tella and Manuel Zymelman, *Las etapas del desarrollo económico argentino,* p. 317.

13. Carl Solberg, "The Tariff and Politics in Argentina," *HAHR* 53, no. 2 (May 1973): 265.

14. *Diputados,* V (February 5, 1917), 4,826–4,836.

15. Ismael Bucich Escobar, *Historia de los presidentes argentinos,* p. 496.

16. Juan B. Justo detailed the Socialist position on provincial interventions in *Diputados,* I (May 29, 1917), 332–341.

17. *Diputados,* I (June 6, 1917), 578.

18. Cúneo's initial proposal can be found in *Diputados,* II (June 15, 1917), 90–91. Law 10,342, permitting "duty-free importation of fresh meat and on-the-hoof beef," is in *Diputados,* VIII (1917–1918), 760–761.

19. *Diputados,* II (June 20, 1917), 152–154.

20. The export tax law submitted by the Yrigoyen administration, although criticized in its particulars, received Socialist support in general. Juan B. Justo, a member of the committee that considered the proposal, noted: "We are going to vote for it in general; we believe that it can be an indirect procedure to achieve a direct and legitimate contribution." *Diputados,* VII (January 3, 1918), 676.

21. Enrique del Valle Iberlucea, *La cuestión internacional y el Partido Socialista,* p. 102.

22. Adolfo Dickmann, *Los congresos socialistas,* pp. 69–71; and *La Vanguardia* (April 29 and 30, 1917).

23. *Diputados,* V (September 11, 1917), 29–42.

24. *Diputados,* V (September 21, 1917), 646.

25. *Diputados,* VI (September 22, 1917), 76–80.

26. *Diputados,* VI (September 24, 1917), 153.

27. *Senadores,* II (September 19, 1917), 962–1,006.

28. *La Internacional: Periódica Socialista Quincenal* (November 30, 1917), p. 1.

29. *La Internacional* (January 23, 1918), p. 5.

30. The UCR slate was composed of Rogelio P. Araya, Carlos A. Becú, Francisco Beiró, Jacinto Fernández, Andrés Ferreyra, Tomás A. Le Bretón, and José Tamborini.

31. Mario Bravo, Francisco Cúneo, Adolfo Dickmann, Angel M. Giménez, Nicolás Repetto, Antonio de Tomaso, and Antonio Zaccagnini made up the Socialist ticket.

32. *La Vanguardia* (January 21, 1918), p. 1.

33. *La Vanguardia* (January 30, 1918), p. 1.

34. *La Vanguardia* (February 9, 1918), p. 1.

35. *La Vanguardia* (February 24, 1918), p. 3.

36. *La Prensa* (March 23, 1918), p. 8.
37. *La Vanguardia* (March 19, 1918), p. 1.
38. Solberg, "The Tariff and Politics," p. 268.
39. *Fuerzas armadas*, I, 376–377.
40. Alfredo L. Palacios, *El nuevo derecho*, p. 190.
41. José Elías Niklison, "La Federación Obrera Regional Argentina," *BDNT* 41 (April 1919): 9–128.
42. Ibid.
43. Martín S. Casaretto, *Historia del movimiento obrero argentino*, pp. 143–163; and Sebastián Marotta, *El movimiento sindical argentino: Su génesis y desarrollo*, II, 207–212. For comments on Yrigoyen's political reasons for settling the strikes as he did, see Winthrop R. Wright, *British-Owned Railways in Argentina: Their Effect on Economic Nationalism, 1854–1948*, pp. 116–120.
44. *La Organización Obrera* 1, no. 20 (January 9, 1918): 1–3.
45. Marotta, *El movimiento sindical*, II, 213.
46. Peter H. Smith, *Politics and Beef in Argentina: Patterns of Conflict and Change*, pp. 71–73.
47. *La Vanguardia* (January 31, 1918), p. 1.
48. *La Organización Obrera* 1, no. 3 (November 1915): 2.
49. This very complicated series of events is described in Niklison, "La Federación Obrera Regional Argentina," passim.
50. *La Organización Obrera* 2, no. 65 (January 23, 1919): 1.
51. Marysa Navarro Gerassi, *Los nacionalistas*, pp. 37–53.
52. Reports of attacks on the Jewish community can be found in *La Prensa* (January 15, 1919).
53. For a description of these events, see Samuel L. Baily, *Labor, Nationalism, and Politics in Argentina*, pp. 36–39.
54. *Diputados*, V (January 14, 1919), 128.
55. Ibid., pp. 137–142.
56. Ibid., pp. 164–165.
57. *Senadores*, II (January 30, 1919), 78–84.
58. *Diputados*, V (January 14, 1919), 139.

Chapter 8: Socialists and Radicals after the "Semana Trágica": 1919–1921

1. *Memoria, 1918–1919* (1919), p. 22. It should also be noted that divisions within the Radical Party in the capital, surfacing in late 1918, also contributed to the UCR loss to the Socialists in March 1919. In municipal elections of October 1918 the Socialists had edged the Radicals by 825 votes. This loss prompted an investigation by the UCR into the state of the electorate and the party in the capital, an investigation that detailed growing differences within Radical ranks at this time, differences that by 1924 would split the UCR into two opposing camps. See *RACP* 17 (1918): 484–487 for the report of the investigating committee.
2. *BDNT* 45 (February 1920): 51.
3. Sebastián Marotta, *El movimiento sindical argentino: Su génesis y desarrollo*, II, 267–268.
4. *La Organización Obrera* 2, no. 87 (June 5, 1919): 2.

5. *La Organización Obrera* 2, no. 92 (August 9, 1919): 1. The three measures ultimately were not approved.

6. *Diputados*, I (June 10, 1919), 427–443.

7. *Diputados*, I (May 28, 1919), 146–155; and *Diputados*, I (June 3, 1919), 297–333.

8. *Diputados*, IV (September 8, 1919), 314–325.

9. *La Vanguardia* (February 11, 1920), p. 1.

10. *La Vanguardia* (February 29, 1920), p. 1.

11. *La Epoca* (February 9, 1920), p. 3.

12. *La Epoca* (February 25, 1920), p. 3.

13. *La Epoca* (March 3, 1920), p. 3.

14. *La Prensa* (March 19, 1920), p. 10.

15. The ten members of the Socialist delegation were Mario Bravo, Juan B. Justo, Federico Pinedo, Antonio de Tomaso, Nicolás Repetto, Augusto Bunge, Enrique Dickmann, Fernando de Andreis, Agustín Muzio, and Héctor González Iramain.

16. Nicolás Repetto, *Mi paso por la política*, pp. 227–230; and *Diputados*, VII (April 27, 1921), 802–803.

17. Yrigoyen's messages and legislative proposals concerning petroleum can be found in a collection of the Radical president's writings: Hipólito Yrigoyen, *Pueblo y gobierno*, XII, 7–45.

18. James E. Buchanan, "Politics and Petroleum Development in Argentina, 1916–1930," pp. 36–128.

19. *Diputados*, IV (August 24, 1920), 452–463; *Diputados*, II (July 20, 1922), 217–226; and *Diputados*, II (July 26, 1922), 367–396.

20. *Diputados*, IV (September 22, 1921), 201–235.

21. *Diputados*, I (June 8, 1921), 343–406.

22. Félix Luna, *Yrigoyen*, p. 260.

23. *Diputados*, IV (September 20, 1922), 166–177.

24. For more detailed information about the strikes in Santa Cruz, see the first-hand account by José María Borrero, *La Patagonia trágica*. A recent and extensive treatment is Osvaldo Bayer, *Los vengadores de la Patagonia trágica*.

25. *Diputados*, V (February 1, 1922), 54–62.

26. *La Organización Obrera* 4, no. 150 (September 25, 1920): 1–2.

27. Marotta, *El movimiento sindical*, III, 20–22.

28. *La Organización Obrera* 4, no. 197 (September 3, 1921): 1–2.

29. *La Organización Obrera* 4, no. 169 (February 19, 1921): 3.

30. Diego Abad de Santillán, *La F.O.R.A.*, p. 279.

31. *La Vanguardia* (June 14, 1916), p. 5.

32. Partido Socialista, *Anuario Socialista: Año 1930*, p. 70.

33. Darío Cantón, *Materiales para el estudio de la sociología política en la Argentina*, I, 85–89.

34. Jacinto Oddone, *Un año de intendencia municipal: Recuerdos anécdotas*, pp. 8–15.

35. *La Vanguardia* (January 1, 1920), pp. 8–9; ibid. (January 2 and 3, 1920), p. 5.

36. *La Vanguardia* (November 1, 1918), p. 1.

37. For more information on the role of the Socialist Party in Buenos Aires city government, see my "Municipal Politics and Government in Buenos

Aires: 1918–1930," *Journal of Inter-American Studies and World Affairs* 16, no. 2 (May 1974): 173–197.

38. Juan B. Justo, *Internacionalismo y patria*, pp. 15–49.

39. *Germinal* 2, no. 3 (January 1921): 74–81.

40. *Democracia Socialista* 1, no. 1 (November 5, 1920): 3.

41. Justo, *Internacionalismo y patria*, pp. 52–64.

42. De Tomaso made a detailed critique of the Russian Revolution and the Third International in "El Bolshevikismo," *Almanaque del Trabajo* (1921), pp. 111–213.

43. Enrique del Valle Iberlucea, *La revolución rusa.*

44. *La Vanguardia* (January 10, 1921), p. 4.

45. *La Vanguardia* (January 11, 1921), pp. 1–2.

46. The debates on del Valle Iberlucea's actions in Bahía Blanca and the charges brought against him are in *Senadores*, I (July 19, 1921), (July 25, 1921), and (July 26, 1921).

Chapter 9: Socialists and the Alvear Administration: 1922–1927

1. *La Epoca* (March 20, 1922), p. 5.

2. *La Vanguardia* (February 5, 1922), p. 1.

3. *La Vanguardia* (March 14, 1922), p. 1.

4. *La Vanguardia* (January 1, 1922), p. 1.

5. *RACP* 12 (June 12, 1922): 227–229.

6. *La Prensa* (April 21, 1922), p. 10.

7. The Socialist deputies were Fernando de Andreis, Augusto Bunge, Adolfo Dickmann, Enrique Dickmann, Héctor González Iramain, Juan B. Justo, Agustín S. Muzio, Nicolás Repetto, Alfredo L. Spinetto, and Antonio de Tomaso.

8. *Diputados*, I (May 10, 1922), 7–24.

9. This measure was sent to and remained in committee. *Diputados*, II (July 19, 1922), 23–25.

10. These included projects on suppression of religious instruction in public schools, popular selection of school board members in the federal capital, an end to artificial stimulation of immigration, prohibition of the sale of alcoholic beverages, and a long, detailed, and comprehensive social security law.

11. *Diputados*, IV (September 27, 1922), 801–817.

12. For a sympathetic written and pictorial description of Alvear, see Ramón Columba, *El congreso que yo he visto*, II, 179–207. For additional biographical information, see Félix Luna, *Alvear.*

13. Guido Di Tella and Manuel Zymelman, *Las etapas del desarrollo económico argentino*, pp. 356–379.

14. Luna, *Yrigoyen*, p. 295.

15. Ismael Bucich Escobar, *Los presidentes argentinos*, pp. 521–525.

16. For more information on the Alvear-Yrigoyen split and the alignment of party figures, see Gabriel del Mazo, *El radicalismo*, II, 21–49; Luna, *Yrigoyen*, pp. 309–314; and Peter G. Snow, *Argentine Radicalism*, pp. 41–43.

17. *Diputados*, V (December 20, 1922), 317. From the 1890s, Minister Herrera Vegas served as consultant and eventually president for several important banks. At the same time he busied himself with the administration of an

estancia and the breeding of prize-winning cattle. William Belmont Parker, ed., *Argentines of Today*, II, 915–916.

18. A united bloc of 86 Radicals overrode the 30 votes of the combined opposition and sent the project on to the Senate. *Diputados*, VI (March 15, 1923), 700. The proposed intervention then became a bone of contention between Alvearists and Yrigoyenists, the latter of whom had initiated the intervention to weaken the grip of Córdoba's conservative governor, Julio A. Roca. The pro-Alvear faction in the Senate refused to pass the chamber resolution, and the president did not force the matter. Carlos Ibarguren, *La historia que he vivido*, pp. 334–335.

19. *Memoria, 1922–1923* (1923), pp. 147–148.

20. Carl Solberg, "The Tariff and Politics in Argentina, 1916–1930," *HAHR* 53, no. 2 (May 1973): 275.

21. Peter H. Smith, *Politics and Beef in Argentina*, p. 80.

22. *Diputados*, III (June 11, 1923), 213–227.

23. *Diputados*, V (August 23, 1923), 346.

24. *Diputados*, VII (October 18, 1923), 556–559.

25. *La Vanguardia* (February 20, 1924), p. 1.

26. *La Vanguardia* (February 22, 1924), p. 1.

27. *La Vanguardia* (March 2, 1924), p. 1.

28. *La Época* (March 21, 1924), p. 5.

29. *Fuerzas armadas*, I, 398–399.

30. *La Vanguardia* (March 31, 1924), p. 1.

31. *RACP* 14, no. 151 (April 12, 1924): 131–135.

32. Joaquín Coca, *El contubernio: Memorias de un diputado obrero*, pp. 19–22.

33. *Fuerzas armadas*, I, 400.

34. *Diputados*, III (August 14, 1924), 333–334.

35. Luna, *Yrigoyen*, p. 308.

36. The Socialist deputies in 1924 were Fernando de Andreis, Ricardo Belisle, Augusto Bunge, Raúl Carballo, José D. Castellanos, Joaquín Coca, Adolfo Dickmann, Enrique Dickmann, Héctor González Iramain, Agustín S. Muzio, Jacinto Oddone, José Luis Pena, Francisco Pérez Leirós, Juan F. Remedi, Pedro Revol, Alfredo L. Spinetto, Edmundo S. Tolosa, and Antonio de Tomaso. Nicolás Repetto, elected in 1922, resigned his seat in late 1923. Eugenio Albani, elected in 1924, died before assuming office.

37. *La Vanguardia* (October 15, 1923), p. 1.

38. *Acción Socialista* 1, no. 1 (November 20, 1923): 5–6.

39. Nicolás Repetto, *Mi paso por la política: De Roca a Yrigoyen*, p. 259.

40. Federico Pinedo, *En tiempos de la república*, I, 61.

41. *La Prensa* (March 26, 1924), p. 14.

42. *Acción Socialista* 1, no. 22 (April 15, 1924): 352–353.

43. *Diputados*, V (August 28, 1924), 30–63.

44. *Diputados*, VI (September 26, 1924), 767–772.

45. *Diputados*, VI (September 29, 1924), 897–898.

46. *Diputados*, I (May 27, 1925), 355–360.

47. *Diputados*, V (September 23, 1925), 31–32.

48. *La Vanguardia* (October 12–14, 1925).

49. Enrique Dickmann, *Recuerdos de un militante socialista*, p. 231.

50. *La Vanguardia* (January 11, 1926), p. 1.

51. *La Vanguardia* (January 31, 1926), p. 1.
52. *Acción Socialista* 3, no. 22 (May 15, 1926): 689–690.
53. Coca, *El contubernio*, p. 72.
54. *La Epoca* (February 20, 1926), p. 1.
55. *La Prensa* (March 31, 1926), p. 14.
56. The Socialist deputies in 1926 were Fernando de Andreis, Ricardo Belisle, Augusto Bunge, Raúl Carballo, José D. Castellanos, Joaquín Coca, Adolfo Dickmann, Enrique Dickmann, Héctor González Iramain, Agustín S. Muzio, Jacinto Oddone, José Luis Pena, Francisco Pérez Leirós, Juan F. Remedi, Nicolás Repetto, Pedro Revol, Alfredo L. Spinetto, Edmundo S. Tolosa, and Antonio de Tomaso.
57. Coca, *El contubernio*, pp. 80–84.
58. *Diputados*, I (June 16, 1926), 458.
59. *Diputados*, III (August 6, 1926), 567.
60. *Anuario Socialista: 1930*, p. 70.
61. Darío Cantón, *Materiales para el estudio de la sociología política en la Argentina*, I, 93–100.
62. See pp. 191–192.
63. Diego Abad de Santillán, *La F.O.R.A.*, p. 281.
64. *Revista de Ciencias Económicas* 15, no. 72 (July 1927): 874–878.
65. *Revista de Ciencias Económicas* 15, no 73 (August 1927): 972–976.
66. José Panettieri, *Los trabajadores*, p. 205.
67. *La Confederación: Organo de la Confederación Obrera Argentina* 1, no. 1 (May 1, 1926): 1.
68. Jacinto Oddone, *Gremialismo proletario argentino*, p. 316.
69. Ibid., pp. 316–317.

Chapter 10: Schism: 1927–1930
1. *Senadores*, II (September 20, 1925), 307–318.
2. *Diputados*, I, (May 19, 1927), 102–121.
3. *RACP* 17, no. 163 (June 12, 1927): 358–360.
4. Enrique Dickmann, *Recuerdos de un militante socialista*, p. 233.
5. *Crítica y Acción* (July 1, 1927), p. 1.
6. *Diputados*, II (July 20, 1927), 385.
7. *Diputados*, III (July 27, 1927), 72–150.
8. *La Prensa* (August 8, 1927), p. 10.
9. Arturo Frondizi, *Petroleo y política*, p. 195.
10. Joaquín Coca, *El contubernio: Memorias de un diputado obrero*, pp. 92–93.
11. *Diputados*, IV (September 1, 1927), 362–363.
12. *Diputados*, IV (September 8, 1927), 478.
13. For a review of the 1927 petroleum debate, see James E. Buchanan, "Politics and Petroleum Development in Argentina," pp. 193–250; and Frondizi, *Petroleo y política*, pp. 195–222.
14. *Senadores*, I (September 15, 1927), 792.
15. Dardo Cúneo, *Juan B. Justo*, pp. 309–313.
16. *Acción Socialista* 5, no. 18 (March 31, 1928): 626–627.
17. The candidates were Héctor González Iramain, Augusto Bunge, Agustín S. Muzio, Federico Pinedo, Antonio Zaccagnini, Roberto F. Giusti, José Rouca

Oliva, Fernando de Andreis, Raúl Carballo, Carlos Manacorda, Manuel González Maseda, and Jacinto Boix. *Crítica y Acción* 1, no. 21 (March 1, 1928): 1–2.

18. *La Época* (March 18, 1928), p. 12.

19. República Argentina, Municipalidad de la Ciudad de Buenos Aires, *Cuarto censo general, 1936*, II, 3–11.

20. Ibid., p. 12.

21. Darío Cantón, *Materiales para el estudio de la sociología política en la Argentina*, I, 101.

22. *Fuerzas armadas*, I, 433.

23. *La Prensa* (May 6, 1928), p. 14.

24. *La Vanguardia* (April 16, 1928), p. 1.

25. *Acción Socialista* 6, no. 7 (October 13, 1928): 194.

26. *Diputados*, I (June 12, 1929), 316–326.

27. Carl Solberg, "Rural Unrest and Agrarian Policy," *Journal of Inter-American Studies and World Affairs* 13, no. 1: 50.

28. *Diputados*, II (August 22, 1929), 823–887.

29. *Diputados*, III (September 5, 1929), 180.

30. Partido Socialista, *Anuario Socialista: 1932*, p. 222.

31. Nicolás Repetto, *Mi paso por la política: De Roca a Yrigoyen*, pp. 295–301.

32. *La Vanguardia* (October 12–14, 1929).

33. *La Vanguardia* (February 25, 1930), p. 1.

34. *Libertad!* (January 30, 1930), p. 2.

35. *Libertad!* (March 8, 1930), p. 1.

36. *La Prensa* (March 22, 1930), p. 15.

37. Yrigoyen supported these increases, which ultimately were approved. The Socialist objections are in *Diputados*, V (September 24 and 25, 1928), 71–129.

38. The pages of *Acción Socialista* from 1923 to 1929 contained many articles on the rise of fascism in Europe and the implications for Argentina. Also, the twentieth party congress in 1929 issued a resolution in sympathy with the "victims of fascist barbarism" in Europe and America. *La Vanguardia* (October 13, 1929), p. 3.

39. *Diputados*, II (August 28, 1930), 523–539.

40. Robert A. Potash, *The Army and Politics in Argentina, 1928–1945: Yrigoyen to Perón*, pp. 55–59.

41. Partido Socialista, *Anuario Socialista: 1932*, p. 158.

42. Cantón, *Materiales* I, 103.

43. *La Vanguardia* (November 27, 1928), p. 1.

44. *La Confederación* 2, no. 14 (December 1927): 1.

45. *La Confederación* 2, no. 16 (July 1928): 2.

46. *La Confederación* 2, no. 17 (September 1928): 4.

47. Jacinto Oddone, *Gremialismo proletario argentino*, pp. 327–331.

Chapter 11: Conclusion

1. Three works by revolutionary nationalist authors extremely critical of the Socialist Party are Rodolfo Puiggrós, *Historia crítica de los partidos políticos argentinos*; Jorge Abelardo Ramos, *Revolución y contrarevolución en la*

Argentina: Las masas en nuestra historia; and Jorge E. Spilimbergo, *El socialismo en la Argentina.*

2. For information on the role of political parties in the process of political development, see the introductory and concluding chapters in Joseph La Palombara and Myron Weiner, eds., *Political Parties and Political Development.*

3. For descriptions of immigrant life and attitudes in the federal capital at the turn of the century, see James R. Scobie, "Buenos Aires as a Commercial-Bureaucratic City, 1880–1910: Characteristics of a City's Orientation," *American Historical Review* 77, no. 1 (October 1972): 1,035–1,073.

Bibliography

REPÚBLICA ARGENTINA

Boletín del Departamento Nacional del Trabajo. Buenos Aires, 1907–1920.
Cámara de Diputados de la Nación, *El parlamento argentino: 1854–1947.*
Buenos Aires: Imprenta del Congreso de la Nación, 1948.
*Censo general de población, edificación, comercio e industrias de la ciudad
de Buenos Aires, Capital Federal de la República Argentina, levantado en
los días 11 y 18 de setiembre de 1904.* Buenos Aires: Compañía Sud-
Americana de Billetes de Banco, 1906.
*Censo general de población, edificación, comercio e industrias de la ciudad de
Buenos Aires, Capital Federal de la República Argentina, levantado en los
días 16 al 24 de octubre de 1909.* Buenos Aires: Compañía Sud-Americana
de Billetes de Banco, 1910.
Congreso Nacional, *Diario de sesiones de la Cámara de Diputados.* Buenos
Aires: Imprenta del Congreso de la Nación, 1904–1930.
Congreso Nacional, *Diario de sesiones de la Cámara de Senadores.* Buenos
Aires: Imprenta del Congreso de la Nación, 1913–1929.
Constitución de la Nación Argentina. Buenos Aires: Imprenta del Congreso
de la Nación, 1961.
Crónica mensual del Departamento Nacional del Trabajo. Buenos Aires,
1922–1923.
*Memoria del Ministerio del Interior, presentada al Honorable Congreso de
la Nación.* Buenos Aires, 1904–1930.
Ministerio del Interior, *Boletín demográfico argentina* 5, no. 11. Buenos Aires,
January–July, 1904.
Ministerio del Interior, Subsecretaria de Informaciones, *Las fuerzas armadas
restituyen el imperio de la soberanía popular: Las elecciones generales de
1946.* 2 vols. Buenos Aires: Imprenta de la Cámara de Diputados, 1946.
Municipalidad de la Capital, Dirección General de Estadística Municipal,
Anuario estadístico de la Ciudad de Buenos Aires, 1910 y 1911. Buenos
Aires, 1913.
Municipalidad de la Capital, Dirección General de Estadística Municipal,
Anuario estadístico de la Ciudad de Buenos Aires: Año 1914. Buenos Aires,
1915.
Municipalidad de la Ciudad de Buenos Aires, *Cuarto censo general, 1936,*
vol. 2, *Población.* Buenos Aires, 1939.

Primer censo de la República Argentina, verificado en los días 15, 16, 17 de setiembre de 1869. Buenos Aires, 1872.

Registro cívico de la nación: Padrón definitivo de electores: Distrito electoral de la Capital, 1917–1918. 4 vols. Buenos Aires, 1918.

Segundo censo de la República Argentina, Mayo 10 de 1895. 3 vols. Buenos Aires: Taller Tipográfico de la Penitenciaría Nacional, 1898.

Tercer censo nacional, levantado el 1° de junio de 1914. 10 vols. Buenos Aires, 1916.

Versiones taquigráficas de las sesiones del Concejo Deliberante de la Ciudad de Buenos Aires. Buenos Aires, 1919–1930.

NEWSPAPERS AND PERIODICALS

La Acción: Organo del Partido Socialista Argentino. Buenos Aires, 1915–1916.

Acción Socialista. Buenos Aires, 1923–1929.

Adelante: Organo de la Circunscripción 10a. Buenos Aires, January 24, 1904–November 1, 1911.

El Alba: Organo Socialista de la Circunscripción 20a. Buenos Aires, May 1904–August 1904.

La Antorcha: Organo del Centro Socialista de la Circunscripción 2a. Buenos Aires, October 1903–December 1903.

Boletín de la Unión Industrial Argentina. Buenos Aires, 1896–1924.

El Ciclón: Organo Oficial del Centro Socialista de la Sección 1a. Buenos Aires, September 20, 1912–July 1, 1913.

La Confederación: Organo de la Confederación Obrera Argentina. Buenos Aires, 1926–1929.

Crítica Socialista: Revista Mensual del Socialismo Científico. Buenos Aires, 1915–1916.

Crítica y Acción: Publicación Socialista Quincenal. Buenos Aires, 1927–1928.

Democracia Socialista. Publicación Decenal. Buenos Aires, 1920–1921.

El Diario del Pueblo. Buenos Aires, 1899.

La Epoca. Buenos Aires, 1918–1930.

Germinal: Publicaciones Mensuales. Buenos Aires, 1920–1921.

Humanidad Nueva: Revista del Ateneo Popular. Buenos Aires, 1910–1917.

La Internacional: Periódico Socialista Quincenal. Buenos Aires, 1917–1918.

Libertad! Buenos Aires, 1928–1930.

Lucha de Clases: Organo del Partido Socialista, Sección Mendoza. Mendoza, 1912–1914.

La Luz: Periódico Socialista. Buenos Aires, November 15, 1901–March 24, 1905.

La Montaña: Periódico Socialista Revolucionario. Buenos Aires, 1897.

Nueva Era: Revista Socialista Ilustrada. Buenos Aires, 1914.

Nuevos Tiempos: Revista de Buenos Aires. Buenos Aires, 1916–1917.

El Obrero: Defensor de los Intereses de la Clase Proletaria; Organo de la Federación Obrera. Buenos Aires, 1890–1892.

La Organización Obrera: Organo Oficial de la F.O.R.A. Buenos Aires, 1915–1921.

Partido Socialista, *Almanaque del Trabajo*. Buenos Aires, 1918–1925.

———, *Anuario Socialista*. Buenos Aires, 1928–1938.

Polémicas: Publicación Mensual Socialista. Buenos Aires, 1928–1929.

La Prensa. Buenos Aires, 1904–1930.
La Protesta: Suplemento Semanal. Buenos Aires, 1922.
Revista Argentina de Ciencias Políticas. Buenos Aires, 1910–1928.
Revista de Ciencias Económicas. Buenos Aires, 1914–1929.
Revista Socialista Internacional: Publicación Mensual de Exposición del Socialismo Científico, Crítica Social e Información del Movimiento Obrero de Ambos Mundos. Buenos Aires, 1908–1910.
The Review of the River Plate. Buenos Aires, 1919–1930.
El Socialista: Organo del Centro Socialista Juventud Obrera, Circunscripción 8a. Buenos Aires, September 15, 1903–January 1, 1904.
La Vanguardia: Periódico Socialista Científico: Defensor de la Clase Trabajadora. Buenos Aires, 1894–1930.
Vida Nueva: Revista Socialista. Buenos Aires, 1906–1907.
La Voz del Pueblo. Buenos Aires, 1928.

BOOKS, PAMPHLETS, AND ARTICLES

Abad de Santillán, Diego. *La F.O.R.A.: Ideología y trayectoria del movimiento obrero revolucionario en la Argentina.* Buenos Aires: Ediciones Nervio, 1933.
———, ed. *Gran enciclopedia argentina.* 9 vols. Buenos Aires, 1956–1963.
A.B.C. *La política argentina: Bosquejos de crítica y de historia contemporánea.* Buenos Aires: Robles & Cía., 1904.
Agnelli, Francisco, and Chiti, Juan B. *Cincuentenario de 'La Fraternidad'— Fundación, Desarrollo, Obra—1887–1937.* Buenos Aires: Talleres Gráficos Revashino Hnos., 1937.
Aguilar, Louis E., ed. *Marxism in Latin America.* New York: Alfred A. Knopf, 1968.
Alba, Victor. *Politics and the Labor Movement in Latin America.* Stanford, California: Stanford University Press, 1968.
Alberdi, Juan Bautista. *Bases y puntos de partida para la organización política de la República Argentina.* Buenos Aires: Editorial Luz del Día, 1952.
Alberti, M. H., et al. *Concepto humanista de la historia.* Buenos Aires: Ediciones Libera, 1966.
Alexander, Robert. *Labor Parties of Latin America.* New York: League for Industrial Democracy, 1942.
Alexander, Robert J. *Communism in Latin America.* New Brunswick, New Jersey: Rutgers University Press, 1957.
———. *Latin American Political Parties.* New York: Praeger, 1973.
———. "The Emergence of Modern Political Parties in Latin America." In Peter G. Snow, ed., *Government and Politics in Latin America: A Reader.* New York: Holt, Rinehart and Winston, 1967.
———. *Organized Labor in Latin America.* New York: The Free Press, 1965.
Amadeo, Octavio R. *Política.* Buenos Aires: Librería Mendesky, 1916.
———. *Vidas argentinas.* Buenos Aires: Emecé Editores, 1965.
Arenas Luque, Fermín V. *Roque Sáenz Peña: El presidente del sufragio libre.* Buenos Aires, 1951.
Ayarragaray, Lucas. *La anarquía argentina y el caudillismo: Estudio psicológico de los orígenes nacionales, hasta el año XXIX.* Buenos Aires: Félix Lajouane y Cía., 1904.

————. *Socialismo argentino y legislación obrera.* Buenos Aires: Librería Nacional, 1912.

Bagú, Sergio. *Vida ejemplar de José Ingenieros: Juventud y plenitud.* Buenos Aires: Claridad, 1936.

Baily, Samuel L. *Labor, Nationalism, and Politics in Argentina.* New Brunswick, New Jersey: Rutgers University Press, 1967.

Balestra, Juan. *El noventa.* Buenos Aires: La Facultad, 1935.

Baliño, José P. "El socialismo en la Provincia de Buenos Aires." In Partido Socialista, *Almanaque del Trabajo* (1919).

Bayer, Osvaldo. "1921: La Masacre de Jacinto Arauz." *Todo es Historia* 4, no. 45 (January 1971): 40–55.

————. *Los vengadores de la Patagonia trágica.* 3 vols. Buenos Aires: Editorial Galerna, 1972–1974.

Belloni, Alberto. *Del anarquismo al peronismo: Historia del movimiento obrero argentino.* Buenos Aires: A. Peña Lillo, 1960.

Bialet Massé, Juan. *El estado de las clases obreras argentinas a comienzos del siglo.* Córdoba, Argentina: Universidad Nacional de Córdoba, 1968.

Bonet, Carmelo M. "El Diputado Antonio de Tomaso." *Nosotros* 8, no. 60 (April 1914): 97–101.

Borkenau, Franz. *World Communism: A History of the Communist International.* Ann Arbor, Michigan: University of Michigan Press, 1962.

Borrero, José María. *La Patagonia trágica.* Buenos Aires: Editorial Americana, 1967.

Bosch, Mariano G. *Historia del partido radical: La U.C.R., 1891–1930.* Buenos Aires, 1931.

Bravo, Mario. "Canciones colectivas." *Nosotros* 5, no. 35 (December 1911): 461–467.

————. *Capítulos de legislación obrera.* Buenos Aires: A. García & Cía., 1927.

————. *La ciudad libre.* Buenos Aires: Ferro & Gnoatto, 1917.

————. "Leopoldo Lugones en el movimiento socialista (1896–1897)." *Nosotros* 2, no. 26–28 (May-July 1938): 27–47.

————. "Organización, programa y desarrollo del Partido Socialista en la Argentina." *Revista Argentina de Ciencias Políticas* 10 (1915): 119–150.

Bryce, James. *South America: Observations and Impressions.* New York: Macmillan, 1912.

Bucich Escobar, Ismael. *Buenos Aires Ciudad: Reseña histórica y descriptiva de la capital argentina desde su primera fundación hasta el presente, 1536–1936.* Buenos Aires: Editorial Tor, 1936.

————. *Historia de los presidentes argentinos.* 4th ed. Buenos Aires: El Ateneo, 1927.

Bunge, Alejandro E. *Una nueva Argentina.* Buenos Aires: Editorial Guillermo Kraft, 1940.

Bunge, Augusto. *El culto de la vida.* Buenos Aires: Juan Perrotti, 1915.

Bunkley, Allison W. *The Life of Sarmiento.* Princeton, New Jersey: Princeton University Press, 1952.

Burgin, Miron. *The Economic Aspects of Argentine Federalism, 1820–1852.* Cambridge, Massachusetts: Harvard University Press, 1946.

Burnett, Ben G., and Troncoso, Moisés Poblete. *The Rise of the Latin American Labor Movement.* New York: Bookman Associates, 1960.

Caballero, Ricardo. *Yrigoyen: La conspiración civil y militar del 4 de febrero de 1905.* Buenos Aires: Editorial Raigal, 1951.

Cantón, Darío. *Materiales para el estudio de la sociología política en la Argentina.* 2 vols. Buenos Aires: Editorial del Instituto Torcuato Di Tella, 1968.

———. *El parlamento argentino en épocas de cambio: 1890, 1916 y 1946.* Buenos Aires: Editorial del Instituto Torcuato Di Tella, 1966.

———. *Los partidos políticos argentinos entre 1912 y 1955.* Buenos Aires: Instituto Torcuato Di Tella, 1967.

———. *La primera encuesta política argentina.* Buenos Aires: Instituto Torcuato Di Tella, 1967.

———. *El sufragio universal como agente de movilización.* Buenos Aires: Instituto Torcuato Di Tella, n.d.

Cárcano, Miguel Angel. *Sáenz Peña: La revolución por los comicios.* Buenos Aires: Librería y Editorial Nuevo Cabildo, 1963.

Carew Hunt, R. N. *The Theory and Practice of Communism: An Introduction.* New York: Macmillan, 1962.

Carrasco, Angel. *Lo que yo ví desde el 80: Hombres y episodios de la transformación nacional.* Buenos Aires: Editorial PROCMO, 1947.

Casaretto, Martín S. *Historia del movimiento obrero argentino.* Buenos Aires: Vescovo, 1946.

Chaquesien, Donato. *Los partidos porteños en la vía pública.* Buenos Aires: Araújo Hnos., 1919.

Coca, Joaquín. *El contubernio: Memorias de un diputado obrero.* Buenos Aires: Claridad, n.d.

Cohen, Carl, ed. *Communism, Fascism, and Democracy: The Theoretical Foundations.* New York: Random House, 1963.

Columba, Ramón. *El congreso que yo he visto: 1906–1913,* I. Buenos Aires: Editorial Ramón Columba, 1948.

———. *El congreso que yo he visto: 1914–1933,* II. Buenos Aires: Editorial Ramón Columba, 1949.

Compañía de Tranvías Anglo Argentino Ltda. Buenos Aires. *Historia de los medios de transporte y de su influencia en el desarrollo urbano de la ciudad de Buenos Aires.* Buenos Aires, 1925.

Corbiere, Emilio J. "Socialistas y Anarquistas," *Polémica* 42 (1971): 29–56.

Costa, Julio A. *Hojas de mi diario.* Buenos Aires: Cabaut & Cía., 1929.

Crawford, William Rex. *A Century of Latin-American Thought.* Cambridge, Massachusetts: Harvard University Press, 1961.

Cúneo, Dardo. *Juan B. Justo.* Buenos Aires: Editorial Americalee, 1943.

———. *El primer periodismo obrero y socialista en la Argentina.* Buenos Aires: La Vanguardia, 1945.

———. *El romanticismo político: Leopoldo Lugones, Roberto J. Payró, José Ingenieros, Macedonio Fernández, Manuel Ugarte, Alberto Gerchunoff.* Buenos Aires: Ediciones Transición, 1955.

Dealy, Glen. "Prolegomena on the Spanish American Political Tradition." *Hispanic American Historical Review* 48, no. 1 (February 1968): 37–59.

Dell'Acqua, Amadeo. *La caricatura política argentina.* Buenos Aires: Editorial Universitaria de Buenos Aires, 1960.

del Valle Iberlucea, Enrique. *See* Valle Iberlucea, Enrique del.

Díaz Alejandro, Carlos F. *Essays on the Economic History of the Argentine Republic.* New Haven, Connecticut: Yale University Press, 1970.

Dickmann, Adolfo. *Los congresos socialistas: 40 años de la acción democrática.* Buenos Aires: La Vanguardia, 1936.

―――. *Nacionalismo y socialismo.* Buenos Aires: Porter Hnos., 1933.

―――. *El socialismo y el principio de nacionalidad.* Buenos Aires: Talleres Gráficos de L. J. Rosso y Cía., 1916.

Dickmann, Enrique. *La conquista del gobierno comunal.* Buenos Aires, 1914.

―――. *Democracia y socialismo.* Buenos Aires: Serafín Ponzinibbio y Cía., 1917.

―――. *Ideas e ideales.* Valencia, Spain: Editorial Prometeo, n.d.

―――. *Páginas socialistas.* Buenos Aires, 1928.

―――. *Población e inmigración.* Buenos Aires: Editorial Losada, 1946.

―――. *Recuerdos de un militante socialista.* Buenos Aires: La Vanguardia, 1949.

El diputado Palacios: Su separación del partido socialista. Buenos Aires, n.d.

Di Tella, Guido, and Zymelman, Manuel. *Las etapas del desarrollo económico argentino.* Buenos Aires: Editorial Universitaria de Buenos Aires, 1967.

Di Tella, Torcuato S.; Germani, Gino; and Graciarena, Jorge. *Argentina, sociedad de masas.* 3rd ed. Buenos Aires: Editorial Universitaria de Buenos Aires, 1966.

Dorfman, Adolfo. *Historia de la industria argentina.* Buenos Aires: Solar/Hachette, 1970.

Duverger, Maurice. *Political Parties: Their Organization and Activity in the Modern State.* Translated by Barbara and Robert North. New York: John Wiley, 1955.

Echeverría, Esteban. *Dogma socialista.* Buenos Aires: Talleres Gráficos Argentinos, 1928.

Falcoff, Mark. "Raúl Scalabrini Ortiz: The Making of an Argentine Nationalist." *Hispanic American Historical Review* 52, no. 1 (February 1972): 74–101.

Farías Alem, Roberto. *Alem y la democracia argentina.* Buenos Aires: Editorial Guillermo Kraft, 1957.

Ferns, H. S. *Britain and Argentina in the Nineteenth Century.* London: Oxford University Press, 1960.

Ferrer, Aldo. *The Argentine Economy.* Translated by Marjory M. Urquidi. Berkeley, California: University of California Press, 1967.

Fiorito, Susana. "Un drama olvidado: Las huelgas patagónicas de 1920–21." *Polémica* 54 (May 1971): 89–112.

Fried, Albert, and Sanders, Ronald, eds. *Socialist Thought: A Documentary History.* New York: Doubleday & Co., 1964.

Frondizi, Arturo. *Petroleo y política.* 2nd ed. Buenos Aires: Editorial Raigal, 1955.

Galletti, Alfredo. *La realidad argentina en el siglo XX: La política y los partidos.* Buenos Aires: Fondo de Cultura Económica, 1961.

Gálvez, Manuel. *Vida de Hipólito Yrigoyen: El hombre del misterio.* Buenos Aires: Editorial Tor, 1959.

Garganigo, John F. *El perfil del gaucho: En algunas novelas de Argentina y Uruguay.* Montevideo: Editorial Sintesis, 1966.

Germani, Gino. *Estructura social de la Argentina: Análisis estadístico.* Buenos Aires: Editorial Raigal, 1955.

———. "Mass Immigration and Modernization in Argentina." In Irving Louis Horowitz, et al., *Latin American Radicalism: A Documentary Report on Left and Nationalist Movements.* New York: Random House, 1969, pp. 314–355.

———. *Política y sociedad en una época de transición: De la sociedad tradicional a la sociedad de masas.* Buenos Aires: Editorial Paidos, 1962.

Ghioldi, Américo. *Juan B. Justo: Sus ideas históricas, socialistas, filosóficas.* 3rd ed. Buenos Aires: Ediciones Monserrat, 1964.

Goldberg, Harvey. *The life of Jean Jaurès.* Madison, Wisconsin: University of Wisconsin Press, 1962.

Goldstraj, Manuel. *Años y errores: Un cuarto de siglo de política argentina.* Buenos Aires: Editorial Sophos, 1957.

Goldwert, Marvin. "The Rise of Modern Militarism in Argentina." *Hispanic American Historical Review* 48, no. 2 (May 1968): 189–205.

Grela, Plácido. *El grito de Alcorta: Historia de la rebelión campesina de 1912.* Rosario, Argentina: Ediciones Tierra Nuestra, 1958.

Grote, Padre Federico. *El socialismo: Breve exposición y crítica de sus doctrinas económicas y morales.* Freiburg, Germany, 1921.

Guerrero, Américo R. *La industria argentina: Su origen, organización y desarrollo.* Buenos Aires, 1944.

Hasbrouck, Alfred. "The Argentine Revolution of 1930." *Hispanic American Historical Review* 18 (August 1938): 285–321.

Herrero, Antonio. *Alfredo L. Palacios: Carácteres, valores y problemas de su personalidad y su acción: Política social, reforma universitaria, iberoamericanismo.* Buenos Aires: M. Gleizer, 1925.

Ibarguren, Carlos. *La historia que he vivido.* Buenos Aires: Editorial Universitaria de Buenos Aires, 1969.

———. *Juan Manuel de Rosas: Su vida, su drama, su tiempo.* Buenos Aires: Ediciones Theoría, 1961.

Ingenieros, José. *Antología: Su pensamiento en sus mejores páginas.* Buenos Aires, 1961.

———. *El hombre mediocre.* Madrid, 1913.

———. *Los tiempos nuevos: Reflexiones optimistas sobre la guerra y la revolución.* Madrid: Editorial America, 1921.

———. *Sociología argentina.* Buenos Aires: Talleres Gráficos de L. J. Rosso y Cía., 1918.

Joll, James. *The Second International: 1889–1914.* New York: Harper & Row, 1966.

Justo, Juan B. *Discursos y escritos políticos.* Buenos Aires: W. M. Jackson, Inc., n.d.

———. *Internacionalismo y patria.* Buenos Aires: La Vanguardia, 1925.

———. *La moneda.* Buenos Aires: La Vanguardia, 1928.

———. *Obras de Juan B. Justo: La realización del socialismo.* Edited by Dardo Cúneo. Buenos Aires: La Vanguardia, 1947.

———. *Socialismo.* Buenos Aires: La Vanguardia, 1920.

———. *Teoría y práctica de la historia.* 2nd ed. Buenos Aires: Lotitio & Barberis, 1915.

Kamia, Delia. *Entre Yrigoyen e Ingenieros: Un episodio de la historia contemporánea*. Buenos Aires: Ediciones Meridión, 1957.

Kautsky, John H., ed. *Political Change in Underdeveloped Countries: Nationalism and Communism*. New York: John Wiley, 1962.

Kennedy, John J. *Catholicism, Nationalism, and Democracy in Argentina*. Notre Dame, Indiana: University of Notre Dame Press, 1958.

Kraft, Guillermo, ed. *Quién es quién en la Argentina: Biografías contemporaneas: Año 1939*. Buenos Aires, 1939.

La Palombara, Joseph, and Weiner, Myron, eds. *Political Parties and Political Development*. Princeton, New Jersey: Princeton University Press, 1966.

Larra, Raúl. *Lisandro de la Torre: El solitario de Pinas*. 7th ed. Buenos Aires: Editorial Futuro, 1961.

———. *Roberto J. Payró: El novelista de la democracia*. 3rd ed. Buenos Aires: Editorial La Mandrágora, 1960.

Larroca, Jorge. "Un anarquista en Buenos Aires." *Todo es Historia* 4, no. 47 (March 1971): 45–57.

Levene, Ricardo. *A History of Argentina*. Translated and edited by William Spence Robertson. New York: Russell and Russell, 1963.

Luna, Félix. *Alvear*. Buenos Aires: Libros Argentinos, 1958.

———. *Yrigoyen*. 2nd ed. Buenos Aires: Editorial Desarrollo, 1964.

Lynch, John. *Spanish Colonial Administration, 1782–1810: The Intendant System in the Viceroyalty of the Río de la Plata*. London: The Athlone Press, 1958.

Macdonald, Austin F. *Government of the Argentine Republic*. New York: Thomas Y. Crowell Company, 1942.

McGann, Thomas F. *Argentina: The Divided Land*. Princeton, New Jersey: D. Van Nostrand Co., 1966.

———. *Argentina, the United States, and the Inter-American System, 1880–1914*. Cambridge, Massachusetts: Harvard University Press, 1957.

Marianetti, Benito. *Las luchas sociales en Mendoza*. Mendoza, Argentina: Ediciones Cuyo, 1970.

Marotta, Sebastián. *El movimiento sindical argentino: Su génesis y desarrollo, Período: 1857–1907*. Buenos Aires: Ediciones Lacio, 1960.

———. *El movimiento sindical argentino: Su génesis y desarrollo, Período: 1907–1920*. Buenos Aires: Ediciones Lacio, 1961.

———. *El movimiento sindical argentino: Su génesis y desarrollo, Período: 1920–1935*. Buenos Aires: Editorial Calomino, 1970.

Mazo, Gabriel del. *Breve historia del radicalismo: Desde sus orígenes y su fundación en 1891 hasta nuestros días*. Buenos Aires: Compañía Editora y Distribuidora del Plata, 1964.

———. *El radicalismo: Ensayo sobre su historia y doctrina*, II. Buenos Aires: Ediciones Gure, 1957.

———. *El radicalismo: Ensayo sobre su historia y doctrina*, II. Buenos Aires: Ediciones Gure, 1959.

Melo, Carlos R. *Los partidos políticos argentinos*. 3rd ed. Córdoba, Argentina: Universidad Nacional de Córdoba, 1964.

Michels, Robert. *Political Parties: A Sociological Study of the Oligarchical Tendencies of Modern Democracy*. Translated by Eden & Cedar Paul. New York: Dover Publications, 1959.

Montes de Oca, O. Del Pino. *La revolución del 90.* Buenos Aires: Editorial La República, 1956.

Moreau de Justo, Alicia. *El socialismo según la definición de Juan B. Justo.* Buenos Aires: Editorial Polis, 1946.

Morey, Ramón. "El Partido Socialista en Mendoza." In Partido Socialista, *Almanaque del Trabajo* (1919).

Mouchet, Enrique. *Juan B. Justo: Ensayo preliminar sobre su vida, su pensamiento, y su obra.* Buenos Aires: La Vanguardia, 1932.

Navarro Gerassi, Marysa. *Los nacionalistas.* Buenos Aires: Editorial Jorge Alvarez, 1968.

Needler, Martin C. *Latin American Politics in Perspective.* Princeton, New Jersey: D. Van Nostrand Co., 1963.

Neumann, Sigmund. *Modern Political Parties: Approaches to Comparative Politics.* Chicago, Illinois: University of Chicago Press, 1956.

Niklison, José Elías. "Acción social católica obrera." *Boletín del Departamento Nacional del Trabajo* 46 (March 1920): 15–286.

"Nómina de socios." *Anales de la Sociedad Rural Argentina* 52 (February 1918): 116–134.

Oddone, Jacinto. *Un año de intendencia municipal: Recuerdos anécdotas.* Buenos Aires: La Vanguardia, 1933.

———. *La burguesía terrateniente argentina.* Buenos Aires: Ediciones Libera, 1967.

———. *Gremialismo proletario argentino.* Buenos Aires: La Vanguardia, 1949.

———. *Historia del socialismo argentino.* 2 vols. Buenos Aires: La Vanguardia, 1934.

Olguín, Dardo. *Lencinas, el caudillo radical: Historia y mito.* Mendoza, Argentina: Ediciones Vendimiador, 1961.

Palacio, Ernesto, *Historia de la Argentina: 1835–1943.* Buenos Aires: A. Peña Lillo, 1965.

Palacios, Alfredo L. *Discursos parlamentarios.* Valencia, Spain: F. Sempere y Cía., 1910.

———. *Dos años de acción socialista en el parlamento argentino.* Valencia, Spain: Prometeo, n.d.

———. *Estadistas y poetas.* Buenos Aires: Claridad, 1951.

———. *La evolución argentina y la patria.* Buenos Aires, 1910.

———. *La justicia social.* Buenos Aires: Claridad, 1954.

———. *La miseria en la República Argentina.* Buenos Aires: Sesé Larranaga y Renovales, 1900.

———. *El nuevo derecho.* 3rd ed. Buenos Aires: Claridad, 1927.

———. *Por las mujeres y los niños que trabajan.* Valencia, Spain: F. Sempere y Cía., n.d.

———. "Socialismo ético." *Cuadernos Americanos* 17, no. 4–5 (July-October 1958): 201–224.

Pan, Luis. *Juan B. Justo y la fundación del partido socialista.* Buenos Aires: La Vanguardia, 1956.

———. *Justo y Marx: El socialismo en la Argentina.* Buenos Aires: Ediciones Monserrat, 1964.

———. *Visión socialista del medio siglo argentino.* Buenos Aires: La Vanguardia, 1947.

Panettieri, José. *Los trabajadores.* Buenos Aires: Editorial Jorge Alvarez, 1967.

———. *Los trabajadores en tiempos de la inmigración masiva en Argentina, 1870–1910.* La Plata, Argentina: Universidad Nacional de La Plata, 1965.

Parker, William Belmont, ed. *Argentines of Today.* New York: Kraus Reprint Corporation, 1967.

"El Partido Radical en el gobierno." *Nosotros* 10, no. 90 (October 1916) : 5–8.

Partido Socialista. *La reforma universitaria y el partido socialista.* Buenos Aires: La Vanguardia, 1945.

Patroni, Adrián. *Los trabajadores en la Argentina.* Buenos Aires, 1897.

"Personal administrativa y docente de la Universidad de Buenos Aires en 1° de diciembre de 1904." *Revista de la Universidad de Buenos Aires* 1, no. 2 (1904): 519–532.

Pinedo, Federico. *En tiempos de la república,* vols. 1 and 2. Buenos Aires: Editorial Mundo Forense, 1946.

Potash, Robert A. *The Army and Politics in Argentina, 1928–1945: Yrigoyen to Perón.* Stanford, California: Stanford University Press, 1969.

Puiggrós, Rodolfo. *Historia crítica de los partidos políticos argentinos.* Buenos Aires: Editorial Argumentos, 1956.

———. *Las izquierdas y el problema nacional.* Buenos Aires: Editorial Jorge Alvarez, 1967.

———. "Los partidos políticos del 90." *Polémica* 46 (1971): 141–168.

———. *El yrigoyenismo.* Buenos Aires: Editorial Jorge Alvarez, 1965.

Ramos, Jorge Abelardo. *El partido comunista en la política argentina: Su historia y crítica.* Buenos Aires: Coyocán, 1962.

———. *Revolución y contrarevolución en la Argentina: Las masas en nuestra historia.* 2nd ed. Buenos Aires: La Reja, 1961.

Ratzer, José. *Los marxistas argentinos del 90.* Córdoba, Argentina: Ediciones Pasado y Presente, 1969.

Ravines, Eudocio. *The Yenan Way.* New York: Charles Scribner & Sons, 1951.

Rennie, Ysabel Fisk. *The Argentine Republic.* New York: Macmillan, 1945.

Repetto, Nicolás. *Como nace y se desarrolla una cooperativa.* 3rd ed. Buenos Aires: La Vanguardia, 1944.

———. *Juan B. Justo y el movimiento político social argentino.* Buenos Aires: Ediciones Monserrat, 1964.

———. *Mi paso por la agricultura.* Buenos Aires: Santiago Rueda, 1959.

———. *Mi paso por la medicina.* 2nd ed. Buenos Aires: Santiago Rueda, 1955.

———. *Mi paso por la política: De Roca a Yrigoyen.* Buenos Aires: Santiago Rueda, 1956.

———. *Mi paso por la política: De Uriburu a Perón.* Buenos Aires: Santiago Rueda, 1957.

———. *Mis noventa años: Escritos e intervenciones parlamentarias.* Buenos Aires: Bases, 1962.

Rock, David. *Politics in Argentina, 1890–1930: The Rise and Fall of Radicalism.* Cambridge, England: Cambridge University Press, 1975.

Rodríguez, Germinal. *La crisis política del socialismo argentino: Partido socialista o partido de vanguardia?* Buenos Aires, 1930.

Rodríguez Tarditi, José. *Juan B. Justo y Nicolás Repetto en la acción cooperativa: Sus discípulos.* Buenos Aires: Intercoop Editora Cooperativa Limitada, 1970.

Romero, José Luis. *A History of Argentine Political Thought*. Translated by Thomas F. McGann. Stanford, California: Stanford University Press, 1963.

Sáenz Peña, Roque. *La reforma electoral y temas de política internacional americana*. Buenos Aires: Editorial Raigal, 1952.

Sánchez Sorondo, Matías G. *Historia de seis años*. Buenos Aires, n.d.

Sánchez Viamonte, Carlos. *El pensamiento liberal argentino en el siglo XIX: Tres generaciones históricas*. Buenos Aires: Ediciones Gure, 1957.

Sarmiento, Domingo F. *Life in the Argentine Republic in the Days of the Tyrants, or, Civilization and Barbarism*. New York: Collier Books, 1961.

Scalabrini Ortiz, Raúl. *Política británica en el Río de la Plata*. Buenos Aires: Editorial Reconquista, 1940.

Scobie, James R. *Argentina: A City and a Nation*. New York: Oxford University Press, 1964.

―――. "Buenos Aires as a Commercial-Bureaucratic City, 1880–1910: Characteristics of a City's Orientation." *The American Historical Review* 77, no. 4 (October 1972): 1,035–1,073.

―――. *Buenos Aires: Plaza to Suburb, 1870–1910*. New York: Oxford University Press, 1974.

―――. *La lucha por la consolidación de la nacionalidad argentina, 1852–1862*. Buenos Aires: Hachette, 1964.

Scott, Robert E. "Political Parties and Policy-Making in Latin America." In Joseph La Palombara and Myron Weiner, eds., *Political Parties and Political Development*. Princeton, New Jersey: Princeton University Press, 1966.

Simon, S. Fanny. "Anarchism and Anarcho-Syndicalism in South America." *Hispanic American Historical Review* 26, no. 1 (February 1946): 38–59.

Smith, Peter H. *Politics and Beef in Argentina: Patterns of Conflict and Change*. New York: Columbia University Press, 1969.

Snow, Peter G. *Argentine Radicalism: The History and Doctrine of the Radical Civic Union*. Iowa City, Iowa: University of Iowa Press, 1965.

Solari, Juan Antonio. *Hombres de la República: Maestros, amigos, compañeros*. Buenos Aires: Editorial Afirmación, 1966.

―――. *Mario Bravo: El político, el poeta, el hombre*. Buenos Aires, 1944.

―――. *Recordación de Juan B. Justo: El hombre, sus ideas, su obra*. Buenos Aires: Bases, 1965.

Solberg, Carl. "Farm Workers and the Myth of Export-Led Development in Argentina." *The Americas* 31, no. 2 (October 1974): 121–138.

―――. *Immigration and Nationalism: Argentina and Chile, 1890–1914*. Austin, Texas: University of Texas Press, 1970.

―――. "Rural Unrest and Agrarian Policy in Argentina, 1912–1930." *Journal of Inter-American Studies and World Affairs* 13, no. 1 (January 1971): 18–52.

―――. "The Tariff and Politics in Argentina, 1916–1930." *Hispanic American Historical Review* 53, no. 2 (May 1973): 260–284.

Soler, Ricaurte. *El positivismo argentino*. Buenos Aires: Paidos, 1968.

Sommi, Luis V. *La revolución del 90*. 2nd ed. Buenos Aires: Ediciones Pueblos de América, 1957.

Spalding, Hobart. *Argentine Sociology from the End of the Nineteenth Century to World War One*. Buenos Aires: Instituto Torcuato Di Tella, 1968.

―――. *La clase trabajadora argentina: Documentos para su historia, 1890–1912*. Buenos Aires: Editorial Galerna, 1970.

Spilimbergo, Jorge E. *El socialismo en la Argentina*. Buenos Aires: Ediciones del Mar Dulce, 1969.

———. *Juan B. Justo o el socialismo cipayo*. Buenos Aires, n.d.

Tomaso, Antonio de. *Socialismo, defensa nacional y paz*. Buenos Aires: Atilio Moro, 1925.

Tornquist, Ernesto, and Company. *The Economic Development of the Argentine Republic in the Last Fifty Years*. Buenos Aires, 1919.

Troncoso, Oscar A. *Los nacionalistas argentinos: Antecedentes y trayectoria*. Buenos Aires: Editorial S.A.G.A., 1957.

Valle Iberlucea, Enrique del. *La cuestión internacional y el partido socialista*. Buenos Aires: Martín García, 1917.

———. *La revolución rusa*. Buenos Aires: Claridad, 1934.

Vanger, Milton I. *José Batlle y Ordóñez of Uruguay. The Creator of his Times, 1902–1907*. Cambridge, Massachusetts: Harvard University Press, 1962.

Vazeilles, José. *Los socialistas*. Buenos Aires: Editorial Jorge Alvarez, 1967.

Véliz, Claudio. *The Politics of Conformity in Latin America*. New York: Oxford University Press, 1967.

Verde Tello, Pedro A. *El partido socialista: Su actual forma de organización*. Buenos Aires: Bases, 1967.

Walter, Richard J. "Municipal Politics and Government in Buenos Aires: 1918–1930." *Journal of Inter-American Studies and World Affairs* 16, no. 2 (May 1974): 173–197.

———. *Student Politics in Argentina: The University Reform and Its Effects, 1918–1964*. New York: Basic Books, 1968.

Whitaker, Arthur P. *The United States and Argentina*. Cambridge, Massachusetts: Harvard University Press, 1954.

Williams, John H. *Argentine International Trade Under Inconvertible Paper Money, 1880–1900*. Cambridge, Massachusetts: Harvard University Press, 1920.

Wright, Winthrop R. *British-Owned Railways in Argentina: Their Effect on Economic Nationalism, 1854–1948*. Austin: University of Texas Press, 1974.

Yrigoyen, Hipólito. *Pueblo y gobierno*, vol. 12. Buenos Aires: Editorial Raigal, 1956.

Yunque, Alvaro. *La literatura social en la Argentina*. Buenos Aires: Claridad, 1941.

———. *Leandro N. Alem: El hombre de la multitud*. Buenos Aires: Editorial Americana, 1953.

Zea, Leopoldo. *Dos etapas del pensamiento en Hispanoamérica: Del romanticismo al positivismo*. Mexico City: El Colegio de México, 1949.

Index

Abad, Gabriel, 28
Abad de Santillán, Diego, 55
Acción, La, 132
Acción Socialista, 193–194, 208, 217
"acuerdistas," 29
acuerdos, 7
Agote, Luis, 156
Agrupación Gráfica Socialista, 63
Agrupación Socialista, 17–18, 19–20, 21
Albani, Eugenio, 38, 62, 188
Alegría, Pedro C., 171
Alem, Leandro N., 8–9
Alvárez de Toledo, Federico, 121–122
Alvear, Marcelo T. de: and division within Radical Party, 187, 191–192; and labor movement, 202; as president, 186–187, 189, 191–192; 195–196, 205, 209; as presidential candidate, 181–182
Alvearists, 187, 189, 191–192, 195
anarchists, 15, 31–32; and labor movement, 16–17, 47–49, 50–56, 126–127, 149, 154, 172, 202; repression of, 67–70. *See also* Federación Obrera Regional Argentina del V Congreso
Anastasi, Leónidas, 162 ,171
Anchorena, Joaquín S. de, 154
Andreis, Fernando de, 136, 161, 188
Anuario Socialista, 225
Apellániz, José de, 121–122
Araya, Rogelio, 108, 119, 160–161
Argentine Socialist Party: and congressional elections, 138–139 (table 8), 147–148 (table 9); formation of, 132–133; mentioned, 212
Argerich, Juan, 88
Armas, Domingo de, 38
Asociación del Trabajo, 154, 160, 172
Avellaneda, 58, 129, 152, 173
Avellaneda, Marco M., 77
Avellaneda, Nicolás, 6, 77
Azul, 38, 58

Bahía Blanca, 38, 58, 91, 176
Baliño, José P., 127, 131–132
Barco, Jerónimo del, 156
Barracas, 29, 36, 47
Bas, Arturo M., 108, 111, 120–121
Beazley, Francisco J., 98, 105, 113–114
Becú, Carlos A., 147
Beiró, Francisco, 214
Belisle, Ricardo, 191
Berisso, 127, 151–152
Bernstein, Eduard, 20
Bialet-Massé, Juan, 83
Bogliolo, Rómulo, 197
Bolshevik Revolution, 145, 153, 154–155, 176–180
Bonifacio, Benjamín, 136
Bonifacio, Juan José, 214
Bravo, Mario: biography of, 60–63; as candidate, 96, 105, 147, 181–182, 187, 205, 211, 232; in Congress, 107, 109–110, 232; poem

275